1/13/89

Understanding Microprocessors

Written by: Don L. Cannon, Ph.D.
Assoc. Prof. of Electrical Engineering
University of Texas at Arlington
Staff Consultant, Texas Instruments Information Publishing
Center

Gerald Luecke, MSEE
Mgr. Technical Products Development
Texas Instruments Information Publishing Center

*With
contributions by:* Leslie E. Mansir, Editor
Ken E. Krone, Editor
Texas Instruments Information Publishing Center

D1484716

Howard W. Sams & Co.
A Division of Macmillan, Inc.
4300 West 62nd Street, Indianapolis, IN 46268 USA

This book was developed by:
The Staff of the Texas Instruments Information Publishing Center

With Contributions by:
Tim Shirey

Appreciation is expressed to Jim Muller, Steve Howard and Doug Luecke for their valuable comments.

Artwork and layout by:
Schenck, Plunk & Deason
Plunk Design

ISBN 0-672-27010-2
Library of Congress Catalog Number: 84-51247

Second Edition
Third Printing

About the cover:

Represented on the cover are the components of the technology that makes microprocessors and microcomputer systems possible: individual unpackaged microprocessor chips and their parent silicon slices in various stages of production, an open packaged microprocessor, interconnecting cable and an unassembled subsystem printed wiring board.

Printed in the United States of America

Table of Contents

Preface

This book is written for the person that has a curiosity about how microprocessors and microcomputers work. Microprocessors that are being used in appliance and automotive controls; microcomputers that are used in toys and games; microprocessor systems that seem to be able to do so much in such a small space.

With this book some knowledge of how digital electronics work and how they are used is beneficial. However, it is not necessary. Basic concepts and fundamentals are a prime ingredient of the book content to provide the overall understanding desired. An understanding that should serve the reader well whether working directly with or on the fringe of microprocessors, or just wishing to be fully aware of the digital evolution sweeping over us.

Microprocessors and microcomputers are causing a change in the design of digital electronic equipment. Where prior systems might have consisted of a set of hardware designed especially for a particular job, now common hardware will be used for many different types of jobs. The only thing that changes is the program of operations that causes the hardware to perform its task. Understanding how this can be done – from idea to completed hardware – is a prime purpose of this book.

This book, like the other Understanding Series™ builds the understanding of the subject step by step. For this reason, the book should be read a chapter at a time starting at the beginning. Don't skip around to get details on individual subjects but study the chapters until the basic concepts are understood, then move on to a higher level of understanding in the next chapter. The book also encourages the reader, through examples and exercises, to actually try to use a microprocessor system.

Quizzes and exercises are provided for checks on the understanding received from each chapter.

A glossary and index help to further expand the understanding of the subject.

The world of digital electronics is very exciting. We hope this book helps you to understand and enjoy it.

D.C.
G.L.

The World of Digital Electronics

We are all surrounded by examples of electronic devices that make our lives simpler and more enjoyable. In the past, these devices were limited to radios, televisions, stereos, tape recorders – so-called analog systems that did not use digital electronics. More recently, electronic calculators have brought the world of digital electronics to our very fingertips. Now there are a variety of games, "smart" appliances, and even computers for the home that are being made available to us through the use of a special type of digital electronic device called a microprocessor.

ABOUT THE BOOK

Computers originally were mechanical devices. Today, they are made of electronic circuitry (hardware) which performs a specific task using a set of steps in a predetermined order (the programming).

This is a book about microprocessors, or more specifically, about microcomputer systems which use a microprocessor as the central unit for processing and control. It is a book for the person who is not familiar with digital electronics, integrated circuits, analog systems, computers, microprocessors, microcomputers, software, programs, programming, source code, object code, machine code, assembly language, assembler, high-level language, compiler, cross-support, etc. It is written to provide understanding of the basic concepts and fundamentals surrounding these terms. It is designed to help provide insight into what makes up a microprocessor, how the microprocessor fits into the microcomputer system, what other system units are required for the microcomputer system, and how one gets a microcomputer system to do something.

This all sounds very difficult and complicated. It's not. But to make the task easier let's make sure we all have the same initial understanding by discussing a few of the basic terms.

SOME BASIC DEFINITIONS

Computer

A *computer* is a system made up of units which are pieces of hardware (electronic circuits, printed-circuit boards, switches, lights, etc.) that perform operations on given inputs to obtain required outputs. These operations are performed by a particular set of steps arranged (programmed) to occur in a particular order.

Computers can be made by using mechanical devices such as gears and levers. Babbage's original analytical steam engine was made this way. Or electromechanical devices such as motors and solenoids can be used for systems such as an aircraft autopilot computer. A system such as the handheld calculator can be made by using only electronic devices. This book is about such electronic devices and how they are used to make computers.

Analog vs Digital Systems

In an analog system, the signals used for transmission, computing and controlling vary in a smooth continuous manner.

Computers can be analog systems or they can be digital systems.

When a system such as a computer is an *analog system* the quantities to be computed, transmitted or controlled are represented with physical means that vary in a smooth continuous fashion. The representation is not broken into discrete parts or separated into set levels and the signal is usually carried on one or two wires.

In contrast, *digital systems* represent a system quantity by breaking it into discrete parts, and usually several wires bundled in a group are needed to carry the signals.

Let's look at *Figure 1-1*. A system that plays records or cassette tapes is an example of an analog system. Continuous varying signals of audio tones from the record or tape pass through the pickup head into the amplifier and out the speaker. The sound impulses on the record or tape are converted to continuous electrical signals that are amplified and reconverted to sound by the speaker. The electrical signals have provided an "analog" or analogy of the sound signals. The circuits used to handle analog information electronically are usually called *linear* circuits.

Digital computers operate using signals that are made up of separate parts to provide the necessary functions. These separate parts are called bits and have two possible values, 0 and 1.

Digital systems on the other hand *handle the information in digital form*. The system quantities or system information is made up of a combination of separate parts called bits. The bits can have only set values, usually two – 0 and 1. The particular combination of the bit values provides a code to represent a particular value of the information. In the case of *Figure 1-1*, there is a different code for each number.

**Figure 1-1.
Analog and Digital
Systems**

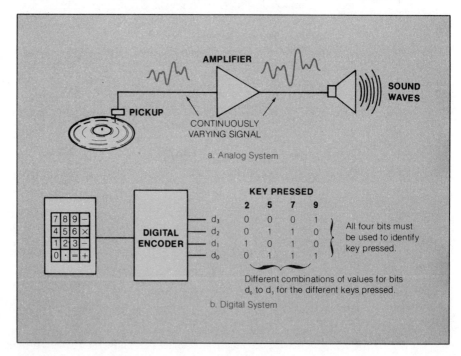

a. Analog System

b. Digital System

Digital Systems and Digital Electronics

Digital systems are systems that handle information in digital form and *digital electronics* are the electronic circuits that make up digital systems to handle the information in digital form.

Digital Functions

A *digital function* is an operation (like adding two numbers, or selecting a code when a switch is thrown, or storing a combination of bits that represent a number) that is performed with digital circuits using digital information.

Digital Integrated Circuits

A semiconductor integrated circuit (called "IC") is an individual, miniature electronic circuit made in one piece which performs all the digital functions required for complete subsystem or system tasks.

Figure 1-2 shows an "IC". That's the shortened name for an *integrated circuit*. It is a means of constructing and manufacturing digital circuits whereby all the circuits can be made very small on one piece of silicon semiconductor material so that the chip, about ¼" (6.35 mm) square, fits on a fingertip. Thus, digital integrated circuits are being called "fingertip electronics". All the digital functions required to perform complete system tasks can be put into such a small space that they fit on the tip of a finger.

**Figure 1-2.
Fingertip Electronics**

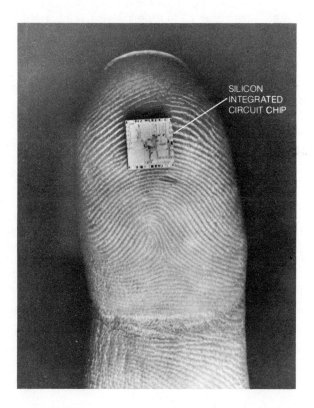

SILICON
INTEGRATED
CIRCUIT CHIP

Microcomputer

The microcomputer is the smallest of the computer systems; single chip ones are contained in one IC. Microcomputers have a microprocessor for their CPU (Central Processing Unit).

A *microcomputer* is a complete digital computer, available in a variety of sizes from one or two printed circuit boards down to all circuitry on a single monolithic (one piece) chip. When all of the functions of a digital computer are available in one integrated circuit, it is called a single-chip microcomputer. It is called a microcomputer because of its small size (micro meaning small). It is usually in the smallest range of size and slowest range of speed when compared with all digital computer systems. On the other hand, it is a complete system and, as more and more digital functions are included as "fingertip electronics" on a single chip, the functions the microcomputer can do in a given size will increase rapidly.

A microcomputer has a microprocessor as its central functional unit. In computer jargon such a circuit is called a CPU (spoken as if you were spelling it – C - P - U) meaning Central Processing Unit.

Microprocessor

The microprocessor is a digital integrated circuit (or a set of IC's) that contains the digital functions necessary to be a CPU. It "processes" information and controls and keeps the system working in harmony as it responds to the step by step program that the CPU follows.

Throughout this book a microprocessor unit is considered to be within a microcomputer and when material is discussed on microcomputers it contributes to the understanding of microprocessors.

Computer-Like Circuits

In many cases digital functions are being accomplished by digital integrated circuits that are not complete computers but use many of the same circuits used in computers. These may be designed especially for a given task (custom designed) or they may be combinations of standard functions. Such circuits are referred to as "computer-like" circuits.

ABOUT THIS CHAPTER

There is no question that digital electronics has made significant strides over the last few years. Take for example *Figure 1-3* which shows the major technology advances that have occurred to impact computer technology since the abacus of 450 B.C. Examining the data shows that the real advances in digital systems have occurred since the early 1940's. The last 4 are directly related to advances in digital electronics and the integrated circuit. In fact, as demonstrated in *Figure 1-4*, it took almost 2300 years to advance from the abacus to Babbage's mechanical calculator, and it has taken only 28 years to advance from the Mark I relay computer to a single-chip microcomputer.

**Figure 1-3.
Advances in Computer
Technology**

450 BC	CHINESE	ABACUS
1642	PASCAL	MECHANICAL +, − MACHINE (GEARS & WHEELS)
1671	LEIBNIZ	MECHANICAL +, −, ×, ÷ MACHINE (BINARY)
1833	BABBAGE	ANALYTICAL ENGINE (STEAM)
1944	MARK I	ELECTROMECHANICAL COMPUTER (RELAYS)
1946	VON NEUMAN	STORED PROGRAM CONCEPT
1948	BELL LABS	TRANSISTOR
1950	UNIVAC I	VACUUM TUBE COMPUTER
1959	TI	INTEGRATED CIRCUIT
1971	TI	ONE-CHIP CALCULATOR
1972	TI	4-BIT MICROCOMPUTER ON A CHIP
1976	TI	16-BIT MICROPROCESSOR
1977	TI	16-BIT MICROCOMPUTER ON A CHIP

**Figure 1-4.
Computer Advances vs
Time**

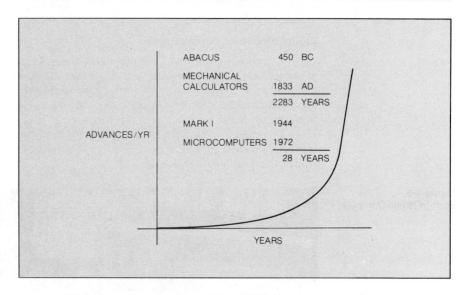

Of the four computer eras shown in *Figure 1-5*, the last three are
tied directly to advances in solid-state technology, more digital functions on
a chip, and lower costs to provide more functions per dollar in a continually
reduced space.

**Figure 1-5.
Typical Computer Eras**

1ST GENERATION	1950'S	VACUUM TUBES
2ND GENERATION	1960'S	SOLID STATE
3RD GENERATION	1970'S	INTEGRATED CIRCUITS
4TH GENERATION	1975	COMPUTER-ON-A-CHIP

This is what's so exciting about microprocessors and microcomputers and computer-like digital circuits in general – they provide such high-powered digital functional capability in such a small space at such a low cost. This has caused an explosion in their use and a change in the approach to digital system design. To understand how and why this has happened is the subject of this chapter. Let's start with the use of digital electronics.

WHO USES DIGITAL ELECTRONICS

Just about everyone uses digital electronics. We may not realize it, but digital electronic systems using microprocessors and microcomputers are appearing in more and more of the equipment that surrounds us each day – in our homes, the place where we work, the places where we shop, the places where we have fun. In our homes, in particular, the evolution is underway. Digital electronic circuits are controlling home appliances. Hand calculators are being changed into hand computers. More extensive fingertip digital electronics are finding their way into the home in the form of complete home systems.

Home computers, which have a wide variety of uses for the household, and in business, are made possible because of the inexpensive integrated circuit microprocessors and microcomputers.

Digital Electronics in the Home

To see how digital electronics in the form of computer-like controls or microprocessors have become part of our everyday lives, let's look in on a modern family just getting settled after moving into their new home. We enter the scene with the man of the house working at his desk. He appears to be typing, but as we move in closer, we see that there is a keyboard and a small TV screen. We realize now that he is working with his home computer *(Figure 1-6)*. He is looking at some family expenses and getting ready to study some possible investments.

**Figure 1-6.
Built-In Home Computer**

A Conversation — About a Home Computer

His son enters and interrupts him with a question: "Hi Dad, what are you doing?" "Working on some bills," replies the father. The son continues, "I was hoping I could play the space game; will you be through soon?" "Fairly soon, then we'll both play," said the father. The son watched the father making his entries and asked, "Dad, I was wondering the other day, are we the only family that owns a home computer?" His father answers, "No, there are many hobbyists who have them. We are probably one of the few families who have a computer that is built-in to help control many things around the house. But that's because we have just built a new house and we invested in a fairly complete home computer system."

"It must have cost a lot," the son commented. "Well, not really. About as much as we paid for Mom's used car," the father replies. "It's an investment that will last us a long time and it makes our lives easier and more enjoyable. We can do a lot of things with it. It helps us keep track of our expenses, supplies, and things we have to do. I can be a better investor, by making more money from investments. It helps us compare quickly things we want to buy so we can be better consumers and spend our money more wisely. It controls our heating and cooling system so that we get the most comfort for the least cost. It keeps our pool heated for the lowest cost."

"It even helps Mom in the kitchen. With the push of a few buttons, she can control her cooking time and temperature to save energy and, of course, time her cooking when she's away. It can keep track of her budget and what she needs to buy and when. It helps her save recipes and to adjust them for different meal sizes."

"It also keeps track of when we should fertilize the yard, when and how long to water the lawn, when we should change our furnace filters, and other simple schedules that we tend to forget without timely reminders."

"I've seen TV ads by companies that make computers and calculators and they talk about these small electronic circuits. I think they call them microelectronics or something like that — maybe integrated circuits," the son responded. "Are there any in our computer?" he asked.

"Oh, yes," said the father, "that's what makes it all possible. If the manufacturer didn't have integrated circuits, they would never be able to do everything in such a small space and at such a low cost. I know there's a central unit in here called a microprocessor. It does the main things, but I understand there are several other units that are just as complicated as the microprocessor that take care of getting the inputs in from this keyboard and from the tape recorder. Remember how we must play in the tape for the space game before we start. That's the program. It tells the computer what to do as we play the game."

About Appliances with Computer-like Controls

"My teacher says it's very unusual for people today to have computers in their homes, but that many people will have them in the future," said the son.

The father remarks, "That's particularly true since more and more people will be buying homes with built-in computers. What many people don't realize is that they already have computers of some form in their homes but don't recognize them as such. Take the microwave oven we have in the kitchen as an example *(Figure 1-7)*. Contained inside it is a microprocessor circuit that controls its operation and provides Mom with many choices for cooking our food. She can tell the oven to defrost frozen food, tell it exactly when she wants it to start cooking, when it is to keep the food warm, and so on. She can program any sequence of these operations that she needs for any meal she wants to cook and the oven does the rest. Then, once the meal is prepared, the oven signals her with a buzzer."

**Figure 1-7.
Microwave Oven**
(Courtesy Litton Microwave)

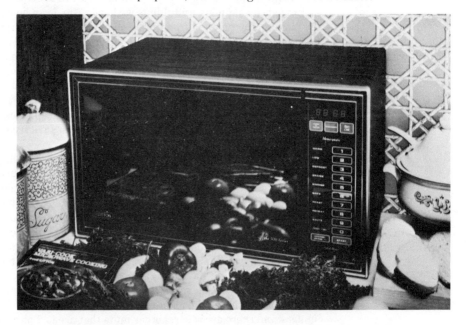

"That's what's so nice about the new microprocessor control. The step-by-step sequence of things that it does can be set-up easily and changed easily; with the older controls you couldn't do that. They weren't *programmable.*"

"The controls in that oven seem quite small," said the son, "I thought computers or controls like that were very large." "Well, they used to be much larger years ago," said the father. "In fact, when computers were first built *(Figure 1-8)*, they required more room than the space in our entire house. But today, digital electronics, and especially digital integrated circuits, have changed that. They provide lots of functions in a very small space and for a very reasonable cost."

**Figure 1-8.
Early Large-Scale Digital
Computer**
(Courtesy IBM Corp)

About Handheld Computers

"Hand me that calculator there on mother's desk," he said. The son reached over and picked up the 4-function hand-held calculator they had purchased at the department store *(Figure 1-9).* "Now here is really a reduction in size," the father continued. "If you were to open this calculator you would find that essentially all the electronics except the keyboard and the display are in one package." "How much did we pay for it?" asked the son. "$9.95," answered the father. "You mean that everything that's needed for all those calculations is made at the same time and put in one package?" asked the son. "That's right" said the father, "and that's why the cost is low. It takes only a small amount of time to put it together and test it."

**Figure 1-9.
Handheld Calculator**

"I know they call these calculators, but is it really a computer?" asked the son. "Yes, somewhat," replied the father, "but it's one designed especially for certain problems and therefore limited in what it can do. It only has a keyboard input and a display as an output. It has no large memory for storing data or programs. It can't be changed in what it does unless the circuits inside are changed."

The father picked up the handheld scientific programmable calculator (*Figure 1-10*) he uses at work. "Now, here is a computer," he said. "It is programmable – that means it can be changed easily to solve many different problems. It has a magnetic card memory so that a program can be saved and used again and it can be attached to a printer to print out what's on its display. It's still limited in inputs and outputs and memory for storage, but it can solve problems as well as some of the better computers of the 1950's which were so large that they would have filled our living room. The size reduction is over 15,000 times." "Gosh, that's some size reduction," replied the son. "It sure is," replied the father.

**Figure 1-10.
Programmable
Calculator**

About A Computer-Controlled Camera

"Here, let me show you something else that really shows what digital electronics can do in a small size," said the father as he found a page in the photography magazine on the desk. "Take a look at the camera in this ad (*Figure 1-11*). It has a computerized control in it. It has a microcomputer with a microprocessor that was designed especially for this camera. It's really something. When you use the camera, you tell the microcomputer in the camera how you want the camera to act by simply setting switches on the camera to certain positions. The microcomputer then sets up the camera and automatically sets the exposure for you so that you get a perfectly

Figure 1-11.
Automatic Exposure
Camera
(Courtesy of Canon Inc.)

exposed picture every time. All you have to do is point the camera, focus, and shoot." "Almost anyone could use one of those," the son observed. The father agreed, "and there's another advantage of using digital circuits. The camera settings can be displayed in number and letter form just as it is on your digital watch." "And look here," the father continued, "here's a picture (*Figure 1-12*) that gives you an idea of the small size of the computerized control circuitry. You see that most of the space in this small camera is used for film, viewfinder, lens, and mechanical controls. Only a very small space is required for the digital electronics that controls all the settings."

Figure 1-12.
Interior View of Camera
(Courtesy of Canon Inc.)

About Electronic Toys and Games

"Dad, do the electronic toys contain computers?" asked the son. "Oh, yes, many of them do. That bowling game that Mary next door got some time ago for Christmas (*Figure 1-13*), that has a microcomputer in it. That ship game you received, *(Figure 1-14)*, what do they call it?" "Code Name: Sector," the son replied. "That has a microcomputer in it and so does the one *(Figure 1-15)* that Steve gave Margo," continued the father, "And I found out something interesting about all of them from our engineer at work. All three of these games use the same single-chip microcomputer. Now, that really shows you the advantage of microprocessors and microcomputers. The same unit can be used to do many different things. Just by making it follow a different step-by-step procedure, the same microcomputer is used to control each of the three games."

Figure 1-13.
Bowling Game
(Courtesy of MARX)

Figure 1-14.
Electronic Game
(Courtesy of Parker Brothers
CODE NAME: SECTOR®
game equipment © 1977
Parker Bros, Beverly, MA.)

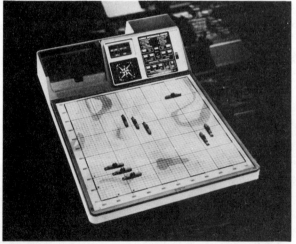

Sams books cover a wide range of technical topics. We are always interested in hearing from our readers regarding their informational needs. Please complete this questionnaire and return it to us with your suggestions. We appreciate your comments.

Book Marker Book

1. Which brand and model of computer do you use?
☐ Apple _____
☐ Commodore _____
☐ IBM _____
☐ Other (please specify) _____
_____

2. Where do you use your computer?
☐ Home   ☐ Work

3. Are you planning to buy a new computer?
☐ Yes   ☐ No
If yes, what brand are you planning to buy? _____

4. Please specify the brand/ type of software, operating systems or languages you use.
☐ Word Processing _____
☐ Spreadsheets _____
☐ Data Base Management _____
☐ Integrated Software _____
☐ Operating Systems _____
☐ Computer Languages _____

5. Are you interested in any of the following electronics or technical topics?
☐ Amateur radio
☐ Antennas and propagation
☐ Artificial intelligence/ expert systems
☐ Audio
☐ Data communications/ telecommunications
☐ Electronic projects
☐ Instrumentation and measurements
☐ Lasers
☐ Power engineering
☐ Robotics
☐ Satellite receivers

6. Are you interested in servicing and repair of any of the following (please specify)?
☐ VCRs _____
☐ Compact disc players _____
☐ Microwave ovens _____
☐ Television _____
☐ Computers _____
☐ Automotive electronics _____
☐ Mobile telephones _____
☐ Other _____

7. How many computer or electronics books did you buy in the last year?
☐ One or two   ☐ Three or four
☐ Five or six   ☐ More than six

8. What is the average price you paid per book?
☐ Less than $10   ☐ $10-$15
☐ $16-$20   ☐ $21-$25   ☐ $26+

9. What is your occupation?
☐ Manager
☐ Engineer
☐ Technician
☐ Programmer/analyst
☐ Student
☐ Other _____

10. Please specify your educational level.
☐ High school
☐ Technical school
☐ College graduate
☐ Postgraduate

11. Are there specific books you would like to see us publish? _____
_____
_____

Comments _____
_____
_____
Name _____
Address _____
City _____
State/Zip _____
27010

SAMS℠

Book Markkram kooB

SAMS™

Figure 1-15.
Computer Toy
(Courtesy of Parker Brothers
MERLIN™ game equipment ©
1978 Parker Bros, Beverly, MA)

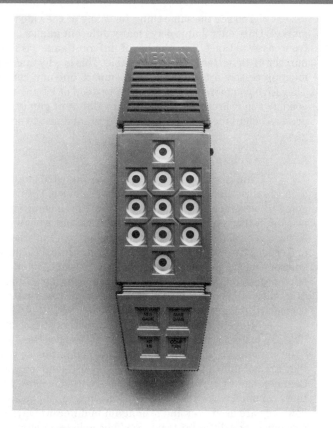

Tremendous cost savings occur when the same microcomputer can be used by programming it uniquely for many different applications. The manufacturer can make large quantities of one unit, rather than small quantities of several units.

"I'm sure you can see the advantages to that. Instead of making three different microcomputers only one is made. The quantity of units for the single unit is now the sum of the units used in each of the three units. This reduces the cost." "Why is that?" asks the son. "It's just cheaper to make one unit in larger quantity than it is to make three units in smaller quantity," replied the father. "The game manufacturers use the same standard part but just change the step-by-step procedure to make their special game."

"That's what you said we do when we play games on our computer," noted the son. "Yes," agreed the father. "We play in a cassette and that programs the computer to: follow the position of the levers on our controls, to keep the score, to keep track of the action and set up the screen so we know what's happening."

"You see the same thing for many of the video games on the market. One central unit plays many different games by reprogramming it from cassette tapes. The number of different games is limited only by the number of cassettes that are available. This is why microcomputers and microprocessors are having such an impact, one unit can do so many things. They give you more for your money. Instead of having to buy a new game, you buy a new program. You get many different games for about the same price as older video games that were designed just to do a given set of games."

About the Future

Thinking back on what they had talked about, the son said, "I didn't realize that electronics was doing so much. If this continues, we are going to be surrounded by electronics." "You're being surrounded already," was the father's reply. "We've just talked about what's going on in our home. Every place – in industry, in business, in the schools – electronics, and especially digital electronics, are doing things cheaper, more efficiently, quicker and are just making our life a lot easier. And it's going to continue. Microprocessors and microcomputers are bringing so much problem-solving capability into our hands at such a reasonable cost that more and more people are going to find ways to use them."

"Have you had anything on computers at school?" asked the father. "We are just starting to get into them in science class," replied the son. "You're going to be learning more about computers as you go on. You'll find they are not difficult to understand. They use common ways of doing things. Common names, terms, and functions are used over and over again. Once these common ways and terms are known, you will be able to understand how they are used over and over again in different ways to solve different problems or do different tasks. You'll be able to understand ––––"

Quite a story, what's behind it? How did it come about? Why is digital electronics used? What made the so called digital electronic evolution happen? Let's start answering these questions by looking at why digital electronics are used.

WHY DO WE USE DIGITAL ELECTRONICS?

In *Figure 1-1* two systems were described. An analog system that has system quantities that vary continuously and a digital system where combinations of bits form codes to represent system quantities.

Although analog systems still have many applications, because of their speed, accuracy, efficiency and low cost, digital systems are replacing analog systems at an ever increasing pace.

Analog systems are all around us. It is the conventional way that has been used for a long time to build systems. For some systems the analog solution is still the most economical and practical way, but because digital electronics can provide system solutions that solve the problem or do the task with less cost, more efficiently, more effectively, quicker, more accurately, digital systems are replacing analog systems.

System Solutions at Lower Cost

I.C. manufacturing techniques have led to a dramatic cost and size reduction of microcomputers while at the same time leading to improved performance, reliable operation, and low power consumption .

Providing system solutions at lower cost has been a prime mover for digital electronic systems. The cornerstone for low cost has been solid-state semiconductor technology and, even more so, integrated circuit technology. *Figure 1-2* showed an integrated circuit. Within such a chip of silicon material (a semiconductor material) enough digital circuits can be made to provide all the digital functions that are needed for a complete computer – a microcomputer. Because the circuits on the chips are made all at the same time, and because thousands of chips are processed together, the cost per function has been reduced up to 2,000 times below the cost when individual parts were wired together. All of this has occurred with improved system performance, smaller size and weight, lower power, wider temperature range operation, and much more reliable operation.

A System Comparison

Perhaps this is best demonstrated by an example. *Figure 1-16* is a comparison of an advanced scientific calculator and a computer of the mid 1950's. The calculator is an earlier model of the type shown in *Figure 1-10*. Within the calculator, which can be held in your hand, there is as much computing capability as the computer – and the computer occupies 270 cubic feet (7.56 m³). It's amazing but, in addition, the handheld calculator has better performance – adding 10 times faster, multiplying 5 times faster and transferring at approximately the same rate. Power is reduced by 100,000 times, volume by 16,000 times, weight by 8,500 times and all this with a cost reduction of almost 700 times. It seems impossible. Let's trace how this capability came about.

**Figure 1-16.
Digital System
Comparison**

	IBM 650 COMPUTER	ADVANCED SCIENTIFIC CALCULATOR	IMPROVEMENT RATIO
Components	2,000 Tubes	166,500 Transistors	1.80
Power, KVA	17.7	0.00018	100,000:1
Volume, cu. ft.	270	0.017	16,000:1
Weight, lbs.	5650	0.67	8,500:1
Air Conditioning	5 to 10 Tons	None	Uses None
Operation	Stored Program, Magnetic Drum With 2,000 Words	Program Steps . . . . . 160-960 Memory Locations . . . . 100-0 Stored Program per Module . . . . 5000 Bytes	Computing Capability Considered Equal
Execution time, milliseconds Add Multiply Transfer	 0.75 20.0 0.5	 0.070 4.0 0.4	 10:1 5:1 Equal
Price	$200,000 (1955 Dollars)	$299.95 (1977 Dollars)	700:1

The Digital Evolution

The smallest and simplest of digital circuits from which other functions are formed is the gate.

The digital codes of *Figure 1-1* that carry the information in digital systems are moved through the system by digital circuits. The simplest of digital circuits is called a *gate*. Combinations of gates make more complex circuits. More complex circuits provide more complex digital functions. When more and more of these digital functions are combined, more complex subsystems and finally full systems result.

Such an evolution of digital electronics is shown in *Figure 1-17, 1-18, 1-20,* and *1-21.*

**Figure 1-17.
Early 1950's — Discrete Devices Wired Together to Form Gates**

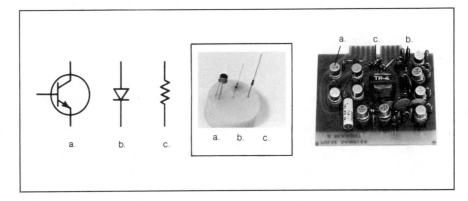

Early 1950's

Diodes and transistors, called discrete solid-state devices, were the state-of-the-art in the early 1950's.

In the early 1950's (*Figure 1-17*), there were individual discrete solid-state devices such as diodes or transistors that had to be combined with separate resistors in order to form a gate. All had to be wired together by hand on terminal boards or printed circuit boards.

**Figure 1-18.
Early 1960's — Small Scale Integration (Up to About 12 Gates)**

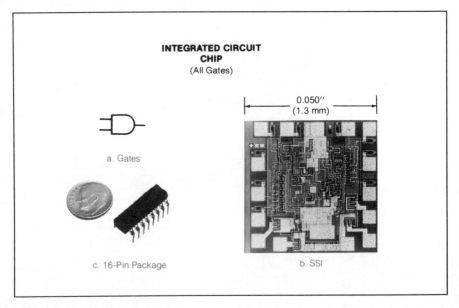

INTEGRATED CIRCUIT
CHIP
(All Gates)

a. Gates

c. 16-Pin Package

0.050″
(1.3 mm)

b. SSI

Early 1960's

The next solid-state development was the integrated circuit itself. It combined all of the components of a circuit onto a single piece of material. This development of the early 1960's was called small-scale integration.

In the early 1960's (*Figure 1-18*), combining such components into one piece of solid-state material called an integrated circuit became a reality. This was called small-scale integration (SSI). Up to 12 gates were put into a piece of square material that was about twice as thick as a piece of paper and about as wide as a pencil lead. To interconnect the small circuits to the outside world, 1 mil diameter (0.0254-mm) wires are bonded from the silicon chip to a package lead frame (*Figure 1-19*). The complete assembly is molded into a plastic package.

**Figure 1-19.
Integrated Circuit
Bonded to Lead Frame
and Molded in Plastic
Package**

Late 1960's

As integrated circuits became smaller, more devices and gates were added to a single chip and subsystems resulted. This was called large scale integration (LSI).

Through the late 1960's (*Figure 1-20*) the number of gates increased to over 1,000 on a single chip. First, using medium-scale integration (MSI), system building blocks were designed; then complete subsystems ushered in the age of large-scale integration (LSI).

**Figure 1-20.
Late 1960's — Medium
Scale to Large Scale
Integration (Up to About
1,000 Gates)**

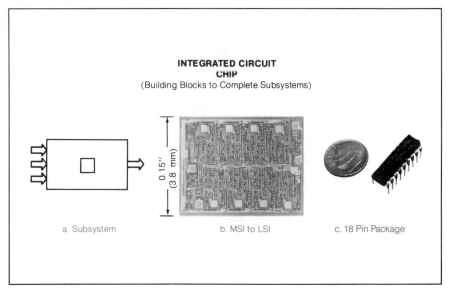

**INTEGRATED CIRCUIT
CHIP**
(Building Blocks to Complete Subsystems)

0.15"
(3.8 mm)

a. Subsystem   b. MSI to LSI   c. 18 Pin Package

Through the 1970's

The integrated circuit has continued to use smaller and smaller devices packed closer together on the chip. When the IC's contain all the circuitry for a complete system, such as a microcomputer, on a single chip it is called VLSI (very large scale integration).

The LSI integration pace, launched by the handheld calculator with all its circuitry on one chip (except the keyboard and the display), continued through the 1970's (*Figure 1-21*). Advances were such that it was not uncommon to put 50,000 gates on the same chip as before — ¼ inch (6.35 mm) on a side and 1/100th of an inch (0.254 mm) thick. All the circuitry for complete microcomputers on a single chip. This is very large-scale integration, VLSI.

Note that the number of package pins increased from 16 in early 1960 to 64 in the late 1970's to handle more bits for inputs and outputs, more bits for addresses and more control signals. The size of the integrated chip on the other hand hardly has increased in size. (It has increased a great deal by integrated circuit manufacturer's standards, but hardly by the user's standards).

**Figure 1-21.
Thru the 1970's — LSI to Very Large Scale Integration (Up to About 1,000 to 50,000 Gates)**

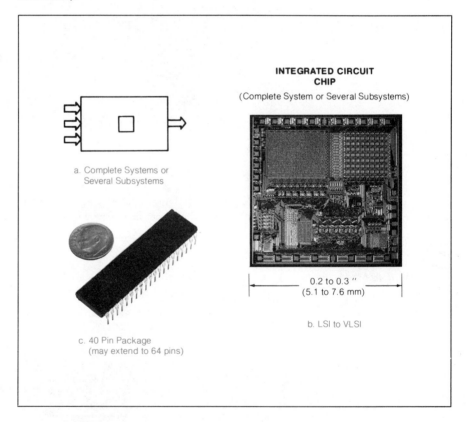

INTEGRATED CIRCUIT
CHIP

(Complete System or Several Subsystems)

a. Complete Systems or
Several Subsystems

0.2 to 0.3 ''
(5.1 to 7.6 mm)

b. LSI to VLSI

c. 40 Pin Package
(may extend to 64 pins)

Results of the Evolution

In *Table 1-1* and *1-2* the evolution is summarized. In *Table 1-1*, the change in the number of gates from early 1960 thru the 1970's means that 5,000 times more information can be handled digitally by VLSI integrated circuits than by SSI integrated circuits.

Table 1-1.
Summary of Digital
Evolution — Change in
No. of Gates

TYPE	TIME PERIOD	NO. OF GATES	CHANGE FROM SSI (ratio)
SSI	Early 1960	10-12	
MSI-LSI	Late 1960	100-1000	100:1
LSI-VLSI	Thru 1970	1000-50,000	5000:1

Table 1-2.
Summary of Digital
Evolution — Change in
Chip Size

TYPE	TIME PERIOD	NO. OF GATES	AUG CHIP SIZE		CHIP AREA (mils²)	CHANGE FROM SSI (ratio)
SSI	Early 1960	10-12	(mils) 50x50	(mm) 1.3x1.3	2,500	
MSI-LSI	Late 1960	100-1000	150x150	3.8x3.8	22,500	9:1
LSI-VLSI	Thru 1970	1000-50,000	250x250	6.4x6.4	62,500	25:1

In contrast, the chip size has only changed by 25 times as shown in *Table 1-2*. This means that the area of solid-state material used per gate has been reduced by 200 times. To get an idea of how small a VLSI digital gate is look at a period on this page. Using MOS (Metal-Oxide-Semiconductor) integrated-circuit technology (this will be discussed in Chapter 3) over 20 logic gates can fit under the period at the end of a sentence.

Even though the IC chip gate density has increased by 200 times, the cost to produce each IC has increased very little due to improvements in design and manufacturing. As a result, the cost per gate has been reduced dramatically.

Because the size of the integrated circuit chip has not increased that much, and because manufacturers have improved the ways the complex integrated circuits are made, the cost for processing each integrated circuit chip has increased very little. But, because there are so many gates per chip, the cost per gate has been reduced drastically!

For example, in the early 1960's, when SSI integrated circuits were first manufactured and there were 10 gates in a package, the cost of the package was $10 and the cost per gate equaled $1.

Contrast this with VLSI circuits with 50,000 gates which may sell at $50 when first manufactured. The gate cost is 0.1¢, resulting in a cost reduction of 1000 times over the SSI circuit. As production volume increases such packages may well sell for $10 and the cost reduction increases to 5,000 times.

Impact on Equipment Cost

The total impact of the digital evolution is best demonstrated by the impact on end equipment costs. *Figure 1-22* illustrates what has happened to the cost of a medium-scale computer. While in the early 1960's the hardware cost was $30,000, in 1980 it will be approximately $1,000, and it is projected to be $100 in 1985. The result of increasing the number of digital functions available in a small space has been the reduction of the cost per function and the resultant lower end equipment cost — by as much as 300 times for the computer example.

**Figure 1-22.
Cost of Medium-Scale
Computer**

```
EARLY 1960 . . . . . . .$30,000
1970 . . . . . . . . . . .$10,000
1977 . . . . . . . . . . . $5,000
1980 . . . . . . . . . . . $1,000
1985 . . . . . . . . . . .  $100
```

In addition, the digital functions are available with the high reliability, low power consumption, increased speed of operation, high accuracy and light-weight features offered by digital integrated circuits. Such advantages are contributing to the explosion in the use of computer-like digital electronic systems and, in particular, microprocessors and microcomputer systems.

WHY DO WE USE COMPUTERS?

Of the digital devices available to us, why do we use computers? What characteristics do these particular combinations of digital electronic subsystems have that make us want to use them? We can get an idea of what these characteristics are by looking at how computers have been used in the past. Refer to *Figure 1-23*.

**Figure 1-23.
Why Do We Use
Computers?**

1. **Computers are Fast and Accurate.**
   A. Handle "Number Crunching" problems with ease.
   B. Handle tedious and routine tasks without error.
   C. Handle "Real Time" problems fast and accurately.

2. **What Computers Can Do is Continually Increasing**
   A. Doing more in a small size with less weight and less power.
   B. Integrated circuit microprocessors and microcomputers.

3. **Computers are Easily Changed (Programmable)**
   A. Applications are changed by changing programs and not hardware.
   B. Expansion is possible by adding to the hardware, not discarding it.

Computers are Fast and Accurate

Number Crunchers

Computers first were used to handle very difficult and lengthy computations required for solutions to scientific problems. Because of their speed of operation, computers can handle "number crunching" problems in minutes that might take weeks or months to compute by hand. In addition, because digital electronic circuits handle information as bits, problem solutions and all computations can be computed with greater accuracy.

Tedious Jobs

Computers can perform a variety of jobs fast and accurately including: complex and lengthy calculations, routine and tedious tasks, and project planning at an accelerated rate.

As computer hardware became more common, the tedious kinds of jobs of keeping track of records became a job for the computer. The same routine of debiting and crediting for checking accounts, credit card accounts, inventory, invoices, and receivables was accurately, consistently, and concisely accomplished by computers. The computer easily handles these routines and tedious tasks for us because it will happily repeat the same procedure over and over again without error.

Fast Real Time

Business and project planning became the thing to do. Business plans were projected for years ahead, and these plans could be changed to try various approaches to determine the impact on profit or cash flow or return on assets. All of this became possible because of the incredible speed of modern computers and the increased computer capability in a given size.

Speed of computation is not critical to such business problems. It just means that the problem solution is obtained quicker.

"Real-time" problem solutions may have requirements where the computation speed is critical. For example, a system that checks that all conditions are GO for a space shot must do so in the last ten seconds. Digital computers do this job routinely with the necessary speed and accuracy.

What Computers Can Do is Continually Increasing

Refer again to *Figure 1-23*. With the increase in the applications came the demand to continue to reduce the size, weight, and power consumption of the computer. The digital integrated circuit fit right in. Systems that could perform the same computations were reduced in size by hundreds and thousands of times (See *Figure 1-16*).

Now microprocessors and microcomputers are available whereby computer systems can be assembled with just a few packages, or often with a single-chip microcomputer. This is enabling computer systems to be applied to almost any task – large or small.

Computers are Easily Changed (Programmable)

Common to all of the applications and advantages of the computer is its programmable nature. This is a main reason why they are so versatile and can be applied to such a wide variety of jobs. Refer again to *Figure 1-23*.

The ability to modify a computer's instructions (called programming) allows them to easily change their application, providing great versatility.

The computer performs exactly the operations we instruct it to. We write down the things we want the computer to do in the order we want them done. This list of instructions is called the program for the computer. By changing the program, we change the behavior and thus the application of the machine. The main difference between a scientific computer and a business inventory computer is in the programs they are given. The scientific computer is given a procedure for calculating some arithmetic function to a desired accuracy. If we want to change the function or the accuracy, we just change the procedure, not the computer. The business computer is given a procedure to keep track of the business inventory as shipments are received and products sold. If we want to change the function or the accuracy, we just change the procedure, not the computer. If we want to expand the computer to handle payroll and timekeeping, the equipment is not changed to handle the job, just new programs are added.

Microprocessor and microcomputer systems bring this same flexibility to their applications, no matter how small the task. With an appropriate program and using basically the same hardware, a microcomputer system can be a toy, an oven controller, a camera control, part of a manufacturing line, etc. All that need be done is to make sure the system is given the right procedure to follow so that it will do the exact task that is required.

ARE COMPUTERS REALLY EASY TO UNDERSTAND?

The computers basic functions can be divided into four areas: sensing, remembering (storing), deciding, and acting.

Since computers have been used to perform very complex tasks, most of us feel that they really must be complicated. In reality, computers offer us a simple, organized way to build almost any electronic system. They behave in ways that are similar to our own behavior. They are made up of circuits or functions that are easily understood and readily available. With microprocessors, we really only have to buy a few types of different circuits and connect them together to make a computer. This is because the computer consists of only a few different types of functional units.

As shown in *Figure 1-24*, all systems (including the human system) can be broken into the functions of *sense, remember (store) , decide*, and *act*. Once we can provide all these features, we can build anything we want. The computer system provides all four of these functions, as shown in *Figure 1-25*, in low cost units that are easy to connect together.

Figure 1-24.
Universal Digital System
Organization
(G. McWhorter, Understanding
Digital Electronics, *Texas*
Instruments Incorporated,
Copyright® 1978)

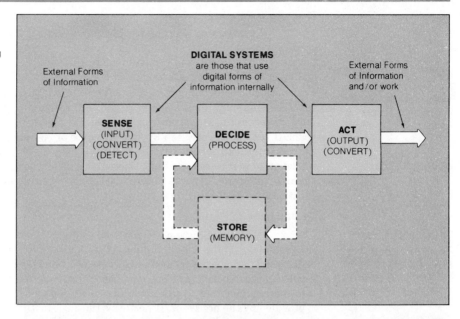

Figure 1-25.
Computer System
Organization

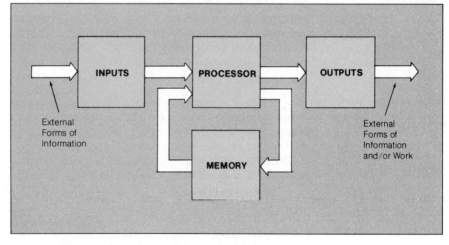

Sense Function

The sense function of the
computer allows it to
receive inputs from people
or other machines and
send the information on to
be processed by the CPU.

In *Figure 1-24,* the *sense* function is what the name implies. It
senses information and transmits it to the machine for decoding
(interpretation) and response. This input information can be data about
surrounding conditions such as temperature, pressure, light, and so on, or it
can be communications and commands that set the machine in a given mode
and tell it where to start. By having such sense elements, the system can
receive information from humans or from other similar equipment. In the
computer system of *Figure 1-25,* the functional units that perform the *sense*
function are simply called *inputs.*

Remember Function

In its memory, the computer stores the information that makes up its program and the data that has been input to it, as well as interim data that it generates as it performs its task.

The *remember (store)* function *(Figure 1-24)* is important to all advanced machines. The machine must remember what it is to do, information for use in what it does, and results of what it has done. It also must remember a number of rules that must be used in making decisions, performing arithmetic and controlling the system. The computer system name for this function is *memory*, for obvious reasons. In the computer *(Figure 1-25)*, the memory serves the same function as the memory portion of the human brain. It remembers the step-by-step sequence of operations (the program) the computer is to perform. It also remembers the instructions and information (data) that are used. Computer memory devices are available as single integrated circuits that can be connected easily to the other functional units of the computer system.

Decide Function

The central processor makes operational decisions, controls the other parts of the system and performs any required logic operations.

The *decide* function *(Figure 1-24)* is much like the reasoning function of our brain. All the computations, logical operations, and operational decisions are made here. These decisions take into account the inputs (commands and information about the surroundings) and the information in memory. In the computer *(Figure 1-25)*, the *decide* function is provided by the processor. It performs the basic arithmetic and logical decisions required by the computer. It also controls the operation of the computer by turning on and off the other functional units in the system at the proper times. The processor in a microcomputer system is a microprocessor. It may be in a separate package or be contained in the single-chip microcomputer that fits on the tip of a finger.

Act Function

Outputs are the actions which the computer performs when the central processor has decided upon the course of action to take.

The *act* function *(Figure 1-24)* is again what the name implies. Once a decision has been made by the processor, the system carries out the decision with the *act* units of the system. These may be devices that display information so it can be communicated to humans. Or the act unit may turn on a motor, or turn off a light, or light the gas in a furnace; or it may be to position a drill bit, or some other similar control operation. The act units allow the system to control something external to the system or to exchange information (communicate) with humans or other machines. In the case of the computer *(Figure 1-25)*, the devices that implement the *act* function are called the *outputs* of the system.

Changes in the function of sense, decide and act are made by changing the program (the step-by-step sequence of instructions) in the desired manner.

The functions of sense or input, act or output, remember (memory), and decide are functions that we can all understand easily. The computer provides all of these functions. The way in which the step-by-step sequence (the program) uses these functions defines the task that a particular system performs. A system can be made a video game by placing the game procedure or program from a magnetic tape cartridge into the system, providing a television screen output, and using game position controls as inputs. We can make a heating unit controller from the same basic set of hardware by providing temperature sensor inputs, furnace fuel and blower controls as outputs, and a program that will monitor temperatures and turn on the furnace at the proper times. The list of such examples is almost endless. We simply have to recall the conversation between the father and son to see how varied the possibilities are.

WHY ARE MICROPROCESSORS SO IMPORTANT?

Look at *Figure 1-26*. Even though we have shown the advances that digital integrated circuits have made in providing more and more digital functions within a single package (curve A), and the reduction in cost per functional unit (curve B), the importance of microprocessors may still not be apparent.

**Figure 1-26.
Summary of
Semiconductor
Technology Evolution**

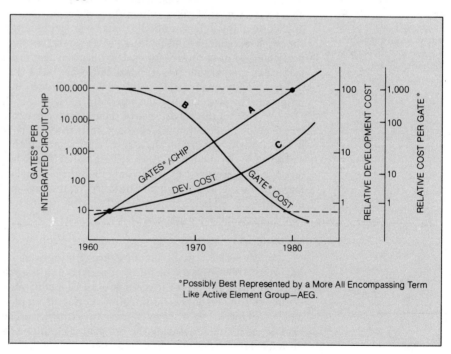

*Possibly Best Represented by a More All Encompassing Term Like Active Element Group—AEG.

Curve **C** will help to understand the final missing link. In the early 1960's the cost of developing an SSI integrated circuit was on the order of $20,000. A 50,000-gate VLSI integrated circuit of the late 1970's may have cost nearly one-half million dollars to develop. Unless the complex integrated circuit with all its functions can be sold in large quantities so that the cost per package can be low, the development costs will not be recovered and the next design will not be financed. When the quantities manufactured are low, the package cost would have to be so high to recover the development costs, that no one would use them. Their end equipment cost would be too high.

There are complex chip designs that are designed for specific applications (custom designs), and the calculator integrated circuit is one of these, where the quantities to be manufactured are large enough to support the high cost of development. However, many systems are used only in small quantity and another solution is necessary. Here is where the microprocessor is so important.

A Standard Unit

A "standard" IC is applied to many different applications simply by changing the programming. This allows large quantities of a single unit to be produced, rather than small quantities of many units.

To meet the needs of large quantity production a "standard" integrated circuit was designed – the microprocessor – so it could be made at low cost. One that many different people could use; one that could be applied to many different applications by programming it differently. Thus, the emphasis changed in the design of a system. Instead of designing a particular set of hardware for each application that is dedicated to a particular system solution, standard hardware units that have many types of functions are made to solve different system tasks by changing the program. The program, not the hardware, varies for each application.

Here is the importance of the microprocessor and its corresponding single-chip microcomputers. They are units that can be told to solve many different tasks by varying the step-by-step sequence they perform. All systems use the same unit. Each system in itself may be produced in small quantity and require only a small number of the standard unit. However, large quantities of the standard unit are required when all of the smaller quantities are added together. Manufacturing the unit in these large quantities results in a low cost unit.

Learning Curve

Experience in the manufacture of integrated circuits is very important. When a large quantity of a given unit is going to be manufactured, the proper investment can be made in the automated equipment, in personnel training, in manufacturing process improvements, and in technical support people. These investments produce a learning experience in manufacturing the integrated circuit which reduces its cost. Such learning-experience cost reduction is shown in *Figure 1-27*, and, is called a learning curve.

**Figure 1-27.
Learning Curve**

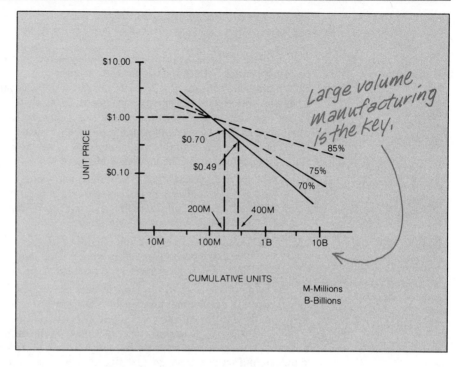

The basic concept of a learning curve is that, after a product is being manufactured in large quantities, each time the total number of units manufactured doubles, the unit price reduces by a constant percentage. The 70% slope of *Figure 1-27* is one that has been typical for the manufacture of SSI and MSI integrated circuits. It says that if the total number of units manufactured was 100 million and the price per package was $1.00, then when the total number of units manufactured reached 200 million the price had reduced to 70% of $1.00 or 70 cents. When the total volume reached 400 million then the price reduced to $0.70x70% or 49 cents.

Learning curve theory is based on the fact that the cost to produce IC's decreases at a steady rate as the quantity produced doubles.

The same learning experience has been true for the LSI and VLSI circuits with the slope ranging from 75 to 85%. It is this kind of regular reductions in the cost of a microprocessor as it is manufactured in large quantities that will help to lower the price and contribute to continued expansion of the applications.

Needless to say, if an integrated circuit is not manufactured in large quantities, then the resulting cost reduction will not occur. But with microprocessors this will be accomplished in a little different way.

They will be manufactured in large quantity even though they are used in small quantities for any one individual design.

They will be made and sold at low cost and the cost will move down a learning curve as the quantity of units manufactured accumulates. Because of the low cost more systems will be designed which, in turn, will lower the cost. The cycle will continue until the unit is replaced with a new and better design.

System Design Trends

A Viable Alternative

Using microprocessors programmed for an application rather than a custom unit provides the large quantity cost advantage to a design.

Providing subsystems or even full systems within one package has certainly changed the emphasis for the designer to a system orientation rather than one concerned with each individual detailed circuit. In addition, when the system design is being considered, if the system designer wants to use VLSI integrated circuits he has several choices that depend on the number of systems that will be manufactured. If the quantity is large, the two choices that are available are listed below. The one chosen should meet the system objectives in the most cost-effective way:

1. Have a special VLSI circuit designed which is dedicated to the specific application. It's likely this will result in the lowest equipment manufacturing cost but it will have limited chance for change without redesigning.

2. Use a microprocessor and the different general purpose packages that have been designed to work with it, and develop a program that guides the system to do the task at hand.

When the quantity is small the same choices are available. The first choice would result in development expenses that usually cannot be justified. In addition, the end cost of the units would be higher.

However, the second choice is a very viable alternative. Because standard units are used with a different program, all the cost advantages of a unit manufactured in large quantity are available even for the system manufactured in small quantity.

System Development Costs

Microprocessor and microcomputer systems are very important because they can be developed at lower total cost due to all the functions that are available within one package. *Figure 1-28* is a curve showing how total development costs have changed since the introduction of integrated circuits.

Since fewer packages are used, fewer assemblies are used. This requires fewer connectors, fewer cabinets, less power distribution, and less air conditioning. The end result is that the hardware costs are reduced as shown.

Software is the term used for the programming instructions developed for the microprocessor based system.

All the programming effort that is used to prepare the step-by-step sequence to get the system to do a particular task is termed "software". The name came about because most software is written or printed material. Because of microprocessors and microcomputers the total development cost has been reduced, even the software costs. Note, however, that the software cost becomes a much larger part of the total development cost.

**Figure 1-28.
System Development
Costs**

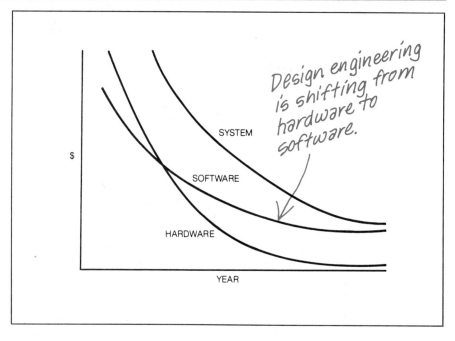

A Shift to Software

Today, as the shift to standard units that can be programmed continues, software rather than hardware requires more effort in system design.

The percent of total costs for software increases because a different program must be developed for each new application. This is a significant change in the way systems are designed. Now the designer must be concerned about how a program is written to make the step-by-step procedure control the system. No longer is the major effort on the design of the hardware. Now it is the creation and checkout of the software.

This change in design procedure is not easy for many designers. However, it is going to be a continuing trend for the future and it is hoped that the fundamental concepts developed in this book will aid in making the change easier.

ADDITIONAL STANDARD UNITS

Computer families have peripheral IC's that are programmable as well. These family units may also be produced as "standard units".

The ability to change the things a system can do by changing the order of the things the microprocessor is told to do will extend to the other units that are needed around the microprocessor to perform the *sense* and *act* functions. *Family* units designed to work with similar types of microprocessors will also be made programmable. Thus, they become "standard" units as with the microprocessor, and are manufactured in larger quantity at a lower cost.

The *family* of units also is an advantage when preparing the software. Because all the family units follow the same instructions, as step-by-step procedures are developed for different applications, the things that are learned and used begin to accumulate to make the next software job easier.

It is difficult to predict the overall impact of microprocessors and microcomputers except to say that it is and will continue to be great. It is hoped that this chapter has given some insight as to why this is so.

WHAT HAVE WE LEARNED?

- An analog system handles information with signals that vary continuously.
- Digital systems handle information with signals in digital form—a combination of separate parts called bits that have set values and occur in codes to represent a particular letter, number, character or symbol.
- Digital electronics has provided the computer controls for many of the products we use.
- The computer is a fast, accurate, and versatile digital electronics system that can be programmed to perform the sequence of operations we need for a given application and can be changed to do different tasks by changing the program.
- Solid-state technology through integrated circuits has made digital electronics the lowest-cost approach to building complex products because it is possible to provide a large number of digital operations in a small area of solid-state material.
- Medium-scale computers have been reduced in cost by 300 times as a result of the digital evolution.
- The central control element of a computer, the processor, is available in integrated circuit form in a device called a microprocessor.
- Connecting memory and input and output circuits to a microprocessor forms a computer.
- A microcomputer is a complete digital system in a small size that is usually in the smallest range of size and slowest range of speed when compared to all digital systems.
- Microprocessors and microcomputers are bringing so much problem-solving capability into our hands at such a reasonable cost that more and more people are going to find ways to use them.
- The existence of programmable standard devices such as the microprocessor and other units that surround it, allows all digital system designers to share the benefits of solid-state technology at reasonable costs.

WHAT'S NEXT?

In this chapter, we have seen some of the characteristics of computers that make them so useful to us. We are now ready to begin looking at the operation of the computer in detail. In the next chapter, we will start by looking at each of the computer functional blocks and how they work together to form a smoothly functioning system that can do almost anything.

Quiz for Chapter One

1. Answer the following statements true or false:
   a. Most of us will never use a microcomputer.
   b. Microcomputers are even found in cameras.
   c. Microcomputers and microprocessors are hard to understand.
   d. Microcomputers are enabling computers to be applied to many tasks.
   e. Computers behave much like we do in many ways.
   f. The microprocessor's main disadvantage is that it is not versatile.
   g. Microprocessors are now found in systems that were originally built with analog electronics.
   h. It is easy to change a computer's behavior or application.

2. Match the following human features with their computer counterpart:

Human	Computers
a. Eyes	A. Sensor Input
b. Ears	B. Memory
c. Memory	C. Control Output
d. Voice	D. Communication Input
e. Muscles	E. Microprocessor
f. Reasoning	F. Communication Output

3. Over the years solid-state technology has:
   a. Provided more digital functions in a smaller area of material.
   b. Increased the cost per digital function.
   c. Has made it harder to understand and build electronic systems.
   d. None of the above.

4. Microprocessors and single-chip microcomputers are important because:
   a. They allow all of us to use the same functional blocks in building our systems so that we can use low-cost units which contain a large number of digital functions.
   b. They allow us to bring the advantages of the computer to all products, large or small.
   c. They can replace calculators.
   d. a and b above
   e. a and c above
   f. None of the above.

5. Computers offer the following advantages:
   a. High speed operation
   b. Accurate operation
   c. Versatility
   d. Programmability
   e. All of the above

6. The purpose of a microcomputer system is defined by its program, inputs, and outputs. Show which inputs and outputs would be used to make the following systems:

System	Inputs	Outputs
a. Home Computer	**A.** Temperature Sensor	**1.** Motor
b. Camera	**B.** Typewriter	**2.** Water Valves
c. Furnace Controller	**C.** Moisture Sensor	**3.** Television Screen
d. Lawn Watering System	**D.** Radio Receiver	**4.** Gas and Air Flow Valves
e. Garage Door Opener	**E.** Light Sensor	**5.** Aperture, Shutter Speed, and LED Indicator Control

7. A device is said to be programmable if:
  a. Its behavior or operation can be changed by changing commands or instructions it is given.
  b. It can be adapted to many applications by giving it a suitable program.
  c. Its operation is fixed and unchangeable.
  d. a and b above.

8. 100 million VLSI circuits are produced at a cost of $2.00. If the production is increased to 400 million, what will be the new cost per device (Assume an 80% learning curve slope)?
  a. $1.00
  b. $1.28
  c. $1.60
  d. None of the above

9. Match the computer subsystems with the system function:
  a. Sense   **A.** Outputs
  b. Decide **B.** Memory
  c. Act   **C.** Inputs
  d. Store   **D.** Processor

10. Software for microcomputers:
  a. Is mainly the computer program
  b. Is less expensive to design than the hardware
  c. Can be used only once
  d. None of the above

Basic Concepts
in Microcomputer Systems

ABOUT THIS CHAPTER

As we saw in the last chapter digital systems have the basic functions of sense, remember, decide and act.

In this chapter we will examine how the computer system satisfies these functions and how the functional blocks work together – all the while searching for understanding of the basic concepts.

WHAT ARE THE MICROCOMPUTER BUILDING BLOCKS?

The microcomputer performs three basic computer system functions — sense, decide and act.

Microcomputer components can be purchased and interconnected to provide a computer system with the functions of sense, remember, decide and act. For the computer system, as shown in *Figure 2-1*, the sense function is the inputs, the remember function is the memory, the decide function is the processor or control, and the act function is the output. Inputs and outputs, even though they perform different detailed functions, are handled very similarly in the microcomputer system and can be classified as a basic communications function. As a result three basic computer system functions result: Processor or control, memory and communications.

Microprocessor — The Central Control Function

The microprocessor is the decision-maker and control center.

The microprocessor tells all the other system components what to do and when to do it. It does all the arithmetic and makes all the decisions for the rest of the system. It is much like the control center of any other system such as the brain of humans, the boss of a company, or the master switching center of a train yard. All of those tell each part of their system what to do and when to do it. As an example, the subconscious part of our brain regulates all of our vital systems in correct order. The reasoning part provides our decision making and other higher intellectual capabilities to help us do what we want when we want.

The boss of a company assigns tasks to all the workers and makes sure that each of them performs his job on time and in cooperation with the other workers in the firm.

The train yard switching center selects and connects boxcars, freighters, flatcars, tank cars, and so on, into cross-country trains by the flick of a lever which controls train yard switches.

Similarly, the microprocessor turns on and turns off all the system components in the proper order and at the proper time to make sure the entire system works in harmony.

All of these systems, as shown in *Figure 2-1*, are not independent of the outside world. They require inputs from the outside world to sense and react to. They give outputs to the outside world to provide action as a result of the inputs. They *sense* inputs and *act* on these inputs to provide outputs. Even the memory of the system may receive inputs or provide outputs to the outside world.

**Figure 2-1.
The Building Blocks of
Computers**

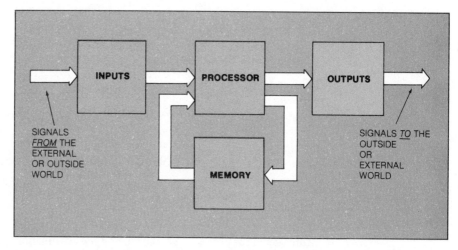

Memory

The memory stores data in units called bits. Each bit can be in either of two states - high or low, 1 or 0.

Let's look at memory. The microcomputer memory performs the rather obvious function of remembering or storing information needed by the system, the same function as the human memory. It is also similar to the file systems and note pads that humans use to store information that they want to refer to later but can't keep completely within their brain at all times. Numbers, words or characters that the microcomputer system must use in performing its tasks — its data — is stored in its memory. It stores this information as bits, "1's" and "0's" as shown in *Figure 2-2*. The arrangement of bits form codes to identify each number or character.

**Figure 2-2.
Information Stored as
Groups of Bits**

	16-BIT WORDS	8-BIT BYTES	4-BIT NIBBLES
MEMORY WORD #1	1 0 0 0 0 0 0 0 1 0 0 0 0 0 0 0	1 0 0 0 0 0 0 0	0 0 0 0
MEMORY WORD #2	0 0 0 0 0 0 0 0 1 0 0 0 0 0 0 1	0 1 1 0 0 1 1 0	0 0 0 1
MEMORY WORD #3	0 0 0 0 0 0 0 0 1 0 0 0 0 0 1 0	0 0 1 1 1 1 0 0	0 0 1 0
MEMORY WORD #4	0 0 0 0 0 0 0 0 1 0 0 0 0 0 1 1	1 1 0 0 0 0 1 1	0 0 1 1
MEMORY WORD #5	0 0 0 0 0 0 0 0 1 0 0 0 0 1 0 0	1 1 1 0 0 1 1 1	0 1 0 0
MEMORY WORD #6	0 0 0 0 0 0 0 0 1 0 0 0 0 1 0 1	0 1 0 1 0 1 0 1	0 1 0 1

The sequence of operations that the microprocessor must perform is stored in the program memory.

The memory is also used to store or remember the instructions or sequence of operations the processor is to perform. Such a memory is called a program memory. The instructions also are coded with "1's" and "0's". The sequence of instructions, stored in order one word after another as shown in *Figure 2-2*, is called the computer program.

Input and Output

Input and output blocks allow the computer to interact with the outside world. The input allows data to be brought into the chip and the output allows the computer's decisions to control a device or to be displayed via a terminal.

Every system must have input and output blocks to provide the sensing, action, and communications functions for the computer. The sense input elements keep track of the system conditions such as temperature, pressure, light levels, and so on. This is similar to the way our human senses of seeing, hearing, smelling, tasting, and feeling make us aware of the conditions around us. The output action elements enable the microcomputer to turn on or off power units such as motors, relays, lights, and so on, much like our brain can control our muscles to do work for us. The communications inputs allow human operators to send information or instructions to the computer using typewriter keyboards, calculator-like keyboards, position controls, telephones, and so on. These devices are much like our ears and eyes, since we use these organs to receive speech and to read printed characters. The communications outputs allow the computer to send information to human operators through character displays or typewriters. These devices are similar to our speech, writing and printing capabilities used for sending information to others.

HOW DO THESE BUILDING BLOCKS WORK TOGETHER?

Microprocessor instructions, like a cake recipe, must be followed in every detail, and in the exact sequence, for the desired end to occur.

The individual function of each block is evident from its name: memory remembers, inputs and outputs communicate with the outside external world, and the microprocessor processes information and controls the operation of the entire system. How these functions work together to achieve their assigned tasks is not so evident. The way the blocks work together can be seen better by looking at the way we do our jobs. We, as humans, act as a computer in many of our activities. We are given a list of instructions in the form of a recipe and get the cake baked by following the recipe instructions step-by-step. We are given a list of jobs that must be done and get the jobs done by doing each in proper order. We behave exactly like a microprocessor behaves in a microcomputer, following each instruction and doing each job a step at a time.

An Example Program

Before making a recipe, we must read the recipe and understand what is to be done. Likewise, the computer performs initial operations to learn what it is to do.

Let's take as an example the situation we have when we are trying to follow the instructions in a recipe. Assume we are trying to make chocolate fudge from a recipe of the type shown in *Figure 2-3*. This recipe is a list of instructions that we must follow exactly if the fudge is to be successful. The list of instructions has been saved or stored on a piece of paper. Some recipes are saved in the memory of some cook somewhere, but this one is available to us in written form. This is similar to the use of the memory in a computer. In the computer, the list of instructions, the program, is stored in solid-state devices as a pattern of digital bits of information. Just as the written instructions on paper are meaningful to us, the digital form of instructions is meaningful to the processor of the computer. In either case, the program or plan of operation is saved and ready to be executed. In the case of the recipe, we must execute the instructions in the order listed without making any mistakes if we are to produce fudge and not mud. Similarly, the processor must execute the instructions in the order they are listed in the computer memory if the computer is to behave as it was intended. Failure to execute the instructions in the proper order and without error could cause an automatic lawn mowing machine to become a berserk public menace or a furnace control system to become a device that burns down the house.

**Figure 2-3.
Chocolate Fudge
Program**

1. Get a mixing bowl.
2. Get 5 pounds of granulated sugar.
3. Get two 8-ounce cans of evaporated milk.
4. Get 12-ounce jar of white corn syrup.
5. Get 1 package of pecans.
6. Get 1 package of chocolate chips.
7. Get 1 stick of butter.
8. Get 2-ounce bottle of vanilla extract.
9. Measure 2½ cups of sugar into the mixing bowl.
10. Measure ¾ cup evaporated milk into the mixing bowl.
11. Measure ⅓ cup white corn syrup into the mixing bowl.
12. Measure 2 tablespoons butter into the mixing bowl.
13. Get a separate container.
14. Measure 1 cup of nuts and 12 ounces of chocolate chips into the separate container and set aside for later use.
15. Mix all ingredients except nuts and chips together in the mixing bowl.
16. Pour this mixture into a pan and bring to a boil.
17. Boil for exactly 5 minutes. Slowly stir mixture as it boils.
18. Remove from heat and stir in one teaspoon of vanilla extract.
19. Stir in nuts and chips (from Step 14) until chips are melted.
20. Pour fudge into buttered pan.

Getting Started

Since we have the program of instructions stored in some suitable form (on paper or in the computer memory), we must read and interpret (decode) the first instruction in the program. In the case of the recipe we actually read the instruction with our eyes and find out its meaning with our brain. The processor in a computer does the same thing by bringing (transferring) the instruction code (in the form of a group of digital signals or bits) into the processor and using the digital electronic circuits inside of the processor to decide what operations the instruction wants done. In the recipe, we see that once we have gotten together the supply of goods that we need, the first thing we must do is measure 2 1/2 cups of sugar into a mixing bowl. Once we do this, we go down to the next instruction, which is to measure 3/4 cup of evaporated milk into the bowl. These types of operations continue until all of the basic ingredients are combined and the result placed into a pan for cooking. Up to this point, most of our activities have been in the form of inputs and initializing the components of our cooking system. The computer usually goes through these types of operations early in the operation of the machine. It steps through instructions that tell it to receive inputs which are digital code commands or which set up system switch conditions that tell the system where to start, when to stop, the limits of memory, etc. Also, it will save needed numbers in some memory locations and clear others, just as certain quantities of specified ingredients were measured into the 'storage locations' of the mixing bowl and, after everything was combined, poured from the bowl into the cooking pan.

Setting Aside Results for Later Use

When following a recipe, some of the ingredients must be mixed and temporarily stored. Likewise, the computer memory temporarily stores data (called "writing into memory") and retrieves it when needed.

The act of measuring the nuts and chips and setting them aside for later use is similar to the way computers save (store) numbers or characters in memory that are important to the operation of the computer. Just as a file cabinet can be used to save important letters for us, part of the computer memory can be used to save information important to the computer. Of course, we must be careful not to save this information in the same cells of the memory as the ones saving our program, for we would lose the program. A memory cell only has room for one piece of information at a time. The act of saving (storing) such information in memory is called "writing into memory." This operation is done by having the processor do an instruction that will bring (transfer) information from the processor to a selected location in memory. In like fashion, "write to output No. 3" causes the processor to perform an output instruction which transfers information and control signals from inside the processor to an output device Number 3. Both operations are similar to the way we use notepads to jot down telephone numbers or other messages that we need to save for later reference.

Doing the Work

Once our system has been set to start at the proper state, the processor starts following instructions that actually begin performing action or work to produce the desired end result. In the case of the recipe we are instructed to boil the mixture in the pan for exactly 5 minutes stirring it so it doesn't burn. Instructions that the processor might be receiving and doing that are comparable could be: perform addition or subtraction of two numbers, turn on some heater element, measure some temperature, decide that a switch should be closed, and so on. In fact, we could program the computer to do any or all of the operations in our recipe, in which case it would turn on the heat to the pan, regulate the heat as it checked the temperature of the mixture in the pan, and boil the mixture for five minutes. After it finished this sequence of operations, it would go to the next instruction, read it from memory, and execute it. The next instruction the cook reads from the recipe is to remove the pan from the heat and stir in one teaspoon of vanilla. If the cook continues to read and do these instructions in order and without error, excellent fudge will result. If the processor continues to read instructions from the proper places in the computer memory and interpret and execute them without error, a perfectly operating machine will result.

Delivering the Results

Notice in the recipe, the last instruction is an output operation. We output the product to a buttered pan for use by the outside world. This type of operation must also be performed by the processor if the computer is to do useful work for us. Thus, some of the last instructions in a program sequence will be output instructions. For example, it might print out what it has done so that humans can understand the result. It might control some motor, or switch, or light located outside the computer.

Summary

The basic microprocessor operations for each instruction are:
1. address location,
2. fetch instructions from memory,
3. interpret the instruction and
4. perform the instruction.

This example has served to illustrate the basic relationships between the functional blocks of the computer. Just as we work down through a list of instructions saved in written form on a piece of paper, the processor goes down step-by-step through a sequence of instructions saved in computer memory, doing each instruction in order. The processor must do the following things for each new instruction:

- It must locate (address) the instruction in memory.
- It must read (fetch) the instruction from memory, i.e. it must bring (transfer) the instruction from memory to inside the processor.
- It must interpret the instruction to understand (decide) what must be done.
- It must then do the operations required by the instruction (act) to actually execute the instruction.

These activities of locate, read, interpret and execute the instruction are repeated for each instruction in sequence throughout the program. These activities are exactly what we do when we follow a list of instructions to do a job.

Throughout this discussion of the operation of processors and computers we have used the action of humans as an example. We will return to this tool later in the book in an exercise that is designed to further show the operation of the various functional blocks of the computer. In the meantime, let's turn our attention to how these blocks communicate with each other.

HOW IS THIS INFORMATION TRANSFERRED IN MICROCOMPUTERS?

Each bit in a digital signal has either a one or zero value.

Since the microcomputer is a digital system, the information within the system must be in digital form, that is, in binary form. Binary signals are signals that can have only one of two values, on or off, present or not present, a 1 or a 0, true or false, etc. These abstract concepts are provided physical meaning by assigning one voltage or current value to be a 1 signal and another value to be or represent a 0 signal.

Single Digital Signals

Since a single binary signal can exist in only two states, several simultaneous binary signals are needed to provide a greater number of combinations. Each combination could represent a command, a number or letter.

A digital signal, shown in *Figure 2-4a*, changes from the 0 level to the 1 level and back as time passes. In *Figure 2-4b*, the 1 level is represented by a +5 volt value and the 0 level by 0 volt value. In *Figure 2-4c* this is done with a switch. Each second the switch position is changed. Note that the 1 level is a more positive voltage than the 0 level. This is a common approach to assigning the 0 and 1 levels and is called positive logic. This is the approach we will use throughout this book. Thus, all of our digital signals will be of the form of those shown in *Figure 2-4*. These signals will be carried on electrical conductors called wires from one part of the system to another. By measuring (sensing) the signal level on these wires at the proper times, the system parts can determine which is being sent, a 1 or a 0.

Figure 2-4.
**Digital Signals Changing
between Two Levels with
Time**

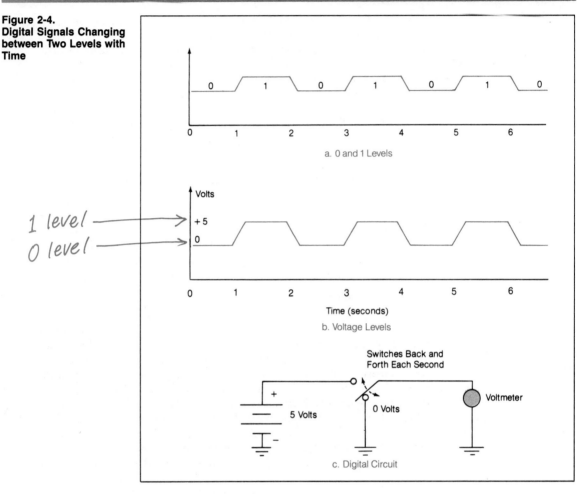

1 level

0 level

a. 0 and 1 Levels

b. Voltage Levels

c. Digital Circuit

Multiple Digital Signals

In a binary code, the more bits available, the greater the number of one and zero combinations possible. Microprocessors usually use 8 or 16 bit wide signals.

While a single digital or binary signal is good for indicating an ON or OFF state or a "yes" or "no" command, it is not enough to represent entire numbers or letters. Several binary signals must be sent at once to transmit this more complicated information. Suppose, for example, that three binary signals are sent along three wires as shown in *Figure 2-5a* and that the voltage on the three wires is measured every second and a record made of the measurements. The record is shown in *Figure 2-5b*. Different combinations of these signals every second have been used to represent the numbers 0 through 7. Since there are 8 different patterns of digital signal combinations, eight different things could be assigned arbitrarily to these eight possibilities. Not only numbers but, as shown in *Figure 2-5b*, the code patterns can be assigned to represent commands or alphabetical characters. In addition, the same given combination of digital signals could mean different things at different times.

Figure 2-5.
Digital Codes for Various
Cases

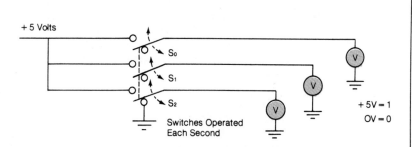

a. Three Binary Digital Signals Sent Along Wires at the Same Time.

TIME (SECS)	BINARY SIGNALS S_2 S_1 S_0	DECIMAL NUMBER EQUIVALENT	OTHER POSSIBLE EQUIVALENCES
1	0 0 0	0	A
2	0 0 1	1	STOP
3	0 1 0	2	GO
4	0 1 1	3	B
5	1 0 0	4	OFF
6	1 0 1	5	ON
7	1 1 0	6	RIGHT
8	1 1 1	7	LEFT
EIGHT DIFFERENT TIMES	EIGHT DIFFERENT SIGNAL PATTERNS	EIGHT DIFFERENT DECIMAL NUMBERS	EIGHT DIFFERENT CHARACTERS OR COMMANDS

b. Using Binary Signals to Represent Numbers, Characters, Commands, or Time

8 Bits

MSB-Most Significant Binary Bit
LSB-Least Significant Binary Bit

MSB							LSB
d_7	d_6	d_5	d_4	d_3	d_2	d_1	d_0
0	1	0	0	1	1	0	0

c. 8-Bit Digital Signal

Figure 2-5b shows that three digital signals (bits) offers only 8 different bit patterns, which is not really enough for use in a computer. In general, if there are N bits, there are 2^N different bit patterns of 0 and 1 combinations for these bits. In present day microprocessors, 4-bit, 8-bit, and 16-bit digital signals are used. Eight different digital signals can exhibit 256 different bit patterns and 16 bits of digital information can exhibit 65,536 different bit patterns. As shown in *Figure 2-2*, a 4-bit group is usually called a nibble, an 8-bit group of signals is usually called a byte; a 16-bit group is usually called a word. Microprocessors typically use 8-bit and 16-bit digital signals to transfer information to and from the other subsystem functional blocks of the computer.

WHAT DO DIGITAL SIGNALS MEAN TO THE COMPUTER?

Digital signals may be encoded to represent whatever is required for microcomputer operation. They could represent memory locations, date, time limits, instructions, etc.

Digital signals can mean different things to different subsystem functional blocks. Generally, a given pattern of digital signals is assigned to represent a given number, alphabetical character, or a command or instruction. When the patterns of 0's and 1's represent numbers, further definition is required to tell what the number means. The number can mean a subsystem location or a memory address in the computer; it can represent a quantity to be used in some arithmetic operation, or it can represent a time limit or other system limit that must not be exceeded. In all cases, the pattern of 0's and 1's is a digital code that means a certain thing to a certain functional subsystem. The subsystem must provide the circuitry that will decipher the code and interpret its meaning, just as a spy must interpret coded messages he receives in order to carry out his intended mission. Since codes often are being used to send messages and instructions, let's first look at this application of the digital signals within a computer.

Instruction Codes

The microprocessor responds to a series of command words in binary coded form. Each command has a mnemonic to help the programmer in developing the program.

The 8-bit digital code of *Figure 2-5c*, 01001100, could represent an instruction. Suppose it is the instruction to add one to a number stored at a known memory location. Since one is added each time, a series of numbers will be generated, each greater than the other by one. In other words, the system is counting by ones. The instruction INCREMENT means the same thing so it is the shortened code word to add one to a number. Thus, the instruction INCREMENT A will add one to a number at location A. A is some storage location inside the processor or in memory. Usually the description of the instruction is shortened to simply INC A to make it easier to write the instruction. While this shorthand code of INC A might be easy for us to recognize, it would not be understood by the microprocessor, which is a digital device and can only understand digital signals. Thus, the digital code 01001100 is used to tell the processor that it is to increment the number stored at location A. The digital circuits inside the processor then sense and decode this pattern of 0's and 1's to decide that it is the instruction INC and proceed to do the desired INCREMENT operation by adding one to the number at location A. Thus, the 01001100 is a machine or processor code, or a code that the digital circuits inside the processor can understand. The shorthand code INC A is a human oriented code (called an instruction mnemonic or abbreviation) that humans can understand. Of course, the machine code 01001100 will mean different things to different processors. Some processors won't even have a device at location A inside of them. To help anyone work with a given processor, the processor data sheet includes a complete table that relates each machine code pattern of 0's and 1's to the corresponding instruction mnemonic or abbreviation for the total set of instructions.

The instruction codes are stored in the computer memory in the order selected by the programmer. Each one is given a separate address.

Usually both the pattern of 0's and 1's and the instruction descriptions are presented in abbreviated form, but one can still see how the digital signal patterns for a given processor have been assigned to represent all of the instructions it is capable of performing.

Different codes then mean different instructions. These instruction codes are what are stored in the computer memory in the order they are to be read (fetched), interpreted (decoded), and executed (acted on) by the processor. This is the program the processor follows. A small segment of a program with instructions and codes is shown in *Figure 2-6*. After the first instruction is sensed, decided on, and acted on, the steps are repeated for the next instruction. The processor must then locate the instruction code within the memory that is to be read next and bring that code inside the processor for the decoding operations. As assigned in *Figure 2-6*, the first instruction is at memory word location #1, the second at memory word location #2, and so forth in sequence in the memory for the length of the program. Again, since the processor is a digital device, it must locate the instruction in memory by sending digital signals to the memory to identify which instruction it wants next. The process of locating the instruction is called addressing and the digital code that represents the location of the instruction in memory is called the address of the instruction.

**Figure 2-6.
Instructions and Their
Digital Codes in
Sequence in a Portion
of a Program**

INSTRUCTION LOCATION	INSTRUCTION	CODE
MEMORY WORD #1	LOAD REFERENCE REGISTER	0000 0010 1110 0000
MEMORY WORD #2	LOAD REGISTER 0	0000 0010 0000 0000
MEMORY WORD #3	LOAD REGISTER 1	0000 0010 0000 0001
MEMORY WORD #4	LOAD REGISTER 2	0000 0010 0000 0010
MEMORY WORD #5	DECREMENT REGISTER 0	0000 0110 0000 0000

Address Codes to Indicate Memory Locations

The address in a computer's memory is similar to a street address. When the address is represented by a 16 bit code, over 64,000 separate addresses can be produced.

The concept of an address is not new to us. We each have a street address or a post office box number where mail can be sent to us. That address is our location in the postal system. Our street address is our location on earth. Similarly, the address of a memory location in a computer is the code that represents where in the computer that memory location can be found. Typically, the address code in microprocessors consists of 16 bits which can exhibit 65,536 different combinations of 1's and 0's. Thus, such an address code can directly distinguish one of 65,536 memory locations. To illustrate how the address code is recognized, think of the part of memory that contains the program or list of instructions as a residential street as shown in *Figure 2-7*. The address in memory of a given instruction is represented by a particular combination of 1's and 0's in the address code. The memory device must be able to sense and decide which address the code represents so that it will know which instruction is being asked for by the processor. This deciding or decoding process is similar to the way a postman determines a house location by correctly figuring out the street address. Let's look at *Figure 2-7*. A package is to be picked up from 1000 Instruction Avenue in a city. First the street is located, Instruction Avenue, then locations along the street are checked until the 1000 address is found. Similarly, if the information stored in location 1000 in memory is to be read, an address code that represents location 1000 must be sent to memory. The memory must have the digital circuitry to sense and decide on the address code and send back the digital bits that are stored at location 1000 to the processor.

**Figure 2-7.
Instruction Location -
Street Address Analog**

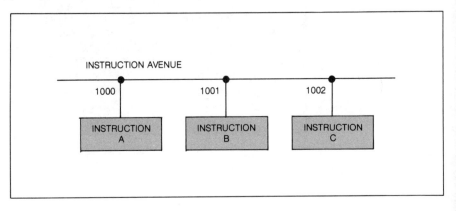

The microprocessor sends an instruction over the address bus to fetch the code located at a certain memory location.

The procedure that is used in reading or "fetching" an instruction from memory is illustrated in *Figure 2-8*. The microprocessor sends out the 16-bit binary pattern of 1's and 0's that represents decimal location 1000 to the memory (a straight binary code for this would be 0000 0011 1110 1000, as shown). At the same time, it sends out a control digital signal to turn on the memory so that the memory will read and transfer to the processor the digital bits for the coded number in the bit cells of the word at the memory location. As indicated in *Figure 2-8*, this control signal is a 1 if the memory is to read the contents of the addressed word. The memory address decoder is the digital circuitry that interprets the address code and sends back the stored information. In the case shown in *Figure 2-8*, the memory word contains an instruction which has the 16-bit code, 0000 0010 0000 0010. Once the instruction code is inside the processor, the address code and the memory will be turned off.

Sixteen parallel lines interconnect memory and microprocessor, because the codes used are 16 bits wide.

You must understand that the single lines going from microprocessor to memory and back are really cables of 16 wires, each carrying one of the bits of the code. That's why they are called buses — address bus and instruction or data bus. As shown in *Figures 2-1*, *2-8*, and *2-9*, buses that have a large number of wires are indicated on a diagram with a broad arrow rather than just a line, usually with the number of bits shown within or near the bus.

**Figure 2-8.
Instruction Fetch
Operation**

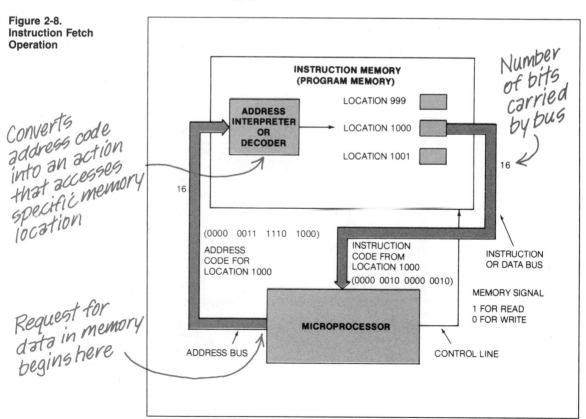

Converts address code into an action that accesses specific memory location

Number of bits carried by bus

Request for data in memory begins here

Address codes are also used to locate which memory location is to be used to save information until the processor is ready to use it. The latter is called "writing into memory" and the addressing and sensing of the address code are the same as for reading from memory. However, now the digital code is to be stored in the memory word that has been addressed. Therefore, the code is sent to the memory from the microprocessor rather than from memory to the microprocessor. The memory knows it is going to receive a code to be stored because the control line is now a zero to put the memory in the "write" state.

Address Codes to Indicate Input or Output Locations

Inputs or outputs may be given addresses just like memory locations. An address code decoder interprets the address and initiates control signals to activiate the proper location.

Addressing or locating a given input device is illustrated in *Figure 2-9*. Let's suppose the microprocessor receives the following instruction: "Bring in information from input device number 10." It might have an abbreviation of IN #10. The microprocessor decodes the instruction and acts on it by sending out to the input functional blocks an address code for location 10 over the address bus. At the same time, as shown in *Figure 2-9*, it will send out a 1 signal on the control line to turn on the input units. Inside the input subsystem is an address code decoder, just as in the memory blocks. This circuitry will sense and decide that the address code is requesting the information from input device 10. The input information, 1111 0000 1111 0000 in the example of *Figure 2-9*, will then be sent (transferred) from input device 10 into the processor. Once the processor has received the information, the address code and input-on signals will be removed by the processor, turning the input blocks off. This will complete the execution of the INPUT LOCATION 10 instruction. Notice that within the instruction, the *sense*, *decide*, and *act* functions occur in a set sequence.

**Figure 2-9.
Input Instruction
Operation**

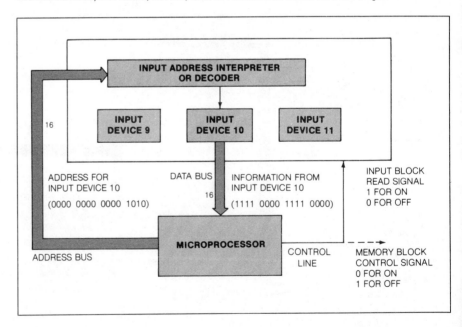

A similar sequence of events would occur on an output instruction except the input-on signal would be replaced with an output-on signal. In all of these cases, the address code is used to specify which location in the computer is to be involved in a transfer of information to and from the processor. In many cases for input and output, another memory control line is involved shown dotted in *Figure 2-9*. When this control line is a 0 the memory is ON. When it is 1 memory is OFF. The use of this control line allows the same address bus to be used for both memory and the input functional block. If the control line is a 1, the input block is ON, memory is OFF and the address code on the address bus will be sensed, decided upon, and acted on by the input block. The reverse occurs if the control line is a 0 – input is OFF, memory is ON and the address locates information in memory.

Number and Character Data Codes

The microprocessor is at the hub of data transfer, data manipulation, and data control.

If the information transferred to a processor is not an instruction code, it will be a set of digital signals that represents either a number, an alphabetical character, or the on-off status of some aspect of the computer system. All of these types of information are called data. As shown in *Figure 2-10*, there are a number of paths for the transfer of data. Data is transferred *to* the processor from the input or from memory, or *from* the processor to an output device or to a memory location for storage.

**Figure 2-10.
Typical Data Paths
Within a Microcomputer**

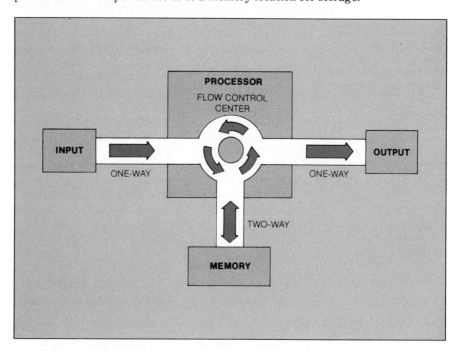

The accuracy of computer calculations is directly related to the number of bits in word size, just as the accuracy of a decimal number is determined by the number of digits available.

When digital codes represent numbers, the more bits in the code, the more accurate the arithmetic. With three bits, only one of 8 different numbers can be used; while with 16 bits, 65,536 different numbers can be used. The three-bit signals would be suitable only for very rough numerical information, while the 16 bit group would be accurate enough for many tasks, such as checkbook balancing or simple arithmetic operations. If more accuracy is necessary, as might be required for scientific calculator type applications, digital signals with more bits are used to represent the numbers. For example, the 17 bit code in *Figure 2-11* would provide 6 place decimal accuracy or 1 part in 131,072 parts. By adding one more bit to a 16-bit code, the accuracy is doubled.

**Figure 2-11.
Some Typical Number Codes**

Binary Code	Decimal Equivalent
0000 0000 0000 0000	0
0000 0000 1000 0000	128
0001 0100 0100 0010	5186
1111 1111 1111 1111	65535
1 1111 1111 1111 1111	131071

The American Standard Code for Information Interchange (ASCII) uses a 7-bit code to represent each letter and character.

The digital signals that represent characters, are generally one of the standard codes that are available. One such code is the ASCII code (American Standard Code for Information Interchange) which uses a seven-bit code to cover the upper and lower case characters of the English alphabet, as well as the common typewriter key symbols and operations. To store or transfer entire sentences or paragraphs of such information, long strings of such 7-bit codes are used and contain all the information needed to send or receive. In microprocessor systems, as shown in *Figure 2-12*, 8-bit bytes are used to handle this seven-bit code. The ASCII code is listed on pg. 2-27 in a table that identifies which character has been assigned to a given pattern of seven 1's and 0's. Other codes or assignments could be used but this is the most common one.

**Figure 2-12.
Example Use of the ASCII Code**

CHARACTER	BINARY CODE
S	0101 0011
T	0101 0100
O	0100 1111
P	0101 0000

STOP can be sent as 0101 0011 0101 0100 0100 1111 0101 0000

HOW DOES THE COMPUTER CONTROL THESE DIGITAL SIGNALS?

Clocks and Other Timing Signals

A timing device, called a clock, precisely synchronizes the transfer, manipulation, and storage functions of the microprocessor.

We'll look at how the microprocessor system uses these signals, but before we do, let's clarify one additional requirement of the functional blocks of such systems. They must be timed (synchronized) to work together. What does this mean? To assure accurate transfer of data and proper operation, digital electronic circuits must have signals present and signals must change at specific points in time. *Figure 2-13* illustrates the idea. The digital circuit, shown in a, is a register. It can store 1 or 0 levels on its outputs to provide a temporary storage place for the digital codes as they are moved from one place to another in the microprocessor system. This is a 4-bit register. It is made up of digital circuits called clocked "flip-flops" (They will be discussed later in more detail) which have a very important property. The outputs will not change until the clock signal is applied. For example, in *Figure 2-13b*, inputs 1, 2, 3 and 4 have the following digital code on their lines at time zero on the time scale: 1,1,1,0 respectively. They have these same values when the clock signal arrives at time period one on the time scale. At time period zero, the output code is 0,0,0,0 on the respective outputs 1, 2, 3 and 4. At time period one, triggered by the clock signal, the output code changes to 1,1,1,0 the same as the inputs. Note, however, no change occurred until the clock signal triggered it.

Figure 2-13.
System Timing

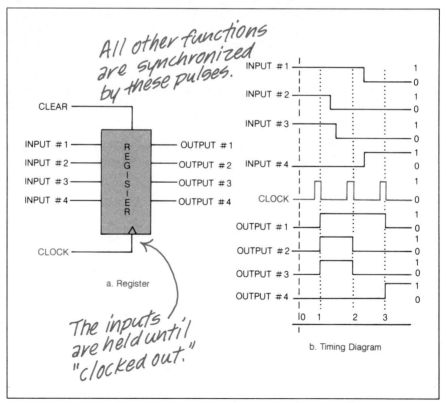

a. Register

b. Timing Diagram

Now look at time period 2, the input code is now 1,0,0,0. The output code does not change to 1,0,0,0 until the clock triggers it, even though the input lines changed at different times between period 1 and period 2. Further changes in the input cause a code of 0,0,0,1 at the outputs triggered by the clock signal at time period 3.

Note that the clock signal occurs at a regular time period. That's why it is called a clock. It keeps the system time and all events are made to happen at the time when the clock signal appears. Just like the register changes its outputs at the clock signal, control line signals, address codes, input data, output action in the other functional blocks of the system do not occur until a clock signal appears. Thus, in the following discussions on how the microprocessor system uses the digital codes, the operational steps are occuring in a timed sequence.

Signal Flow in a Microcomputer

The microcomputer sends out timing and control signals to regulate the flow of data words and address codes between the functional blocks.

Figures 2-8 and *2-9* show that the microcomputer functional blocks get their addresses from the microprocessor. In a time sequence like the one just talked about, the microprocessor sends out timing signal information turning on or off the functional blocks that need to send back signals in response to the address code. One time the microprocessor will receive an instruction code, another time, a data code from memory, or another time a data code from the input block. At other times the microprocessor will send data out to other functional blocks rather than receiving it. In order to provide these information transfers within the microcomputer, the signal paths must be connected between the functional blocks as shown in *Figure 2-14*. Pins that carry the address signals coming out of the microprocessor must be connected to the pins of the memory that receive the address signals and to the connecting pins for the address lines of the input/output digital circuits. (Remember all of these will be integrated circuits.) The timing signal lines coming out of the microprocessor must be connected to the timing signal lines of the other functional blocks. The control signal lines must be connected to the on-off and read-write control lines of the memory and, as required, to the input/output units in the system. The data code and instruction code signal lines must be connected between input/output, memory and microprocessor.

**Figure 2-14.
Signal Flow in a
Computer**

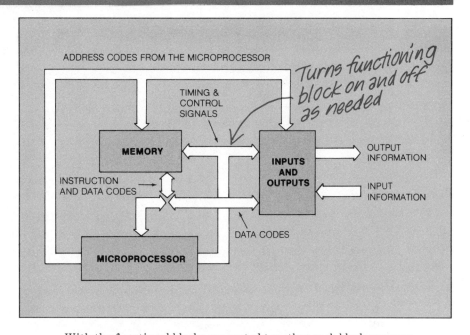

Turns functioning block on and off as needed

The microcomputer input-output blocks send and receive information to the microprocessor and may store information temporarily. The memory block holds information for longer periods of time.

With the functional blocks connected together each block can now be looked at in more detail. The use of the signals in the input, output, and memory blocks is fairly straight forward as shown in *Figures 2-15, 2-16* and *2-17*. They receive addresses and timing and control signals from the microprocessor. They may receive or send information to the processor, depending on what the processor tells them to do. The memory block is for storing information for relatively long periods of time. It may be read from or written to. The other blocks also have storage circuits, but ones that only hold or store information temporarily. For the ones with address lines, each must contain circuits that will determine when it has been addressed by the microprocessor and if its storage circuits can be read from or written into. The latter occurs at the time set by the control signals being sent by the microprocessor.

**Figure 2-15.
Signal Flow at the Input
Block**

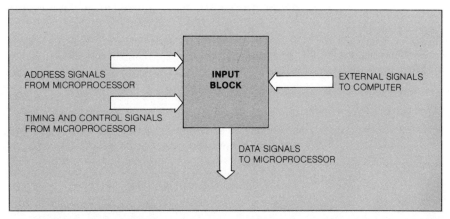

**Figure 2-16.
Signal Flow at the
Output Block**

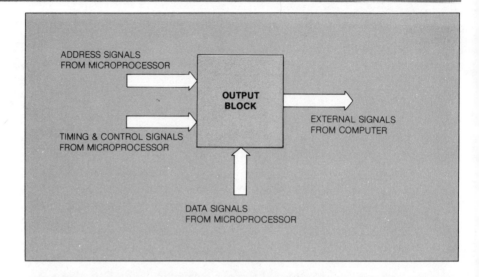

**Figure 2-17.
Signal Flow at the
Memory Block**

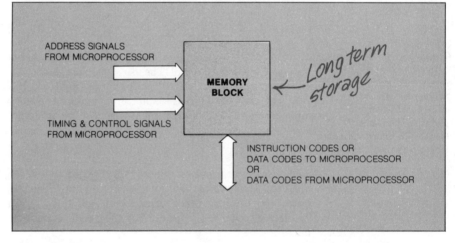

HOW DOES THE MICROPROCESSOR USE THESE DIGITAL SIGNALS?

The microprocessor gener-
ates address timing and
control signals and senses
and decodes instructions.

    The units around the microprocessor have been discussed. Now let's
look inside the microprocessor. It's more complicated than the other blocks.
The addresses and timing and control signals, sent out to the other
functional blocks, are generated by circuits in the microprocessor. In
addition, it has circuits to sense instructions, decide on which instruction it
is (decode), and action circuits that cause appropriate events to occur in
order to execute the instruction. If the microprocessor is not receiving
instruction codes, then it is receiving or sending data codes between
memory and input and output units. All of these are synchronized (kept in
time) by the timing and control signals. How does the microprocessor do all
of this? This can best be understood by looking at each activity in detail in
terms of the microprocessor's internal functional blocks.

Address Circuits

Whenever memory is accessed or data is transferred, the microprocessor sends out an address. The block which holds the address to find the next instruction is called the program counter.

Depending on whether the microprocessor is fetching an instruction from memory or is transferring data to or from the other functional blocks or from memory, the internal circuitry of the processor must generate either an instruction address or a data address. Let's look at *Figure 2-18*. The functional block which contains and sends out the memory address which locates the next instruction is called the *program counter*. It is a temporary storage register whose contents can be incremented (changed by adding one to the value) so that the addresses of successive instructions (next in order) in memory can be generated.

**Figure 2-18.
Address Circuits Inside
Microprocessor**

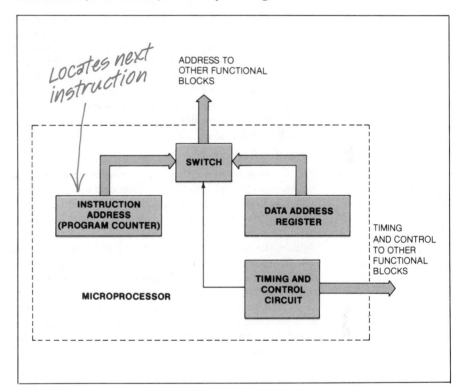

The microprocessor keeps track of the address of the data it must use in executing an instruction. The address is stored in the data address register.

Usually data must be used by the processor when executing an instruction. This data must be located by an address either in memory or from an input. The microprocessor must keep track of this data address. Such a data address may come into the processor as part of the instruction or it may have been saved from an earlier instruction. The functional block shown in *Figure 2-18* that saves the data address is called a *data address register*. As discussed previously, the term register means a storage device that can save a certain number of digital bits. In many microprocessors, the address register and the program counter provide 16-bits of storage, since these microprocessors use 16 address lines to select one of 65,536 different memory locations.

The timing and control circuit, which is regulated by the clock, is the control and coordination of the address circuitry. The instruction address or the data address is put on the address bus at the appropriate time and in the appropriate sequence to execute an instruction.

Either the program counter or the data address register may provide the signals that will be placed on the address lines. Therefore, as shown in *Figure 2-18*, the processor must provide a switch that can select which of these two addresses will be sent to the other functional blocks. This switch is controlled by the timing circuitry *(Figure 2-18)* inside the microprocessor. Thus, if the processor is about to fetch the next instruction from memory, the timing circuit will switch the contents of the program counter onto the address lines. If the processor is about to send data to memory or an output device, the timing circuit will switch the data address registers with the appropriate address onto the address lines. At the same time the timing circuit will output the correct memory or input/output control signal to turn on the functional block involved in the transfer. The instruction that the processor is doing may require a number of steps to complete. Some of these steps require data from one of the various sources. The timing circuit thus is switching the source of the address on the address lines from program counter to data address register in the correct sequence the processor requires. After an instruction has been executed, the timing circuit will add one (increment) to the program counter so that it now contains the memory address of the next instruction to be executed. All of this is handled automatically by the components inside the processor.

Instruction Decoder Circuits

The microprocessor stores the fetched instruction code in the instruction register. The decoder deciphers the code, and causes the timing circuits to produce the sequential signals to perform the required events.

Once an instruction has been transferred from memory to inside the processor, the processor must provide a storage device that will save the instruction code so it can be decoded or interpreted by the decoder. Another register is used, in this case, as shown in *Figure 2-19*, it is called an *instruction register*. With the instruction code saved in the instruction register, the decoder circuit decides which instruction is called for by the code. The decoding circuit does the same decoding operation for the instruction code that the address decoder does for the address code in the memory and input/output blocks. However, as shown in *Figure 2-19*, there is a difference between the two. The output of the instruction decoder must cause the timing circuits to produce signals in a required step-by-step sequence to execute the instruction. Depending on the instruction, this can be a very complicated sequence. However, again, this is all handled automatically by the microprocessor.

**Figure 2-19.
Instruction Fetch
Operation**

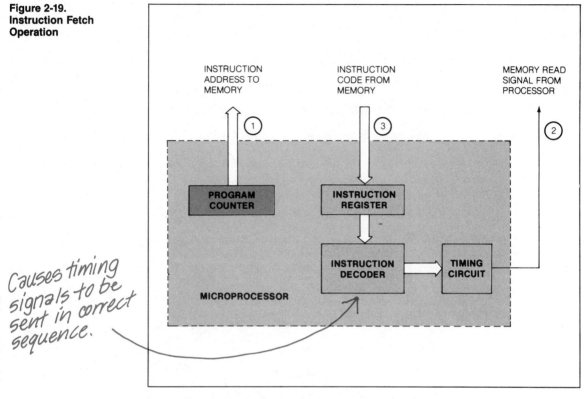

Causes timing signals to be sent in correct sequence.

Arithmetic-Logic Circuits

The arithmetic logic unit (ALU) provides the logic, computation, and decision-making function.

If the processor is to be able to do more than just transfer information around the computer, it must have circuits that will perform arithmetic and logic operations. This group of circuits is called the arithmetic-logic unit or ALU. They are shown in *Figure 2-20*. It provides the logical, computational, and decision-making capabilities of the microprocessor that make it such a powerful digital system element. Typically, the ALU provides addition, subtraction, and the basic logical operations. Some ALU's even provide multiplication and division; if they do not, then these functions are done by successive addition or subtraction under control of a step-by-step sequence. Logic circuits such as AND, OR, NOT will be discussed more later, but for now these circuits allow the processor to make decisions such as greater than, less than, equal to, positive, negative, etc. Data is brought from memory or from input/output units. The ALU has storage devices (again, registers) that provide temporary storage for the often used data. It is to and from these internal data registers that information flows from the other functional blocks within the computer.

**Figure 2-20.
Arithmetic Logic Unit
Features**

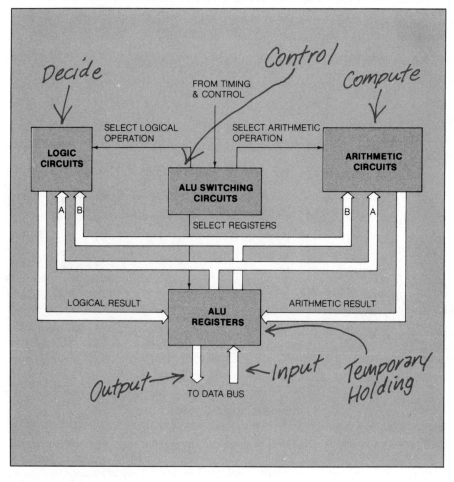

The Overall Structure

To fetch instructions from memory, the program counter sends its address to memory, along with a read signal, thus enabling the memory to put the coded instruction on the data bus.

Now that the individual parts have been examined, let's piece them together into the internal structure of the microprocessor and show how the microprocessor works as a complete unit to perform its job of fetching, interpreting, and executing instructions. First consider the activity of obtaining an instruction from memory, in terms of *Figure 2-19:*

Step 1) The program counter contains the address of the instruction to be executed, so this address is sent to memory.

Step 2) In timed sequence, the timing circuit generates a memory read signal.

Step 3) The instruction code comes from the memory block over the data bus and is stored in the instruction register.

The instruction decoder interprets the instruction code and tells the timing circuits what instruction is to be executed. The timing circuits then generate the needed sequence of operations.

**Figure 2-21.
Input Instruction
Operation**

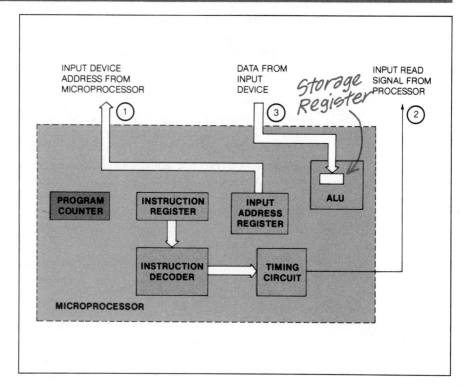

To transfer data from an input or output device to or from the microprocessor, the address of the input/output device is placed on the address bus, along with an input Read or output Write signal.

If the instruction is to transfer data from an input device to the microprocessor, the events of *Figure 2-21* would occur in the following sequence:

Step 1) The address of the input device is obtained from the instruction code and is sent out on the address lines.

Step 2) The timing circuits generate an input read signal.

Step 3) The data comes into the microprocessor and is stored in one of the registers inside the ALU portion of the processor.

Similarly, if the instruction is to transfer data from an ALU register to an output device, the output address would be sent out on the address lines and the timing circuit would generate an output write signal as shown in *Figure 2-22*. At the same time, the data in the ALU register would be placed on the data lines. This would cause the data to be stored in the appropriate output device.

Sending data to and from memory would be handled in similar ways; the main difference being in the source of the address. In memory operations, the address is obtained from a data address register of the type indicated in *Figure 2-18*.

All of these activities are automatically done by the microprocessor. The designer just makes sure that the addresses and instructions used by the processor are correct and occur in the proper order to cause the system to behave in the desired manner.

WHAT HAVE WE LEARNED?

- Microcomputers behave in much the same way that we do, with the microprocessor providing the master control for the system.

- The microprocessor goes down through the list of instructions stored in memory in the proper order, deciding (decoding) and acting on (executing) each instruction in turn.

- The microprocessor must locate (address) the instruction, cause the instruction to be transferred to inside the processor (fetched), decide which instruction it is (decode or interpret it) and act (execute) on it.

- Information is transferred inside the microcomputer system using digital signals. A given pattern of digital signals (bits) can mean an instruction code, an address code, a number, an alphabetical character, or the status of some part of the system.

- The main components of memory and input/output devices are an address decoder and storage locations.

- The term register is used to describe a storage device that saves a group of digital bits such as an address code, instruction code, or a number/character data code.

**Figure 2-22.
Output Instruction
Operation**

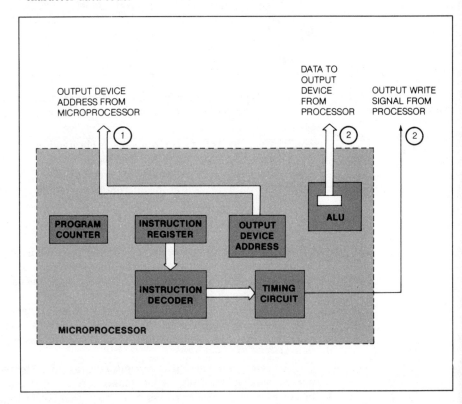

· The main components of the microprocessor are:
  1) The Program Counter
     (The Instruction Address Register),
  2) The Data Address Register
  3) The Instruction Register
  4) The Instruction Decoder
  5) The Timing Circuits
  6) The Arithmetic and Logic Unit.

WHAT'S NEXT?

Now that we are getting an idea of how the various functional blocks in a microcomputer work together to provide a smoothly functioning digital system, we can begin looking at how these devices are built in order to provide these functions. In the next chapter we will go further inside the functional blocks to see how they are designed and manufactured.

The next chapter is designed to promote additional study. It is intended to whet the appetite of the person less familiar with the digital terms that are used and the way digital integrated circuits are made.

"ASCII" (American Standard Code for information Interchange)

BIT POSITIONS:										
7 →				0	0	0	0	1	1	1	1
6 →				0	0	1	1	0	0	1	1
5 →				0	1	0	1	0	1	0	1
4 ↓	3 ↓	2 ↓	1								
0	0	0	0	NUL	DLE	SP	0	@	P	\	P
0	0	0	1	SOH	DC1	!	1	A	Q	a	q
0	0	1	0	STX	DC2	''	2	B	R	b	r
0	0	1	1	ETX	DC3	#	3	C	S	c	s
0	1	0	0	EOT	DC4	$	4	D	T	d	t
0	1	0	1	ENQ	NAK	%	5	E	U	e	u
0	1	1	0	ACK	SYN	&	6	F	V	f	v
0	1	1	1	BEL	ETB	'	7	G	W	g	w
1	0	0	0	BS	CAN	(	8	H	X	h	x
1	0	0	1	HT	EM	)	9	I	Y	i	y
1	0	1	0	LF	SUB	*	:	J	Z	j	z
1	0	1	1	VT	ESC	+	;	K	[	k	{
1	1	0	0	FF	FS	,	<	L	\	l		
1	1	0	1	CR	GS	–	=	M	]	m	}
1	1	1	0	SO	RS	.	>	N	∧	n	~
1	1	1	1	S1	US	/	?	O	—	o	DEL

Quiz for Chapter 2

1. Indicate the order in which
   the microprocessor provides
   the operations on instructions:
   a. Interpret
   b. Fetch
   c. Execute
   d. Address or locate

2. Match the functions shown to
   one of the units from a
   microcomputer
   a. Program Memory
   b. Control Inputs
   c. Data Memory
   d. Control Outputs
   e. Communications Inputs
   f. Communications Outputs
   g. Microprocessor

   A. Store data.
   B. Time and Control System
      Elements.
   C. Store Instructions.
   D. Perform Work.
   E. Monitor external
      conditions.
   F. Receive information from
      operators.
   G. Send information to
      operators.

3. A 14-bit binary signal
   could represent one of ____
   different numbers.
   a. 4096   c. 16384
   b. 8192   d. 32768

4. A 12-bit binary number
   has an accuracy equivalent to
   the decimal fraction:
   a. 1/2048
   b. 1/4096
   c. 1/8192
   d. None of the above

5. The seven bit code 0101 0100 is
   the ASCII code for the letter:
   a. S   c. T
   b. O   d. None of the above

6. Microprocessors examine
   digital input signals:
   a. When they change
   b. All the time
   c. At specific times
      determined by the system
      clock
   d. None of the above

7. A pattern of 0's and 1's could
   represent the following in a
   microcomputer:
   a. An instruction code
   b. A number code
   c. A character code
   d. An address code
   e. Any of the above

8. In a microcomputer,
   data can flow from:
   a. processor to program
      memory
   b. program memory to
      processor
   c. input devices to output
      devices
   d. data memory to and from
      the processor
   e. input devices to processor
   f. processor to output devices
   g. All of the above
   h. a, b, and c above
   i. b, d, e, and f above

9. The program counter of a
   microprocessor contains:
   a. the address of data
   b. the value of the data
   c. the address of an
      instruction
   d. None of the above

How Digital Integrated Circuits Provide the Functions

ABOUT THIS CHAPTER

We now have seen the impact of digital electronics and the key contribution made by integrated circuits – that of providing more and more functions inside a small space at a very reasonable cost. In this chapter, we will learn more about digital integrated circuits. How they are designed and made so that they can provide the basic functions required.

Even though a fair amount of detail is covered, the main purpose of this chapter is to bring into focus the overall concepts of how digital functions are executed using digital integrated circuits. It's not nearly as important to understand the exact values of the resistors and the number of transistors in a particular digital circuit, as it is to come away with the concept of the AND and OR and NOT functions, and that a register is a functional unit that provides temporary storage, and that a decoder selects something as a result of a particular coded input.

The insight into how these basic functions occur will aid a great deal in understanding what a microprocessor does in a microcomputer system.

OVERVIEW

All of the functions performed by a computer are based upon digital codes (made up of 1's and 0's) and are provided by some switching function.

Digital electronic systems send signals made up of 1's and 0's in the form of codes between subsystem parts to accomplish the *sense, decide, store,* and *act* functions of the system. It has been shown that the 1's and 0's of the digital codes can be formed by turning switches on or off. All of these switches can be of the same type. Therefore, one of the advantages of digital electronics is that all components are made up of combinations of simple on-off switches of the same type.

Originally, this basic digital operation was provided by using relays. These are switches that are electrically controlled. These were slow, expensive, and noisy devices. Relays were replaced with faster and less expensive vacuum tubes, operating either ON or OFF. Vacuum tubes were in turn replaced by the very fast, small transistor, also operating as a switch that is either ON or OFF. Using a transistor as a switch in a circuit (called a gate) along with associated components (mainly resistors) had the further advantage that all components could be fabricated at the same time on a small area of silicon material in the form of an integrated circuit. This way of making digital devices offers the ultimate in speed, low cost, and reliability. In this chapter, we will look at how digital integrated circuits are designed and made.

WHAT ARE INTEGRATED CIRCUITS?

In integrated circuits, switching circuits called "gates" provide the switching functions. When combined in unique ways, they provided the various circuit functions required.

Digital electronic circuits are made up of many identical switching circuits called gates. Look at *Figure 3-1*. There are in the order of 12,000 gates on the chip shown. The individual digital gates are made in a space much smaller than the point of a pin or a needle. Therefore, functional blocks such as memory consisting of thousands of such gates can be provided in an area the size of a pinhead, and microprocessors and microcomputers can be made on a chip small enough to fit in the eye of a needle. But all of this is only part of the story of integrated circuits. Let's look in more detail to find out how all this is possible and what it means.

Figure 3-1.
Picture of TMS1000 Chip

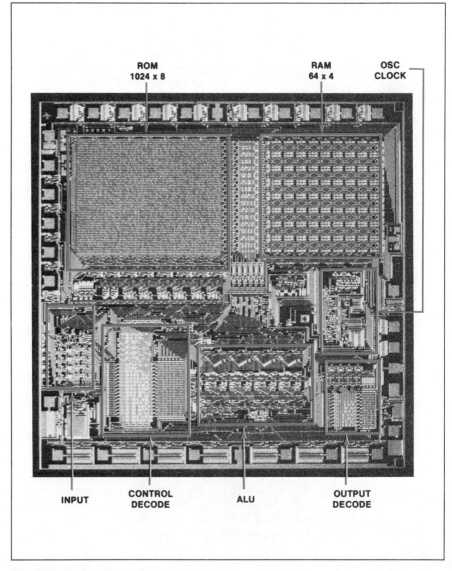

The Overall Process

Integrated circuits are manufactured on silicon slices which have the IC's repeated several hundred times.

The main feature of the overall way (process) of making integrated circuits is that many copies of a given circuit are made at the same time as shown in *Figure 3-2b*. The circuits are made on a round disc *(Figure 3-2a)* of nearly pure crystalline semiconductor material (called a slice) 3 to 4 inches (7.6 to 10.2 cm) in diameter and about one-hundredth of an inch (0.254 mm) thick (about the thickness of five pages of this book). It looks like a round thin piece of gray-blue tinted glass with a highly polished surface on one side. The square or rectangular circuit area is repeated in a regular pattern consisting of many rows and columns to form hundreds of circuits on a single slice as shown in *Figure 3-2b*. By processing many slices at once, thousands of the circuits can be made at the same time. Thus, it costs little more to make thousands of such circuits than it would to make just one. Once these circuits have been formed on the slice, the slice is cut into individual circuit chips about ¼ of an inch (6.35 mm) on a side *(Figure 3-2c)*. Each of these chips is a complex digital component such as a memory, microprocessor, or microcomputer. The one shown in *Figure 3-1* is a complete 4-bit microcomputer. These individual chips are then mounted in a plastic, metal, or a ceramic package *(Figure 3-2d)* so that electrical connection can be made to them through the pins shown on the package of *Figure 3-3*.

**Figure 3-2.
Silicon Slice and Chips**

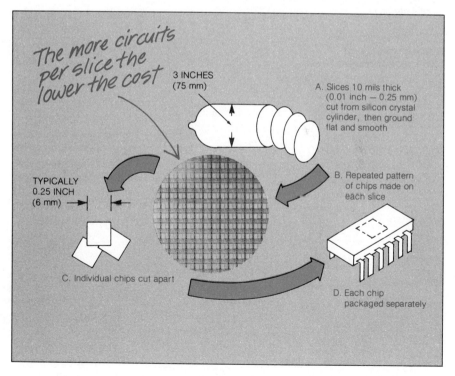

The more circuits per slice the lower the cost

3 INCHES
(75 mm)

A. Slices 10 mils thick
(0.01 inch — 0.25 mm)
cut from silicon crystal
cylinder, then ground
flat and smooth

B. Repeated pattern
of chips made on
each slice

TYPICALLY
0.25 INCH
(6 mm)

C. Individual chips cut apart

D. Each chip
packaged separately

**Figure 3-3.
Picture of 40 Pin
Package**

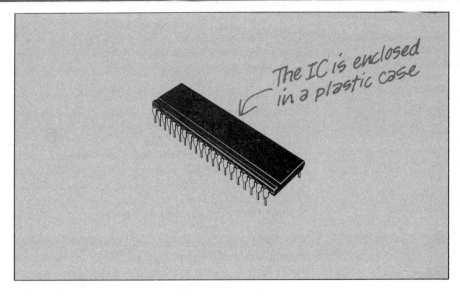

MOS Transistors

The chip contains all the specific digital functions (memory registers, input, output, etc.) which make the microprocessor or microcomputer function.

Let's look further inside the microcomputer chip *(Figure 3-4)*. It consists of digital functions of the types discussed in Chapter 2: memory (program and data), registers, decoders, arithmetic-logic units, and input/output. Each of these functions is made up of thousands of individual transistor switches made from a sandwich consisting of semiconductor material, an insulating layer of glass (silicon oxide) and a coating of metal. This makes a simple MOS (Metal-Oxide-Semiconductor) transistor as shown in cross section in *Figure 3-5*. This transistor consists of a gate input (a metal strip sitting on top of the silicon oxide (glass) which covers the silicon material), source and drain regions, and a substrate. Openings have been made in the oxide surface above the drain and the source regions so that the metal placed on top, which is insulated from the silicon by the oxide layer, can make contact to these areas and electrical current can flow when voltage is applied. The symbol used for this MOS transistor is shown to the right. The substrate material of *Figure 3-5* is the base material of the chip of *Figure 3-2c* and the slice of *Figure 3-2a* that has been cut from the grown crystal. It is one type of silicon (N or P type), the small islands called source and drain regions are of the opposite type. Silicon can be either pure silicon, N-type silicon, or P-type silicon. It is not necessary for us to understand the details of what these different types of silicon are physically. We only have to know that electric current flows easily in a piece of silicon that is all N-type or all P-type, but that electric current cannot flow from an N region to a P region and into another N region. Similarly current cannot flow from a P region into an N region and into another P region.

Figure 3-4.
TMS1000 Chip Showing
Functional Areas

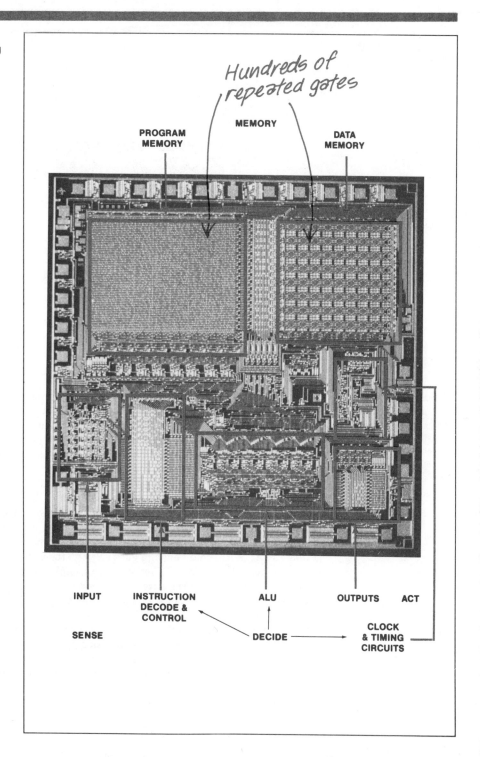

Hundreds of repeated gates

MEMORY

PROGRAM
MEMORY

DATA
MEMORY

INPUT   INSTRUCTION   ALU   OUTPUTS   ACT
             DECODE &
             CONTROL
                                                      CLOCK
SENSE   DECIDE   & TIMING
                                                      CIRCUITS

**Figure 3-5.
Cross-Section of MOS
Transistor**

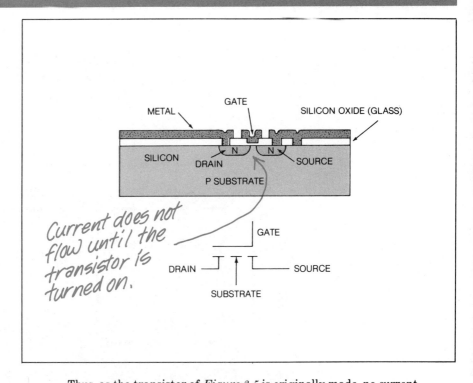

Different areas with different electrical characteristics are defined and modified through patterns of selected openings to form the transistors and other devices which make the chip function.

Thus, as the transistor of *Figure 3-5* is originally made, no current can flow from the drain N region through the P substrate region to the source N region. The P region between the source and drain blocks this flow as shown in *Figure 3-6a*. However, when the transistor is used as a switch, a voltage is applied to the gate terminal that is more positive than the voltage on the substrate. *Figure 3-6b* shows + 10 volts. This causes a thin channel of N material to form between the source and drain N regions. When this occurs, current can flow from the drain to the source region or vice versa provided a voltage is applied between drain and source connections. In other words, the transistor acts like a voltage controlled switch. With no gate voltage, the switch is open and no current flows *(Figure 3-6a)*. With a high enough gate voltage, the switch is closed and the transistor acts like a resistor *(Figure 3-6b)* through which current can flow. Note the dimension W of the gate of *Figure 3-6a*. By making the transistor with a large W dimension for a long gate (which causes the transistor to have relatively large area), this switch will have a low resistance so that it acts almost like a metal wire. By using a short gate and smaller area, the transistor acts like a large value resistor. Just by varying the dimension W, the same type of structure can be used to fabricate the two types of components needed to make all digital devices — switches and resistors.

Figure 3-6.
MOS Transistor as a
Switch

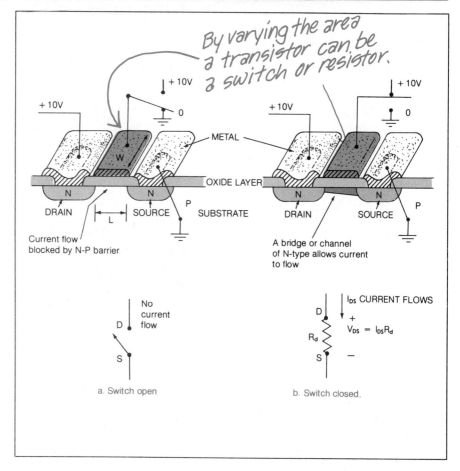

By varying the area a transistor can be a switch or resistor.

a. Switch open

b. Switch closed.

The Detailed Steps

In order to create the very small regions that form the MOS transistors on and in the silicon slice, these basic things need to be done to the material:

1) Oxidation – a furnace process for growing a silicon oxide (glass) layer on the top of the silicon *(Figure 3-7a)*.

3) Photomasking – a photographic process that allows areas of material (such as the oxide layer) to be selectively removed from off the top of the silicon *(Figure 3-7b)*.

3) Diffusion – a furnace process that allows an area of silicon not protected by an oxide layer to be changed to an n type or p type by "diffusing in" other materials (dopants). *(Figure 3-7c)*.

4) Metallization – the process of placing a thin metal layer over the top of the slice *(Figure 3-7d)* for the purpose of connecting the transistors (or diodes, or resistors) together electrically.

**Figure 3-7.
Integrated Circuit
Processes**

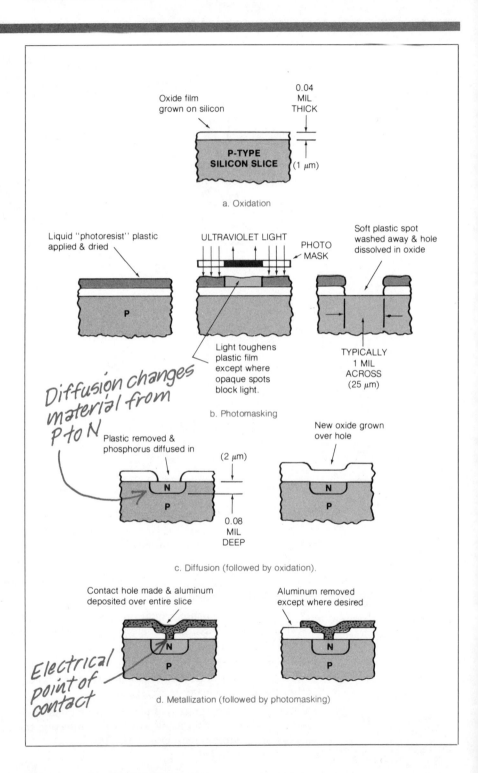

Oxide film
grown on silicon

0.04
MIL
THICK

**P-TYPE
SILICON SLICE** (1 μm)

a. Oxidation

Liquid "photoresist" plastic
applied & dried

ULTRAVIOLET LIGHT

PHOTO
MASK

Soft plastic spot
washed away & hole
dissolved in oxide

P

Light toughens
plastic film
except where
opaque spots
block light.

TYPICALLY
1 MIL
ACROSS
(25 μm)

b. Photomasking

*Diffusion changes
material from
P to N*

Plastic removed &
phosphorus diffused in

(2 μm)

New oxide grown
over hole

N
P

N
P

0.08
MIL
DEEP

c. Diffusion (followed by oxidation).

Contact hole made & aluminum
deposited over entire slice

Aluminum removed
except where desired

*Electrical
point of
contact*

N
P

N
P

d. Metallization (followed by photomasking)

The manufacturing steps required to make an integrated circuit are repeated several times. Each step has a specific purpose in forming the devices that make the circuit function.

When examining *Figure 3-7*, it must be remembered that the cross sectional drawings are greatly magnified. Many dimensions are 1 or 2 mils (0.025-0.05 mm) total (a mil is one thousandth of one inch), and the vertical dimensions are made ten times taller than they really are to more clearly explain the process. To build the MOS transistor within a very small area of a few thousands of an inch on a side on the highly polished slice surface, the basic processes above are used, sometimes more than once. The first step is to oxidize a P-type silicon slice to form a protective and insulating layer of glass (silicon oxide) over the entire surface by placing it in a furnace with oxygen and steam *(Figure 3-7a)*. A photomasking step comes next. A light-sensitive chemical film that hardens wherever ultra-violet light hits it is then spun onto the surface of the slice. This film will protect areas of the oxide layer from being dissolved away. A mask with clear parts that pass light and dark parts that block the light forms these areas on the film surface when placed between the ultra-violet light and the slice. This is shown in *Figure 3-7b*. The oxide is dissolved in the unprotected areas and the hardened film coating removed afterwards by washing the slices in chemical solutions. In this way, the oxide layer is removed over the very small areas that are to become the N-type source and drain regions of transistors *(Figure 3-7b)*. Next, is a diffusion step. The original P-type silicon substrate is now modified in the areas where oxide has been removed. To do this, N-type atoms in a phosphorus gas are passed over the slice while in a furnace at 1200°C to change the open areas of the silicon from P to N type by the diffusion of N-type atoms as shown in *Figure 3-7c*. The oxide layer prevents these atoms from entering the uncovered areas of the silicon.

The final connections are made by depositing a thin layer of metal over the slice and then etching away the undesired areas by using the photomask process.

Now that the very small regions are formed, electrical connections need to be made to them so they will function as a circuit. However, before the metallization step, a photomasking step opens holes in the oxide layer wherever the metal is to contact the silicon areas as shown in *Figure 3-7d*. Then a metal layer is coated over the entire slice. Photomasking is again used. This time to define the pattern of metal that connects the source and drain of the transistors as well as the metal areas to make the gate of the transistors. The plastic film again spun on the slice is exposed to the ultraviolet light through the clear areas of the mask to protect the metal that is to remain on the slice. All other metal will be washed away or dissolved when the slice is dipped in a chemical solution for this purpose. After this step, the forming and connecting together of the digital circuits is complete. To allow for easy use of the circuits, they are cut apart from the slice and packaged separately as shown in *Figure 3-2* and *3-3*.

The Need for Volume Production

The fact that photomasks can be used many times significantly reduces the cost to design and use them.

The design of the circuits and the photomasks to form them is the most expensive part of this entire process. However, this has to be done only once. If the photomasks are used only once, as they would be in making a small number of any one type of circuit, the circuits would cost thousands of dollars each. However, if the photomasks are used over and over again to fabricate millions of circuits, the cost of the circuit and photomask design is only pennies for each circuit made. This is why integrated circuits must be produced in large quantities in order for each to be bought at a low cost.

This quick overview of integrated circuit fabrication and MOS transistor operation should give some understanding of the concepts of integrated circuits and how more and more digital functions are being made in a smaller and smaller space. It is useful to understand how these circuits are designed and how they operate to see how microcomputer building blocks work. Let's begin by reviewing the basic digital operations that are a part of all digital systems.

WHAT ARE THE FUNDAMENTAL DIGITAL OPERATIONS?

Digital circuits can be separated into two different groups or types of units: those that make decisions and those that remember or store information. The storage or memory units are made up of the simpler decision making units. We will first look at the simpler, more familiar decision elements.

Digital Signals

The gate is a digital device which has only two options, on, open, true or a logic 1 level and off, closed, false or a logic 0 level.

Many of these decision elements affect our everyday lives. For example (refer to *Figure 3-8)*, an on-off light switch and the light bulb it controls represents a simple digital system. When the switch is OFF, the light is off; with the switch ON, the light comes on. There are only two possibilities – OFF and ON. Thus, this is a binary circuit because it has two conditions. The light switch allows power to flow or prevents power from flowing to the light bulb. It is a simple digital gate. The term gate is needed since its action is much like the gate to a horse corral. If the gate is in one position, it allows the horses to run out of the corral. If the gate is in the other position, the horses are kept in the corral.

Both of these situations are digital in nature. The flow or no flow of power (electrical or horse) can be represented as a digital signal. Let's arbitrarily give the light power a symbol A. Thus, if power flows, let's say A is a 1 or is ON. If power doesn't flow, let's say A is 0 or is OFF. The A represents the state of the gate. The output is a 1 if the gate allows power flow and is a 0 if the gate does not allow power flow.

**Figure 3-8.
Simple Digital System**

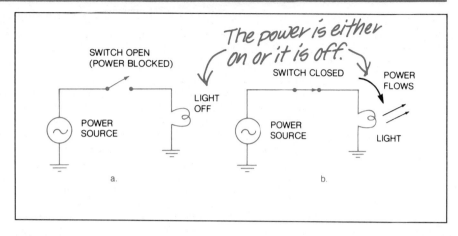

The power is either on or it is off.

AND Gates

The AND gate is one which functions only if *both* conditions for operation are met. It will respond only if both inputs A and B are a 1.

Digital power or signals can be controlled by more complicated gates. The lights in our homes again provide us with a simple example. There is a fusebox or a circuit-breaker box in the house that determines whether power is available to a certain portion of the house. The individual light switch further decides whether or not a given light is to receive this power. The circuit for this is shown in *Figure 3-9*. The light bulb will be ON (power flows) only if both the circuit breaker AND the light switch are ON (in the closed position) to complete the circuit. If either switch is OFF, power will not flow to the light. It will be off. The state of the circuit breaker can be represented with the symbol A, the state of the light switch with the symbol B, and the state of the power flowing to the light bulb (or whether the bulb is lit or not) by the symbol C. A, B and C represent digital signals. In the case of the switches, A or B is a 0 if the appropriate switch is OFF and A or B is a 1 if the appropriate switch is ON. If the light bulb is OFF (no power flow) C is a 0. If the bulb is ON (power is flowing), C is a 1. A and B must be On to make the light be ON. The relationship between these particular signals is called the AND gate in digital electronics.

**Figure 3-9.
Illustration of Simple
AND Digital Operation**

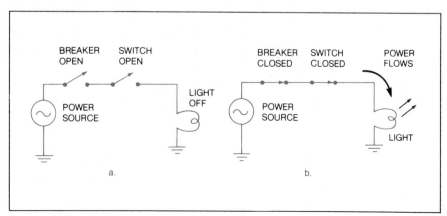

The truth table lists all the possible input/output combinations (expressed as 0 and 1 levels) that occur for a particular logic circuit.

The operation of the AND gate, summarized in words earlier, can also be summarized in table form showing a list of all the input and output combinations. *Figure 3-10a* is such a table using the symbols ON and OFF. *Figure 3-10b* is another choice. Here the 0 and 1 conditions are used to represent the state of the inputs and outputs. This form of the table is called a truth table. Truth tables also are written based upon signal levels. *Figure 3-10c* is a table using L for a low or 0 level and H for a high or a 1 level. Recall that positive logic notation was mentioned earlier. When the H level is a more positive voltage level than the L level in a digital circuit, then *Figure 3-10c* defines the circuit in positive logic notation. All of these tables contain the same information. They all fully describe the operation of the AND gate. The gate has a 1 output only if all inputs are 1. If any or all of the inputs are a 0, the output of the gate will be a 0.

**Figure 3-10.
AND Truth Tables**

INPUTS		OUTPUT
A	B	C
OFF	OFF	OFF
OFF	ON	OFF
ON	OFF	OFF
ON	ON	ON

a.

INPUTS		OUTPUT
A	B	C
0	0	0
0	1	0
1	0	0
1	1	1

b.

INPUTS		OUTPUT
A	B	C
L	L	L
L	H	L
H	L	L
H	H	H

c.

The AND gate is used for a decision to act only if all input conditions are met. For example, in a furnace controller, the heater gas flow is turned ON only if both of the following conditions are true: the house temperature is below the thermostat setting *and* the pilot light is lit. This is the AND decision.

A symbol represents the AND gate when it is used as a circuit element in a digital system. A two-input AND gate is shown in *Figure 3-11*. We should become familiar with this symbol and think of the operation of the AND gate and its truth table everytime we encounter this symbol in diagrams of digital system.

**Figure 3-11.
AND Symbol**

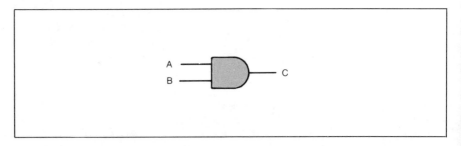

OR Gate

The OR gate will respond if either input is a 1 or if both inputs are a 1. The OR gate just like the AND gate is very small in size and large numbers can be placed on a chip.

Unlike the AND gate which requires all inputs to be a 1 before the output is a 1, the OR gate outputs a 1 if any one of the inputs is a 1. This operation is summarized in the truth table of *Figure 3-12*. The symbol for the OR gate also is included. Familiar OR decisions are involved in driving a car. We must stop a vehicle if we approach a stop sign, or if we approach a stop light which is red, or if we are about to hit something. If any of these conditions arise, we would want to stop.

**Figure 3-12.
OR Gate Truth Table and
Symbol**

INPUTS		OUTPUT
A	B	C
0	0	0
0	1	1
1	0	1
1	1	1

Like the AND gate, the OR gate can be demonstrated by using switches A and B and the light bulb C shown in *Figure 3-13*. Now power flows to the light bulb (C = 1) when A is ON (A = 1) or B is ON (B = 1) or both are ON. Power stops flowing (C = 0) only when both A and B are OFF (A = 0, B = 0). These switches can be made from regular switches, relays, vacuum tubes, or transistors. If the OR gate is made in an integrated circuit form, the entire gate can be made in such a small area that over 2,000 take no more area than that taken by one letter of type in this book. Therefore, many such circuits can be placed on the same chip of silicon to make a complex integrated circuit such as a microprocessor.

**Figure 3-13.
Simple OR Gate**

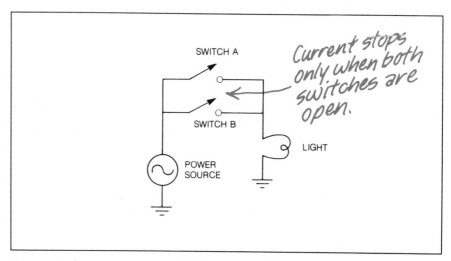

SWITCH A

SWITCH B

Current stops only when both switches are open.

LIGHT

POWER
SOURCE

NOT, NAND, and NOR Gates

The NOT gate will respond with an output that is opposite to the input it receives. Such a device also is called an inverter.

The NOT function is really the simplest digital operation since it has an output of a 1 if the input is a 0 and an output of a 0 if the input is a 1. The circuit represented by the symbol in *Figure 3-14* performs this operation and is called an inverter. The inverter is used when another circuit has an output of 1 but a 0 output is needed. For example, if an AND gate tests to see if all input conditions are 1 at the same time, then an output of 1 will be obtained when this is true. However, due to a system need, the output should be a 0. The AND gate output simply needs to be connected to an inverter as shown in *Figure 3-15.*

**Figure 3-14.
Inverter**

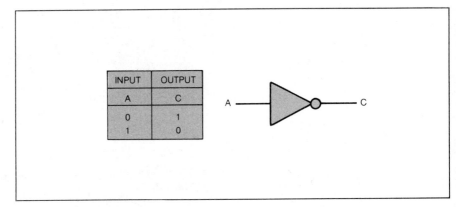

INPUT	OUTPUT
A	C
0	1
1	0

**Figure 3-15.
AND-NOT Combination**

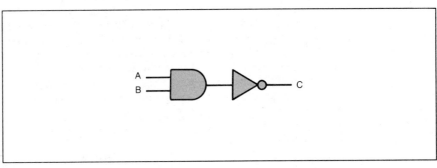

This combination is shown in *Figure 3-16* where it is considered as a complete gate, called the NAND (short for *Not-AND*) gate. The truth table is just opposite (inverted) from that of the AND gate. This is a very important type of gate since, in many cases, it is the easiest type to make in integrated circuit form. Similarly, the OR gate can be followed with an inverter to form the NOR gate of *Figure 3-17* which also is made easily as a complete gate in integrated circuit form.

**Figure 3-16.
NAND Gate Truth Table
and Symbol**

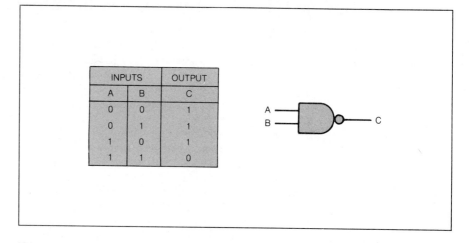

**Figure 3-17.
NOR Gate Truth Table
and Symbol**

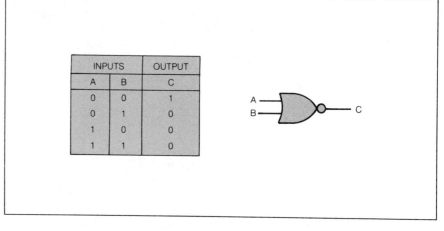

With various combinations of the basic AND, OR, NOT, NAND OR NOR gates one can make any digital device or system perform the desired decision required.

All of these basic digital gates (AND, OR, NOT, NAND, and NOR) share the common feature of being decision elements. They provide certain logical decisions based on their input signals. Any digital device or system can be made by interconnecting enough of any of the following combinations of such basic gate elements:

1) AND, OR and NOT elements

2) All NAND elements

3) All NOR elements

A little later these gates will be combined to form storage or memory elements, complete memories, and even microprocessors and microcomputers. But first, let's see how these elements are fabricated in integrated circuit form.

HOW ARE THE FUNDAMENTAL DIGITAL ELEMENTS MADE?

An Inverter

Two stacked MOS transistors can be combined to form a single inverter. The bottom transistor is the switching transistor and the top transistor acts as a resistor.

A transistor structure that can be used in making a digital gate is the MOS N-channel transistor which has already been discussed. (Refer back to *Figures 3-5* and *3-6;* recall the W and L dimensions.) Using the fact that such transistors can be made so they act as an almost ideal switch or as a resistor component, let's construct a gate. When a MOS transistor is made to be a high-value resistor, it will have a significant voltage drop across it from drain to source when current is flowing. Therefore, two MOS transistors can be connected very simply to form the simplest digital element, the inverter of *Figure 3-18*. The top transistor is used as a resistor (it is a relatively small area device because the ratio of the W over L dimensions of *Figure 3-6* is a small number, one or less) and it is called the load transistor. Because of the way the gate is electrically connected to the drain, the top transistor is always ON, while the bottom transistor is turned ON or OFF by the input signal. The bottom transistor is a relatively large area device (its W/L ratio is usually greater than 10) so that it will act as a good switch. Let's look at *Figure 3-19a*. If the bottom transistor is OFF due to a 0 input (input connected to ground — zero volts on gate), no current will flow in the bottom transistor. It will act as an open circuit, and the output of the inverter gate will be near the V_{dd} supply voltage of + 10 volts - a 1 level.

**Figure 3-18.
N-Channel Inverter
Circuit**

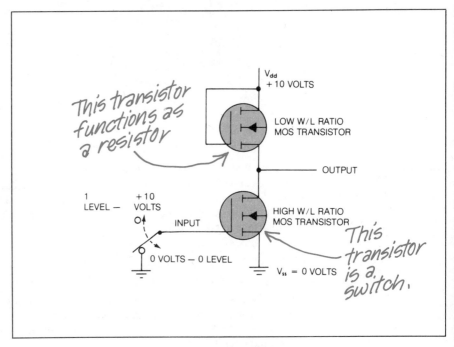

Figure 3-19.
Two States of MOS
Inverters

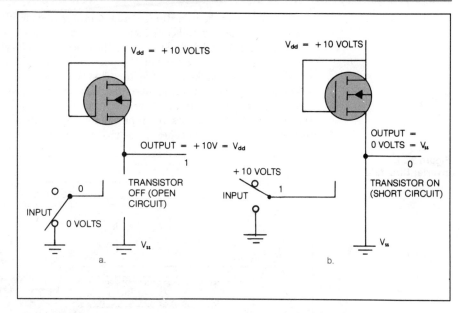

The bottom transistor is ON when the input is a logical 1 level and OFF when the input is a logic 0 level. The output is just the inverse of the input.

If the input is a 1 level (+ 10 volts) so that the bottom transistor is turned ON *(Figure 3-19b)*, the output voltage will be a 0 level, which is close to the V_{ss} voltage of zero volts. The output versus input characteristics of this circuit are shown in *Figure 3-20*. Note that as long as the input voltages are less than a certain value called the threshold level, the output is 1. This satisfies the 0 in 1 out condition of the inverter. Once the gate voltage exceeds the threshold, the gate switches and the output of the inverter drops to a 0 level, which satisfies the 1 in - 0 out condition. The output 1 level is normally designed to be above a minimum level so noise pulses in the system do not falsely trigger the next gate. This difference in 1 or 0 level from the threshold level is called noise margin.

Figure 3-20.
Inverter Characteristics

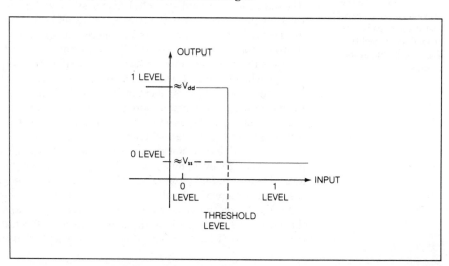

The way the inverter is made in integrated circuit form is shown in *Figure 3-21.* The N islands are formed in the P substrate by diffusion and the metal etched and defined to make the electrical connections as previously described. An area of 12 square mils is required on the surface of the silicon slice to make this inverter. This is a very small area. As an example, the period on this printed page has an area of 219 square mils. 18 of the inverter gates can fit underneath the printed period on this page. The top and bottom transistors and input and output leads are easily identified in *Figure 3-21.* The difference in the size of the two transistors is also obvious.

**Figure 3-21.
Inverter Structure**

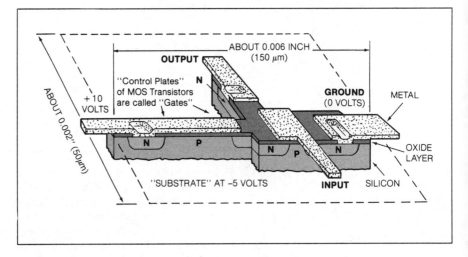

P-Channel Inverter

The P-channel inverter, with P diffusions for source and drain, is similar in operation to the previous inverter except that it operates between ground and a negative V(base-sub)dd(sub-base) voltage.

With little modification, the inverter structure can be converted to a NAND structure. The inverter of *Figure 3-21* used an N-channel MOS transistor which requires positive gate and drain voltages in its operation (the source is at ground -- 0 volts). The positive voltage on the gate, +10 volts for the 1 level, turns the transistor ON and causes the output of the inverter to be a 0 -- a level near V_{ss}. There is a second type of MOS transistor, the P-channel device. This device has P-type diffusions into an N-type substrate, therefore, it has a P-channel formed by applying gate voltage when the unit turns on. The operation of the transistor is the same. When the gate voltage is near the drain voltage, the transistor is ON; when the gate voltage is near the source voltage, the transistor is OFF. However, it uses negative voltages on its gate and drain (with the source grounded) just reverse of the N-channel transistor.

Positive logic notation will still be used where a 1 is the most positive voltage level and a 0 is the least positive (more negative) voltage level. Therefore, for the circuit of *Figure 3-22,* a 0 is a negative voltage near the drain voltage of −5 volts and a 1 is a more positive level near the zero volts, V_{ss}. A 0 on the input gate (−5 volts) turns the transistor ON and pulls the output close to V_{ss}, a 1. With the gate near V_{ss} (0 volts), a 1 level, the transistor is OFF and the output is near −5 volts, the 0 level.

Figure 3-22.
P-Channel Inverter

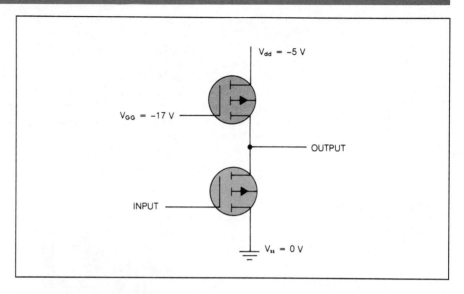

NAND Gate

The simple inverter can be converted to a NAND gate by adding input transistors in parallel with the original bottom transistor of the inverter.

Now by adding additional transistors in parallel with the bottom one of *Figure 3-22*, the NAND gate of *Figure 3-23* results. Compare the truth table with that of *Figure 3-16*. If either or both inputs have a 0 level, a voltage of −5 volts, the output will be near V_{ss}, the 1 level. Only when both inputs are at the 1 level near V_{ss} are the input transistors OFF and the output near −5 volts, the 0 level. Thus, the result is a very simple circuit that provides the NAND decision function.

Figure 3-23.
P-Channel MOS NAND
Gate and Truth Table

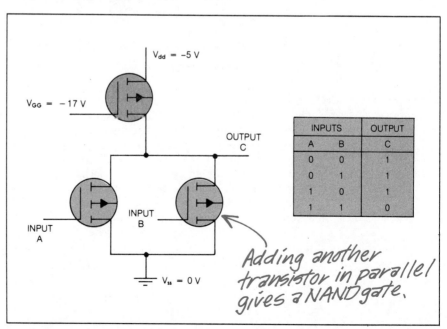

INPUTS		OUTPUT
A	B	C
0	0	1
0	1	1
1	0	1
1	1	0

Adding another transistor in parallel gives a NAND gate.

Small compact areas patterned to make NAND gates are repeated thousands of times on one chip to provide the digital functions that make up memory, input/output, even complete microprocessors.

The structure of this type of circuit in integrated form is shown in *Figure 3-24*. This 4-input NAND gate is fabricated with a very simple geometry and again in a very small area of silicon. In fact, it uses less area than the single inverter of *Figure 3-21*. This simple NAND gate structure, repeated over and over again thousands of times is the secret to making the digital functional blocks required for input/output, memories, microprocessors, and complete microcomputers in integrated circuit form on one chip of silicon. NOR gates structure are made in a very similar way and used when necessary in the circuits. To further examine how circuits are repeated and to look at the remaining type of digital circuit that stores information, lets discuss how memory circuits are made in integrated circuit form.

**Figure 3-24.
4-Input NAND Gate
Structure**

This gate duplicated thousand of times results in many types of digital functions

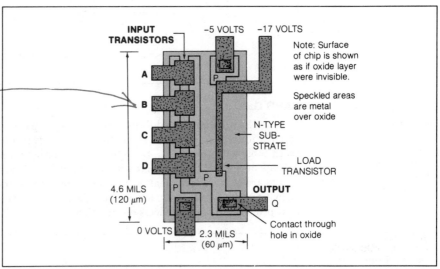

HOW IS MEMORY MADE

Digital information is stored as codes in memory units known as flip-flops for single bits or registers or memory locations for multiple bits.

Recall that memory in a digital system must store digital bits for the system and remember them until the system needs them. The digital bits are in the form of a code. They may be a single bit storing the binary code of 0 or 1 or they may be a string of N bits storing any one of the 2^N codes available when using 0 and 1 to identify the value of each bit. Such storage circuits are required, not only in the main memory of the system, but in the input or output functional blocks and inside the microprocessor itself. These circuits need to store one bit at a time or else several related bits together as a unit to form a register, or a memory byte or a memory word. Here are examples of what might be stored:

$$1 = \text{One-bit code}$$

$$01001101 = \text{8-bit code or byte from register or}$$
memory location

$$1110001110011101 = \text{16-bit code or word from register}$$
or memory location

All three types will be discussed, beginning with the simplest, the single bit storage element, the "flip-flop.' It's called this because it "flips" into one stable state as a result of a control signal and stays there and then "flops" back into another stable state and stays there due again to an input control signal.

Single-Bit Storage

A flip-flop, the simplest memory storage element, can be made from a combination of NAND gates. It holds, or stores, a single bit of information.

Flip-flops can be made from combinations of NAND gates; as a result, they can be made easily in integrated circuit form. The simplest combination that will provide the storage needed is the R-S flip-flop which can be made from just two such gates with inputs and outputs cross-connected as shown in *Figure 3-25*. The operation of such a storage circuit is best understood by examining the outputs, called "true" or Q and "complement" or Q-bar (also called Q-Not), under various input conditions. First, assume there is a 1 on the S input and a 0 on the R input. The output of the S inverter is a 0 and the output of the R inverter is a 1. The 0 on the output of the S inverter causes the output of the Q NAND gate to be a 1. This 1, along with the 1 out of the R inverter, causes the output of the $\bar{Q}$ (Q-Not) NAND gate to be a 0, which will hold Q at a 1 even if the 1 on S is removed. Thus, a 1 on the S terminal sets Q to a 1 and resets $\bar{Q}$ (Q-Not) to a 0. By providing the appropriate S and R signals, the storage circuit will store a 1 or a 0 on the output Q. This 1 or 0 will remain on the Q output even after the S or R signals return to 0. Note that $\bar{Q}$ is the inverted state from Q. Thus, $\bar{Q}$ is said to be the "complement" of Q.

While the R-S flip-flop is simple to build and understand, it does have its drawbacks. First, it responds to a constant 1 on the S or the R inputs. One can't be sure precisely when the outputs on Q and $\bar{Q}$ will change. Secondly, system design must make certain that a 1 is not applied to the S and R terminals at the same time (See truth table of *Figure 3-25*). This is an indeterminate case. More complicated flip-flops overcome these problems by providing additional NAND gates and inverters and an additional signal called a clock or a latch signal. One such device is the D flip-flop, sometimes called the gate-latch flip-flop.

**Figure 3-25.
R-S Flip-Flop and Truth
Table**

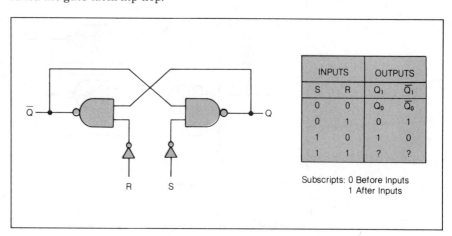

INPUTS		OUTPUTS	
S	R	Q_1	$\bar{Q}_1$
0	0	Q_0	$\bar{Q}_0$
0	1	0	1
1	0	1	0
1	1	?	?

Subscripts: 0 Before Inputs
1 After Inputs

D Flip-Flop

A latch or D flip-flop can be made by using two AND gates and a NOT function along with the simple flip-flop.

To form this type of flip-flop as shown in *Figure 3-26a*, the same R-S flip-flop (called the latch) is used along with two AND gates and a NOT function. The NOT function on the input prevents R and S from being 1 at the same time. The input line is labeled D for data input. The AND gates keep the R and S inputs at a 0, because the gate or clock input is held at 0, so that no input signal changes can change the state of the latch. When the gate or clock signal changes to the 1 level, the input signal present on D will feed thru the AND gates and provide a 1 level at either R or S to set the latch and Q to the correct state: Q = 1 for D = 1, Q = 0 for D = 0, as shown in the truth table of *Figure 3-26*.

**Figure 3-26.
D Flip-Flop (Gated Latch)**

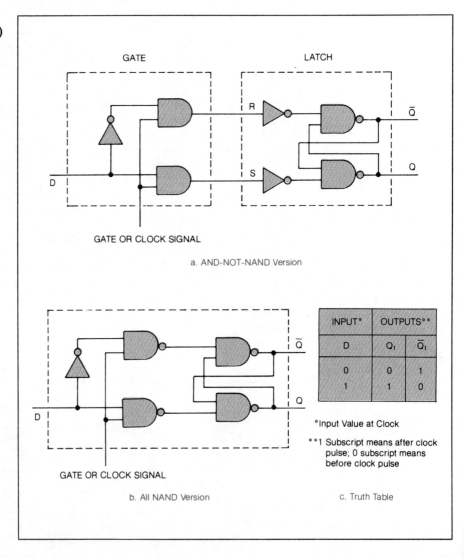

a. AND-NOT-NAND Version

b. All NAND Version

c. Truth Table

INPUT*	OUTPUTS**	
D	Q_1	$\overline{Q}_1$
0	0	1
1	1	0

*Input Value at Clock

**1 Subscript means after clock pulse; 0 subscript means before clock pulse

Making such a flip-flop in integrated circuit form is made easier by using the same type circuit over and over again. *Figure 3-26b* shows how NAND gates are substituted for the AND - NOT function to provide a NAND gate version. Trace through this circuit to verify that the operation is the same.

A "clock" signal is used to precisely time the sequences of events in digital circuit operations.

Perhaps this D flip-flop description provides a better understanding of the term "clock" signal because it determines the *time* at which the data on the D line is accepted and latched or stored into the flip-flop. To make this clearer, refer to what is called a "timing diagram" in *Figure 3-27*. In this diagram, the signal levels at each input or output are plotted against time to show exactly when the data present on the D line is gated in and stored by the latch. The timing diagram begins with all signals at the 0 level. The D level changes first to the 1 level but does not cause a change in the latch output Q until the clock level is a 1. Q then has stored the 1 ("latched it in") even though the clock returns to 0. No other change occurs in the latch output Q until the clock again goes to a 1 and detects that D has changed to a 0. It then gets latched to a 0. Note that the D input in *Figure 3-27* changed during the clock signal time. This is not normal practice in digital circuit design. Most circuits are designed so that signal D would be in a "stable" state before the clock signal arrives so that signals are transferred correctly and there is no chance for error.

Microcomputers use clock signals to time the operation of all their circuits. Clocked flip-flops and other memory elements allow this timing to be precise. The D flip-flop is but one type of clocked flip-flop. All clocked flip-flops can be used individually to hold single bits of information. They can also be used in groups to provide several related bits of storage in devices called registers.

**Figure 3-27.
D Flip-Flop Timing
Diagram**

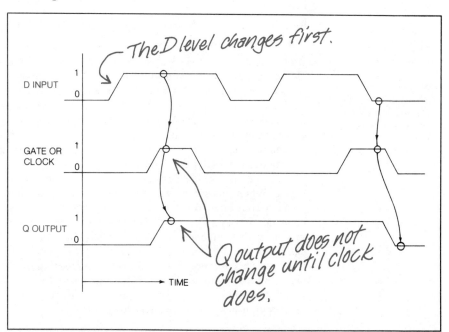

Register

Once a single flip-flop is built that does what is needed, several of these flip-flops can be combined along with additional NAND gates to provide multiple-bit storage in a device called a register as shown in *Figure 3-28.*

**Figure 3-28.
Parallel 4-Bit Register**

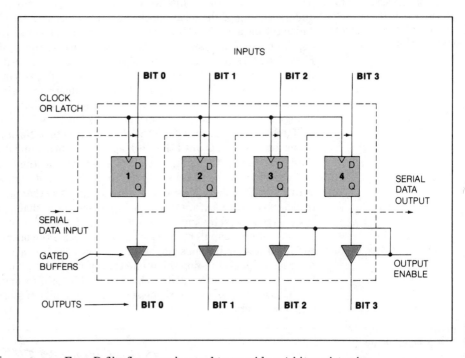

Several flip-flops combined with additional NAND gates form a multiple bit storage unit called a register. A parallel register inputs or outputs all of its information at the same time on parallel lines.

Four D flip-flops can be used to provide a 4-bit register by providing a common clock signal to the clock input of each flip-flop. When this clock signal goes from 1 to 0, the four signals present on the four input lines will be stored in flip-flops one through four. Whenever the code stored in the register is to be read, the outputs of the flip-flops are gated onto the 4 output lines. This type of structure is a parallel register in that the input information is taken 4 bits at the same time (in parallel) and the output information is provided 4 bits at the same time. Control of when the output information is read occurs by turning on an output gate (gated buffer) at the correct time with a signal commonly referred to as an output enable signal. When this signal is active, the outputs of the flip-flops are connected to the output lines. When this signal is inactive, the output lines are in an open circuit state. That is, the wires act as if they were not connected to anything. Such an output control is called "three-state", since the output can be a 0 or a 1 when output enable is active or open circuit when it is inactive. This property is very useful in microcomputers since it allows a very simple interconnection of elements within the structure. Not all registers provide this type of output, but most registers designed for use in microcomputer systems do have this feature.

A serial or shift register transfers all input/output bits one at a time in sequence over a single line.

The register of *Figure 3-28* provides for parallel input and parallel output of data. Not all registers are built this way. Some registers provide for shifting information into the register on a single line or for shifting information out of the register on a single line. (The dotted lines of *Figure 3-28* indicate such a connection.) Bringing in data one bit at a time on a single line is called a serial data transfer, while bringing all bits in at once on several different lines is called a parallel transfer. Thus, there are possibilities for serial input-parallel output registers; parallel input- serial output registers; and so on. Also, there is a completely serial shift register in which the inputs and outputs occur in serial form on a single input and single output line. These special shift registers will come up again in more detail when serial data communication is discussed in later chapters. For now, the main interest for microcomputer systems lies in the parallel data transfers from register to register using the type of registers already discussed.

RAM's

Storing information in a Random-Access Memory (RAM) integrated circuit is called "writing into memory" and retrieving the information is called "reading the memory".

Memories that are used with microprocessors and microcomputers store multiple-bit digital codes representing instructions, data, and control signals. A memory for this purpose can be provided by using many registers, or many lines of multiple flip-flop rows, for the multiple-bit storage locations. An example of a memory to store 16 bits is shown in *Figure 3-29*. Note the regular pattern of such an array consisting of rows and columns. The row lines select 4 stored bits at the same time and the column lines are common to 4 stored bit locations. The column lines can be used as lines to carry inputs to the bit locations for storage or they can be used as lines to read out the bits stored at a location. When the column lines are used as inputs, a clock gate like the one previously described for the D flip-flop, gates the inputs to the bit locations and stores the bit in the latch. When the column lines are used as outputs, an output enable gate reads the stored bit placed on the output lines by the latch. Storing inputs into the bit locations is called "writing into memory"; reading out the stored bits is called "reading memory." This is a Read-Write memory because both functions can be accomplished.

A group of memory bits (in *Figure 3-29* it is 4 bits but it could be an 8-bit byte or a 16 or 32, or 64-bit word) are to be read out or written into in parallel. Therefore, all need to be selected at the same time. This is done by selecting a row in *Figure 3-29*. An address decoder is required for this. Since there are 4 rows, only a 2-bit address is needed to choose any one of 4 rows. In the *Figure 3-29* example, the third row is being selected by the input address 10. A control Read/Write signal, 1 for write and 0 for read, tells the memory to store the inputs, or read the outputs.

**Figure 3-29.
Basic RAM Structure
Using Flip-Flop Elements**

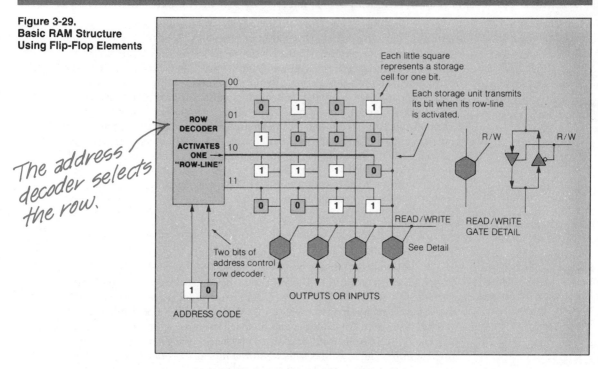

The address decoder selects the row.

Again, a memory, made to store thousands of bits, is realized by combinations of many thousands of NAND gates. *Figure 3-30* shows a typical picture of such a device in its integrated circuit form. The array of flip-flop memory cells and the decoder rectangular area are easy to identify. It is the regular nature of the integrated circuit form of such devices that makes them so economical to produce with high densities.

**Figure 3-30.
Picture of RAM Chip**

A name is given to a read-write memory such as this where any address location can be chosen at random and the bits stored at that location arrive at the output in approximately the same time for any address used. It is called a random-access memory or RAM. It is used for storing both data and program information.

ROM's

A ROM (Read Only Memory) has the information written into it when it is manufactured; therefore, it can't be changed. Every time the same memory location is addressed, the same information will appear at the output.

Some of the memory that is used to store program instructions need not be changed for a system. In this case, a memory that has fixed bits stored in its cells will be used. This is called a read-only memory. When it is addressed, it will always read out the same information from the addressed location. If no writing is required, then the circuitry for the storage cells is much simpler. In fact, in its simplest form, connecting two crossing wires in a matrix or array stores a 1 and leaving them disconnected stores a 0. For example, look at *Figure 3-31*, the same four rows that were used for the RAM are shown here, except now the decoder gates are actually shown. The outputs of the AND gates are the row selection lines and will be 1 when all the inputs are 1. The 1 can be gated to the output line through an OR gate. The only requirement is that the OR input be connected to the row line. The required codes for the output lines for each row are shown in *Figure 3-31*. The OR gate input for each output gate need only be connected or not connected to the row line to produce the code of 1's and 0's for that address location. When the connections are once established, the same code appears on the output lines each time that memory location is addressed.

ROM (Read-Only Memory) means that the memory has a program of bits that is fixed in its array during the time of manufacturing. The connections are made by the photographic masks while the material is processed.

The other types of memories are: PROM (Programmable Read-Only Memory, EPROM (Erasable Programmable Read-Only Memory), EAROM (Electrically Alterable Read-Only Memory).

PROM (Programmable Read-Only Memory) means that the memory bits can be programmed into the array by the user. Usually the full array is made with 1's in each location and then the user burns away the connection between the crossing wires by a pulse of current to make a 0 and get the required code in the array.

EPROM (Erasable Programmable Read-Only Memory) means that the code stored in the memory array can be programmed by the user, erased, and then reprogrammed to a different code. Special equipment (e.g., ultraviolet light fixtures) are required to erase the units. They must be removed from the system to be erased and reprogrammed.

EAROM (Electrically Alterable Read-Only Memory) means that the memory array can be programmed and erased while still in the circuit.

Read-only memories are very important for the microprocessor system or microcomputer system designer because sets of instructions (programs) that are used over and over again are coded into ROM, PROM, or EPROM. They are then connected into the system and used as required.

Figure 3-31.
Read-Only Memory

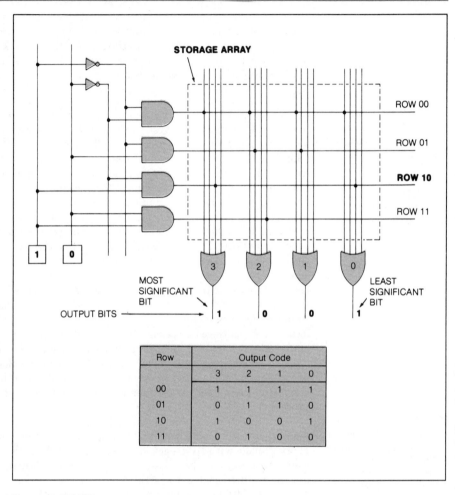

Row	Output Code			
	3	2	1	0
00	1	1	1	1
01	0	1	1	0
10	1	0	0	1
11	0	1	0	0

Dynamic RAMS

The capacitor-like structure of the MOS transistor provides an alternative storage cell for a memory circuit. The level of charge stored by the capacitor structure represents the information stored in the memory.

Integrated circuit designers found out that they didn't have to use a flip-flop to provide the storage cell for RAM storage. MOS transistors provided them with another solution. Recall from *Figures 3-5* and *3-6* that the gate of an MOS transistor is a metal plate over an insulator (oxide layer) which is on top of a silicon substrate. This sandwich of material forms a capacitor. This capacitor stores charge. This charge keeps the voltage on the gate at the signal level until a discharge path changes the charge and thus, the voltage level. *Figure 3-32* shows how this is used for a dynamic RAM cell. T_s is an MOS transistor just like the switching transistor of the inverter circuit previously discussed. C_s is the gate storage capacitor. When a 1 level voltage is placed on the gate of T_s, this gate voltage will turn T_s ON to form a path for current to flow from drain D to source S. If the voltage level on the gate is a 0 level, then T_s would be OFF and no current path is provided.

**Figure 3-32.
Dynamic RAM Storage
Cell**

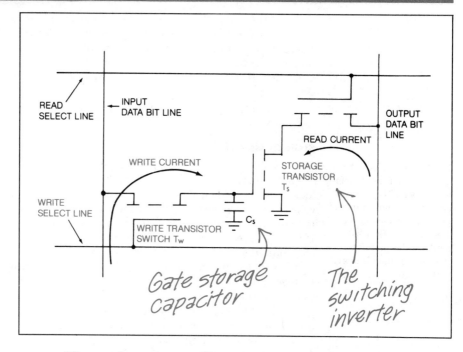

When used as a storage cell, current flow in T_s represents a 1 and no current flow is a 0. To read the storage cell, another transistor T_R, is connected to an output line. T_R and T_S must be ON to have current flow. T_R is turned ON by a 1 level on the READ SELECT line (its gate) to provide a current path to the output data line. If current flows, a 1 is stored in the cell. If no current flows, the bit stored is a 0.

Writing into the storage cell occurs in somewhat the same way. A transistor, T_W, connects the input data line to the gate of T_S. To store a 1 level voltage on C_S of the gate, T_W is turned ON with a 1 level on its gate with the WRITE SELECT line. The 1 level on the input data line then charges the gate of T_S to the 1 level. The operation is similar for a 0 level voltage, except that C_S is discharged to the 0 level voltage.

Much of the information stored in a dynamic RAM cell is lost after a period of time due to stray current and must be refreshed periodically.

The only problem with such a cell is that the charge "leaks off" C_S due to stray current paths and thus the cell loses its information. Designers have determined that the information will stay on C_S without error at least about 0.002 seconds (2 milliseconds). Therefore, the bits stored in the cells must be used in 2 milliseconds after they are stored or else all bits must be brought back to full information level. This is why this memory cell is called a dynamic RAM cell. It must be "refreshed" within a short period of time or it will lose the bits stored. Extra circuitry is required to provide the "refreshing" and sometimes systems must be shut-down during the refreshing period. However, this has presented little problem to system designers and the advantages of the dynamic RAM far outweigh this refreshing requirement, especially for systems where large storage capacity is required.

The main advantages of the dynamic cell over the flip-flop cell are:

1) The dynamic cell occupies a much smaller area so that this approach permits a very high density memory (large number of bits in a single integrated circuit) and thus a very low cost per bit stored. For example, 64K(65,536) bits are available in a package of the size shown in *Figure 3-2.*

2) It requires very little power when it is not being read from or written into.

Static RAMs and Volatility

RAM cells may lose their information if the system loses power. They are volatile, and require standby power to prevent such a memory loss. ROM's do not have this problem, their information is stored permanently.

The main disadvantage of the dynamic cell is the refreshing since the cell looses its charge. In contrast, the flip-flop holds its information as long as power is applied, whether it is used or not. Thus, the flip-flop is called a static memory. However, static memory cells take more silicon area than dynamic memory; therefore, the number of bits per package is less. In many cases, because microprocessor/microcomputer systems tend to require only limited memory, static memory is likely to be more important to these systems than dynamic memory. One other note on semiconductor or solid-state memory - RAM storage is volatile. This means that all data is lost if power is turned off. Thus, system designs may have to include stand-by power to RAM if data is to be saved when the system shuts down. ROM, because of its fixed storage, is usually not volatile.

We've shown that single-bit storage flip-flops, decoder circuits, registers, and memory cells are made of similar types of NAND gates. Besides these, microprocessors and microcomputers also require circuits that do arithmetic – addition, subtraction, multiplication, and division. Let's see how these are formed by using the same basic decision gates.

HOW ARE ARITHMETIC LOGIC UNITS MADE?

A carry results when binary numbers are added just as when decimal numbers are added.

Binary addition is much simpler than the addition of decimal numbers familiar to all of us. If we add one bit to another, there are only four possible results. A 0 plus a 0 is 0, a 1 plus 0 (or 0 plus 1) is a 1, and a 1 plus a 1 is 0 and a carry to the next place A 1 plus a 1 results in the two place binary sum 10. The decimal equivalent of the binary number 10 is 2, which is the decimal sum of the decimal numbers $1 + 1$. The binary 1 plus 1 case requires the existence of a carry; this carry must be considered when a circuit is built from basic gates to add together the 1 and 1 bits. Not only must the adder (the name of the circuit) be able to generate a carry if necessary, but it must provide for adding a carry to a given bit sum if necessary.

The example sum of two 4-bit binary numbers of *Figure 3-33* shows how the two binary numbers are added. It starts with the LSB as with decimal addition. Adding the least significant bits, with no input carry, the sum of $1+0$ is a 1 with no carry. Adding the second two bits, $1+1$ yields a sum of 10. The 0 is the sum for the second bit position and the 1 is the carry to the next (third) bit position. The sum of the third bits must include the carry in the sum. The 1 of the carry and the 1 of the first number give an intermediate sum of 10 with the carry going to the next (fourth) bit position. The 1 of the second number sums with the intermediate 0 in the third bit position to give a final 1 in the third bit position. The fourth bit sum is then the carry 1 plus 0 plus 0 which is a 1 in this bit position.

**Figure 3-33.
Binary Addition
$(7+6=13)$**

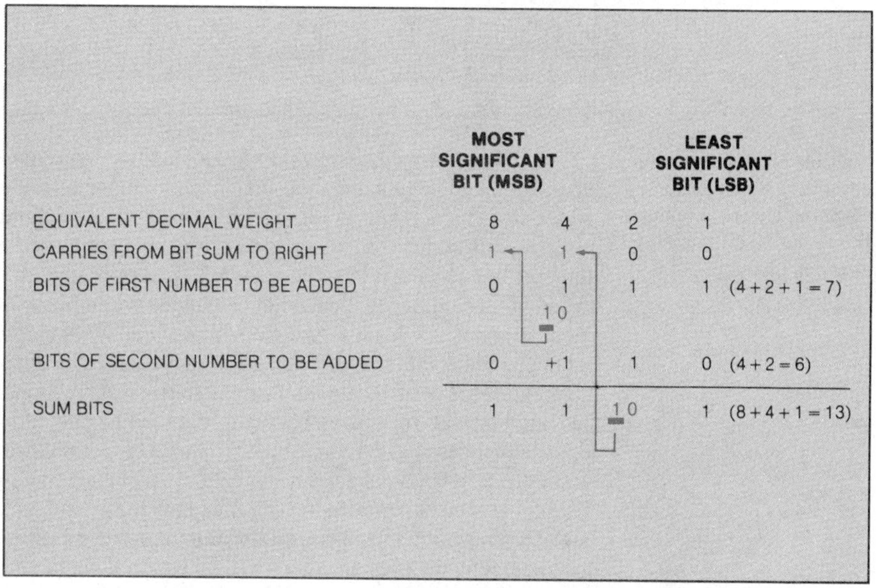

	MOST SIGNIFICANT BIT (MSB)		LEAST SIGNIFICANT BIT (LSB)	
EQUIVALENT DECIMAL WEIGHT	8	4	2	1
CARRIES FROM BIT SUM TO RIGHT	1 ←	1 ←	0	0
BITS OF FIRST NUMBER TO BE ADDED	0	1	1	1 ($4+2+1=7$)
		1 0		
BITS OF SECOND NUMBER TO BE ADDED	0	+ 1	1	0 ($4+2=6$)
SUM BITS	1	1	1 0	1 ($8+4+1=13$)

Binary adder circuits can be constructed which can handle the addition of 2 or 4 binary bits at a time.

This example shows that the functional block that performs the addition must use as inputs the corresponding bits from each of the two numbers being added and a possible carry bit. It must provide for the input of a carry that could come from the sum of the two bits in the bit position to the right of the bits being added. The functional block must provide two outputs to complete the function – the sum bit and a carry bit. It is shown in *Figure 3-34*. The truth table of *Figure 3-34* shows that the sum bit is the result of the addition of the bits inputted into the adder (including the input carry, C_{i-1}, which is from the bit position to the right). The carry output C_i must be sent to the adder handling the summing of the two bits to the left of this adder. This circuit is called a full adder because it takes into account the possibility of a carry from the summing of the two bits to the right. Integrated circuits that add 4-bits at a time are available as separate packaged units. They can be constructed from all NAND gates or they can be fabricated using a mixture of the decision and storage functions that have been discussed. It depends on the type integrated circuit used.

Figure 3-34.
Description of Full Adder

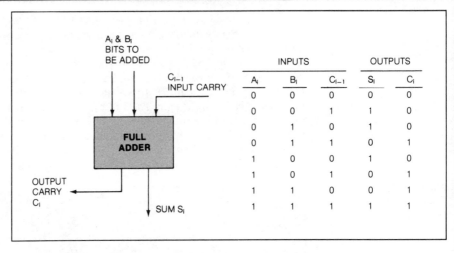

INPUTS			OUTPUTS	
A_i	B_i	C_{i-1}	S_i	C_i
0	0	0	0	0
0	0	1	1	0
0	1	0	1	0
0	1	1	0	1
1	0	0	1	0
1	0	1	0	1
1	1	0	0	1
1	1	1	1	1

Multiple bit adders can be designed by combining single-bit adders in tandem 11.8 to handle as many bits as required.

In microprocessor and microcomputer systems, single-bit, 4-bit, 8-bit, 16-bit and larger multiple-bit numbers must be added. Once the full adder design for a single bit is available, it can be repeated to build a multiple-bit adder that will add two binary numbers of a given length. A four-bit one is shown in *Figure 3-35*. The sum is sent to a result register called an accumulator. Provision is usually made for a flip-flop to hold the input carry to the least significant bit sum S_o. This carry may result from some previous addition of two binary numbers. The output carry from a given adder is sent to the next adder to the left. A flip-flop is usually provided to hold this output carry generated by the addition of the two most significant bits of the two numbers. These two carry flip-flops can be the same flip-flop if the adder timing and control circuitry is designed properly. This control circuitry also determines how many different registers can be used to send numbers to the adder and where the sum is to be sent. The basic concepts of such circuitry will be covered when timing and control functions are covered later in this chapter.

Figure 3-35.
Multiple-Bit Adder
Circuit

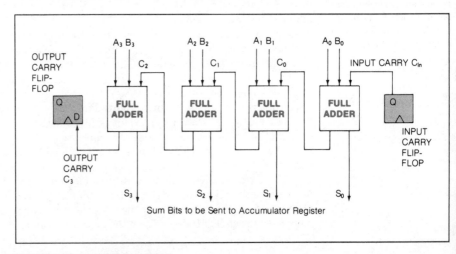

Multiplication and Division

Registers which have the capability to shift numbers to the left or the right are needed to do multiplication and division.

Other arithmetic operations that are needed in microprocessors are multiplication and division of a number by 2. To do these operations, registers and/or control circuitry that will shift a binary number one position to the right (division by 2) or one position to the left (multiplication by 2) are required. One way this could be done is to send the data out of the register, returning it to the same register in the shifted position. A register that shifts left or right is shown in *Figure 3-36*. To perform the shift left, a 1 is placed on the SHIFT-LEFT signal line and the output of a given flip-flop is sent to the input of the flip-flop immediately to the left by the gated buffers. The SHIFT-LEFT signal is timed to the clock. The input carry flip-flop is sent to the first flip-flop to set the LSB bit. An output carry flip-flop saves the MSB that was present before the shift. It may be required for subsequent operation. A shift right is performed by the gating the buffers with a 1 on the SHIFT-RIGHT signal line instead of the SHIFT-LEFT line to send the output of each flip-flop into the input of the flip-flop immediately to the right. If the number stored in the register is 0110 (binary equivalent of decimal 6) before the left shift, the number stored after the shift operation is 1100 (binary equivalent of decimal 12). The shift left has multiplied the number by 2. If the 1100 is now shifted right to become 0110, the 12 would be divided by 2.

**Figure 3-36.
Shift Right or Left
Operation**

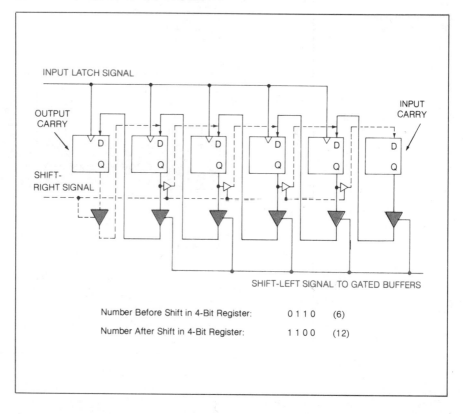

INPUT LATCH SIGNAL

INPUT CARRY

OUTPUT CARRY

SHIFT-RIGHT SIGNAL

SHIFT-LEFT SIGNAL TO GATED BUFFERS

Number Before Shift in 4-Bit Register: 0 1 1 0   (6)

Number After Shift in 4-Bit Register: 1 1 0 0   (12)

Subtraction and Other Logic

Subtraction can be per-
formed by the ALU by
changing some of the
binary numbers in the
adder to 2's complement
numbers. The ALU also
provides other arithmetic
and logic functions.

Other arithmetic operations are provided by the arithmetic logic unit (ALU), such as multiplication and division by numbers other than just 2, decimal code addition, and subtraction. Subtraction can be provided by using a subtractor circuit, just as an adder circuit was used. However, in order to limit the number of different circuits, subtraction in microprocessors (and in most computers in general) is done by using the adder circuit. To do this requires changing some of the binary numbers to "2's complement" numbers. Look at *Figure 3-37* which shows the 4-bit adder of *Figure 3-35* but with inverter gates on the inputs of the B bits. By inverting the B bits before they are input to the adder, and by providing an input carry, the adder subtracts. Notice that sending the number B through inverters cause the bits to the adder to be 1001 instead of 0110 (the binary equivalent of decimal 6). This is the complement or "1's complement" of 0110. Adding 1001 to the A number of 1100 (equal to the binary equivalent of decimal 12) with an input carry of 1 yields the result 0110. Thus, the desired subtraction is obtained $(12-6=6)$ through addition. The added carry provided the 2's complement of number B. With this procedure, integrated circuit area can be saved because the adder circuits are used for more than one function.

**Figure 3-37.
Subtraction Using
Binary Adders**

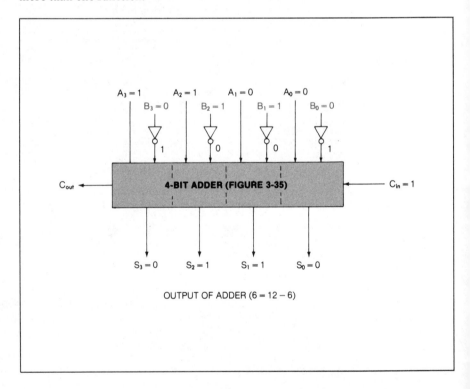

OUTPUT OF ADDER $(6 = 12 - 6)$

In gaining an understanding of the basic arithmetic operations, we have dealt with only 4-bit numbers and have shown most of the circuitry in block diagram form. Further, we have shown only part of the circuitry, just enough to see how that part of the arithmetic logic unit would work. You can well imagine how complicated the drawings would have been if we had drawn all of these circuits out in detail, showing all transistors and resistors. This has to be done by the manufacturers of microprocessors and microcomputers. Not only must the circuit diagrams be complete, but the integrated circuit mask patterns must be drawn and photographed. This is all a very expensive and time consuming process, which is why it would be so expensive for the manufacturer to build just a few thousand of such devices.

HOW DO THE TIMING AND CONTROL FUNCTIONS WORK?

All operations which occur in microprocessors and microcomputers must happen in a specific step-by-step sequence. These sequences are controlled by the timing and control center.

As complicated as the arithmetic logic unit might be when it is finished, there is another portion of the microprocessor that can be even more complicated – the timing and control function. The timing and control center of the microprocessor must turn on and off all the circuits within the microprocessor as well as control all of the memory and input/output functional blocks. The step-by-step way in which these devices come on and off will vary from instruction to instruction. The timing and control circuitry must keep track of it all. This is the reason it is one of the most important portions of the microprocessor and the microcomputer.

Every operation that has been discussed from reading memory to the arithmetic functions requires that certain events occur in a proper step-by-step sequence for the operation to be successful. To successfully read memory, addresses must be sent to memory, a signal must be sent to perform the read, and then, after enough time delay to be sure the information has been read, the bits must be sent to the proper destination. As another example, suppose two numbers are sent to the adder from different places and after the addition is completed, the sum is sent to the proper location. A means of timing and control is required to keep track of all the events in the system. Such timing and control is referenced to a master timing signal called a clock.

The heart of the timing and control function is the clock, which can be two- or four-phase.

This clock provides the heartbeat of the system. One or more clock signals are used for the master timing. Some processors use a two-phase clock as shown in *Figure 3-38a*, and further divide time into smaller intervals as needed. Others use 4 phases to get the required time periods *(Figure 3-38b)*. By having such signals available throughout the microcomputer system, any given element can do a given task in complete harmony with the way all other elements are performing their tasks. Let's look at a couple of typical examples.

Figure 3-38.
Master Clock Signals

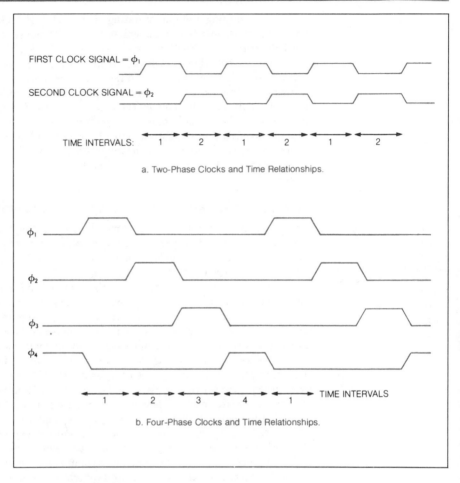

FIRST CLOCK SIGNAL = ϕ_1

SECOND CLOCK SIGNAL = ϕ_2

TIME INTERVALS: 1   2   1   2   1   2

a. Two-Phase Clocks and Time Relationships.

ϕ_1

ϕ_2

ϕ_3

ϕ_4

1   2   3   4   1   TIME INTERVALS

b. Four-Phase Clocks and Time Relationships.

An Instruction Fetch

To carry out an instruction, the microprocessor sends the address of the instruction to memory along with a control signal to read memory. The instruction read from memory is sent to the microprocessor and stored in the instruction register.

The first operation that all processors have to do in order to carry out an instruction is to fetch that instruction from RAM or ROM. To do this, the processor must send out the contents of the program counter (the address of the instruction) to the memory on the address lines and generate a memory read signal. The read signal must last long enough to give the memory time to output the desired instruction code (the contents of the memory location addressed). At the proper time, this information is stored or latched into the instruction register. The timing diagram of *Figure 3-39* summarizes the signals needed at a particular time, all referenced to the microcomputer clock signal. Let's assume that the memory can locate and read out its information in the time between two clock pulses. Therefore, during this period, the address and the memory read signals are on. At the end of this period, but before these signals have returned to zero, a signal must latch the information into the instruction register. The timing of this signal is shown in *Figure 3-39*. *Figure 3-40* shows how functional circuits derive these signals from the clock signal. The memory read signal is formed using a clocked D flip-flop that stores a 1 on the trailing edge of the clock. It will trigger again on the next trailing edge of the clock and return to a 0 output. This control signal is sent to the output enable of the program counter to send the instruction address out on the address lines. It is also sent to memory as a memory enable or memory read signal. MEMORY READ (MR) is NANDed with the clock to cause the instruction register to latch information from memory at the proper time. Thus, the clock signal along with information from the microprocessor controller (that an instruction fetch is to be performed) can be used to provide the control and timing signals needed.

**Figure 3-39.
Timing Diagram for a
Memory Read Operation**

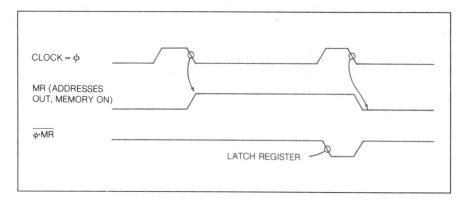

**Figure 3-40.
Timing and Control
Circuit for Instruction
Fetch**

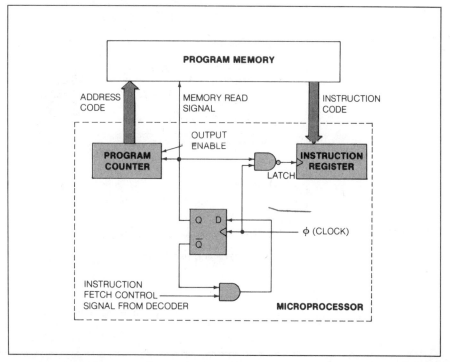

The ADD Operation

To perform the add operation the contents of the A and B registers are inputted to the adder, where the sum is latched into the A register.

The timing signals to control the adder operation behave in a very similar manner as shown in *Figure 3-41*. Again, a signal that lasts from one trailing edge of the clock to another is used to time the addition. It is required when the control center decides that the instruction is an addition. Assume the instruction is to add the contents of register B to register A in the arithmetic logic unit. The sum is to be stored in register A, which acts as an accumulator register. *Figure 3-41* contains the timing diagram and shows how the timing and control signals are derived from the clock. The sequence starts with both numbers already in register A and register B. The control section of the microprocessor outputs a signal ADD B to A as a result of the addition instruction. This signal is used, just as the instruction fetch control signal, to generate the output enables that connect the outputs of registers A and B to the adder. As before a latch signal is provided to store the sum into register A after the addition is completed.

**Figure 3-41.
Simple Add Timing
Within Arithmetic Logic
Unit**

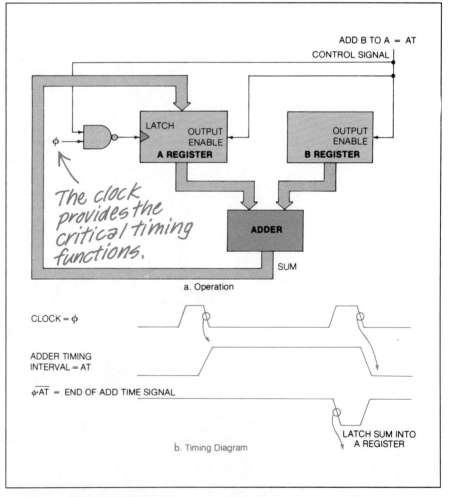

a. Operation

b. Timing Diagram

These two cases are very similar even though one involved a memory operation and the other involved an arithmetic operation. Timing and control signals for hundreds of other operations are similarly generated within the timing and control section of the microcomputer. While each of these timing signals may individually be generated very simply, the overall timing control section can be a very complex and costly digital subsystem. Fortunately, this subsystem is built into the microprocessors and microcomputers and can be used throughout the system to time the components outside the microprocessor. The microprocessor designers have helped by providing signals that are relatively simple to use. All that needs be done is to correctly connect these signals to the memory, input/output, and microprocessor functional blocks.

WHAT HAVE WE LEARNED?

· Modern digital circuits are made in the form of integrated circuits with all components fabricated on a single piece of silicon material called a chip or wafer.

· In integrated circuit manufacture, many chips or wafers are made on a single slice and many slices can be processed at the same time to produce inexpensive complex digital circuits.

· All digital circuits can be made from simple transistor switches, inverters, AND and OR gates. In many cases, using NAND or NOR gates makes it easier to manufacture the circuits in integrated circuit form.

· Data Memory (RAM) is made by using flip-flop storage cells (static memory) or by using the storage effect inherent in MOS transistors (dynamic memory).

· NAND gates are used in RAM memories to decode addresses and thus to select which storage cells (or rows or columns of storage cells) are to be read from or written into.

· ROM Memory is made by using one set of NAND gates to decode address signals and another set of NAND gates to output the instruction codes.

· Registers consist of a row of clocked flip-flops used to store a group of related digital signals.

· The basic arithmetic-logic operations for the microcomputer are made up of adder logic circuits and register transfer circuits,

· The microcomputer has a timing and control section that generates signals that turn on or off all components in the system at the proper time.

WHAT'S NEXT?

We've found out what the basic functional blocks are of a microcomputer system and how the functions are provided by digital integrated circuits. It's time now to understand the system operation of all of the units together as we will do in the next chapter.

Quiz for Chapter 3

1. Any digital system can be completely fabricated using:
   a. All NOR gates
   b. All NAND Gates
   c. AND and OR gates only
   d. None of the above
   e. a and b above

2. All N-channel MOS transistor conducts current from drain to source:
   a. all the time
   b. when the gate voltage is the same as the substrate voltage
   c. when the gate voltage is close to the drain voltage
   d. when a bridge of N-type material forms between the source and drain regions
   e. None of the above
   f. c and d above

3. An MOS transistor acts like a wire when it is on and when:
   a. its width W is large
   b. its length L is large
   c. its width W is small
   d. its length L is small
   e. a and d above
   f. b and c above

4. The purpose of oxidation is to:
   a. form a window to see the silicon through
   b. form an electrically insulating layer over the silicon
   c. provide a protective layer over the silicon
   d. all of the above
   e. b and c above

5. The process of photomasking is:
   a. a photographic process
   b. used to selectively remove areas of unwanted material such as oxide or metal from the top of the silicon
   c. used to define areas that will be diffused into
   d. all of the above

6.. Diffusion is a process in the fabrication of integrated circuits that:
   a. occurs at a high temperature
   b. is used to make a selected area of silicon p-type or n-type
   c. will not change the type of silicon in areas covered by oxide
   d. all of the above
   e. none of the above

7. A register is used to:
   a. store a group of related binary bits
   b. provide random access data memory
   c. store a single bit of binary information
   d. none of the above

8. Indicate which of the following digital gates would output a 1 with an input of a 0 and an input of a 1:
   a. OR
   b. NOR
   c. Inverter
   d. NAND
   e. AND
   f. a and d above

Fundamentals of Microcomputer System Operation

ABOUT THIS CHAPTER

There are certain basic concepts involved in using all microprocessors and microcomputers in systems. The concepts of digital information, digital codes, microprocessors as the central control function, memory, input-output functional blocks, addresses, instructions, timing and control have been developed. This chapter is devoted to the fundamentals of system operation. System fundamentals that are needed to decide what the system must do, what functional units are required for it to do what it should, how the system units are interconnected and what system instructions are normally available.

SYSTEM EVALUATION

System evaluation usually begins with the features available in the microprocessor or microcomputer. Examining these features and what the system must do determines what added functional units must be purchased to complete the system. After purchase, all elements must be connected together so the selected functional blocks will do all the tasks required with efficiency and in harmony. The step-by-step sequence — the program — must then be written, using the basic processor instructions so that the microcomputer behaves in the proper way to perform the tasks.

HOW ARE THE SYSTEM UNITS SELECTED?

Before choosing a micro-processor, one must develop a list of performance objectives.

First of all, before any selection begins, what the end system must do should be thought out carefully. An aid in doing this is to make a list in table form, or in the form of a flow chart, of all the things the system must do in the proper order to complete its tasks. With such a complete understanding of what the system has to do, it will be much easier to match the available microprocessors and other functional units to the system requirements.

System Description

To illustrate the process of describing what the system must do, let's take a simple familiar example and develop such a description. Let's assume the system to be built is a machine that will play Tic-Tac-Toe with another person. Recall that Tic-Tac-Toe is played on a piece of paper divided into nine adjacent spaces formed by three rows and three columns. Each player, in turn, plays either an X or an O in any empty square. The first player to get three X's or O's in line horizontally, vertically, or diagonally is the winner.

The game requirements include: (1) Accept 2 inputs (X and O), (2) Decide the machine's next move (3) Check for winners after each play, (4) Maintain the game board display, etc.

First of all, the system must have some sort of game board that shows the player's move and the state of the game after each play. The system starts in an initial condition where it is waiting for a person to take a turn to begin the game. The microprocessor must then accept the X or O input information when the person takes a turn. It must check to see if that play won the game. Next, the system will have to make a play, and it will have to check for a winner. In fact, the system checks for a winner after each play. It must maintain the game board display in terms of the familiar X and O symbols. It must keep score of the games won with the person playing. It must start each new game with a cleared game board and must have a provision for starting a new series of games with a new player. All of these descriptions show that the normal step-by-step operation of a Tic-Tac-Toe machine is relatively straightforward.

List Or Flow Chart

A flow chart clearly describes the sequence of events. The block describes operations and the diamond describes decisions.

To more clearly understand the sequence, it should be summarized in a flow chart form as shown in *Figure 4-1* or as a list of operations as follows:

1) The machine is turned on. This should cause it to start out at the first game of a series of games, waiting for a person to make a play. A switch is also provided to cause the system to start a new series of games if the machine has been played already.
2) The person's next play (it may be the first one) is received and displayed on the game board.
3) The system checks to see if this is a winning play; if it is, one is added to the player's score and a new game is started (Step 7).
4) If the game is not won, the system makes its play.
5) Again the system checks for a winner; if it has won, it will add one to its score and start a new game (Step 7).
6) If there is no winner at this point, the machine will go to Step 2 to continue play.
7) A new game is started by clearing the game board, displaying the scores, and going to Step 2 to begin play.

In the flow chart form of description, rectangular blocks (☐) are used to define operations and diamond blocks (◇) are used to describe decisions. It provides a graphic overview of what the system must do and how the tasks relate to each other. For this reason it may be easier to use and make reference to than the list form. However, a good descriptive list will aid in defining a good flow chart. Once the system operation is completely defined, the hardware requirements can be examined to see what type of microprocessor is best for the system.

Figure 4-1.
Flow Chart Description
of Tic-Tac-Toe Game

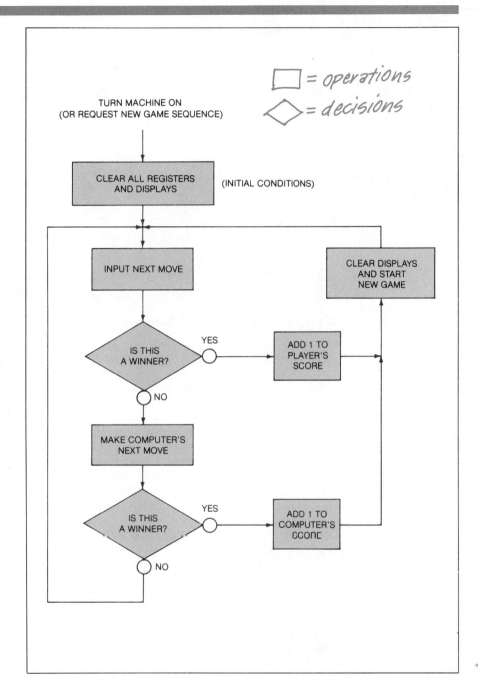

Microprocessor Selection

Key parameters like bit length, speed, instruction set must be taken into account when selecting a microprocessor.

The factors that enter the microprocessor selection are the bit length, the speed at which the system performs the steps in the task solution, the instruction set, the timing and control signals available from the microprocessor for controlling other functional units, and the interrupt procedure. Of course, each must be related to the problem being solved; some may be important, others may not. Let's look at these factors in terms of some specific types of problems *(Figure 4-2)*.

**Figure 4-2.
Features Important in
Processor Selection**

Processor Features	Applications Requirements		
	Simple Controllers	High-Speed Communications	Accurate Arithmetic
Bit Length	4	8 or 16	16
Speed	Low	High	High
Instruction Set Needs	Simple	Efficient Data Transfers & Comparisons	Efficient Arithmetic Operations
Timing/Control	Simple	Simple	Simple
Interrupt Structure	Simple, Slow	High Speed, Multiple Level	Multiple Level

Bit Length

The number of data bits that can be inputted/outputted simultaneously (bit length) determines the accuracy of computation. More bit length usually means more hardware is needed.

The bit length of the processor refers to the number of data bits the processor handles at one time. Typically, microprocessors are designed to handle data signals 4 bits at a time, 8 bits at a time, or 16 bits at a time. For simple problems, such as the Tic-Tac-Toe machine, which require limited accuracy of the numbers it uses and a small number of different input codes, a 4-bit machine is more than enough. For problems requiring higher number accuracy or where long strings of number or character codes are involved, a 16-bit processor would be needed. For requirements in between, with a relatively limited number of different input and output codes, and requiring number accuracies in the 1% range, an 8-bit processor can do the job. The number of different system conditions that an N-bit processor can handle directly and rapidly is 2^N. Thus, a 4-bit processor can handle up to sixteen different numbers or conditions directly, while a 16-bit machine can handle 65,536 such situations if necessary. The numerical accuracy from an N-bit processor in a single operation would be $1/2^N$ or $100/2^N$ per cent. Thus, the 4-bit unit only offers high speed number accuracy of about 6% while an 8-bit processor would have numbers that it used in the system accurate to 0.4%. All processors can be used to any accuracy desired by simply processing more bits, but only with much more hardware and usually at the sacrifice of system speed. Let's look at operating speed *(Figure 4-2)*.

Speed

A microprocessor's speed of operation is determined by the program used, the memory response times, and the input/output functional blocks.

Besides bit length, the speed at which a microprocessor can handle a given type of problem is related to many other factors such as the power of the instruction set, timing and control, interrupt procedures, and the response of memory and/or the input and output functional blocks. Speed of operation is important when sending and receiving information at a high rate. Also, it is usually very important when performing difficult and complex computations. In both of these cases, a processor that offers long-bit-length operation with high-speed clocks and an efficient instruction set is required. For systems, like the Tic-Tac-Toe problem, where the operations are simple and the player is a slow opponent, speed is totally unimportant, and almost any processor would suffice. However, in an automobile control unit, where speed may be critically important, a fast 8-bit or 16-bit processor would need to be selected. This is particularly true if the processor has to respond to external conditions in real time at a rapid rate.

Instruction Set

A microprocessor's instruction set must provide the operations required to perform the applications desired.

Recall that the microprocessor or microcomputer follows steps in a program. These steps are defined in terms of instructions that are recognized by a given microprocessor or microcomputer. Thus, a close check must be made to see that the instructions offered by a processor are sufficient to handle the problem requirements. A calculator type of system needs efficient arithmetic operations including addition, subtraction, multiplication, division, absolute value, and so on. A communications system needs a wide choice of input and output instructions that can transfer information quickly. A logical system such as a chess game would need extensive logical and comparison and decision-making instructions. A simple system such as the Tic-Tac-Toe game would need only a very small set of instructions to do all of its operations. In fact, any microprocessor on the market offers enough instructions to handle the Tic-Tac-Toe problem.

Timing and Control Features

System timing relationships between the microprocessor and connecting units must be evaluated to determine that the system is fast enough to solve the problem in the time required.

The timing features of a microprocessor must be studied to see if its clock and instruction execution times are fast enough to solve the problem at hand in the time available. This must be carried through to include the other functional blocks to be connected to the microprocessor. In addition, the ease with which the microprocessor timing signals can be connected to outside units is very important. If the processor control signals are such that they can be connected directly to the memory and input devices, the system timing is made easier because additional time delays through additional circuits are avoided. Obviously, this also saves system design time and the cost of the additional circuits that would be required if added circuits were needed.

Interrupt Structure

A microprocessor operating in a system goes merrily on its way doing one instruction after another. It would continue this way unless there is a need to stop it at unexpected or at random times for input or output information or at definite terminating times such as STOP or HALT. A control signal that interrupts the processor in its sequence is called an interrupt signal.

Interrupts stop the microprocessor and ask for service; however, some microprocessors will only respond to interrupts at certain points in their program.

Many microprocessors do not accept interrupt signals in an unexpected or random way. The microprocessor continues with its program until it receives an instruction that tells it to check for a signal that would interrupt it if the control signal is present. The system is only interrupted when the microprocessor wants it to be. More advanced microprocessors have an interrupt structure that does respond to the random interrupts at unexpected times.

A microprocessor's speed of response to interrupts may be critical in certain applications.

How fast a processor can respond to an interrupt determines whether it is acceptable for many situations. If input information must be received over and over again into a system at unpredictable or random times, then whatever the processor is doing is interrupted quite often. The processor must be able to get its other jobs done despite the many interruptions. In the case of the Tic-Tac-Toe example, the only time the processor needs to be interrupted is when a person makes a play or when a new game is started. A person is so slow in comparison to the speed with which all processors can respond to an interrupt, that the interrupt structure is unimportant in this problem. On the other hand, if the processor were receiving information from a satellite communications system and had to respond quickly, the interrupt structure would be critical and only a few processors would have the capability needed.

Figure 4-2 provides summary statements about the five features discussed for three types of applications. These statements can be used as guidelines. In general, the capability of the system increases as the bit length increases.

Single-chip Microcomputer Versus Microprocessor

Recall that to provide the *sense, decide, remember* and *act* functions of a computer system, the microprocessor (the decide function) must have input, output, and memory functional blocks surrounding it to complete the system.

If a single chip microcomputer with the required operational parameters can be substituted for a microprocessor, a system should require less packages.

A single-chip microcomputer, on the other hand, has all of these functions self-contained. As processors are evaluated for a given application, available single-chip microcomputers should also be considered. If the bit length, speed, instruction set, timing and control, and interrupt structure that satisfy the system needs can be found in a single-chip microcomputer, the system might be constructed using only one package instead of many. Of course, the microcomputer chosen must supply enough memory and enough input and output circuitry to meet the system needs; otherwise, separate functional blocks must be added to meet these needs.

Memory

The system program must be stored in memory and data to be used by the system must be stored in memory. Estimates must be made to determine how much memory will be required and, in addition, what type of input and output circuits are needed. It may be difficult to accurately estimate the memory needed for program requirements until the program steps have been decided upon in some detail. However, the data memory and the input and output requirements are fairly well determined by the description of the system behavior. For example, the Tic-Tac-Toe machine should only need 18 bits of information to keep track of the X's, O's, and squares that haven't been played. As indicated in *Figure 4-3*, 9 bits are needed to indicate if a position is open (0 for used and 1 for unused). Another 9 bits are used to indicate the play (0 for a O and 1 for an X played). 4 bits of memory will hold the player's score (up to 16 games) and similarly, 4 bits would hold the machine's score. Thus, 26 bits of memory would meet the requirements of this simple game. If a 4-bit processor with at least 7 internal 4-bit storage locations is used, there is no need for external RAM. Similarly, if a microcomputer has this much on-chip storage, there wouldn't be a need for any external memory devices. More complicated systems require much more random access memory and, in those cases, external RAM circuits must be provided.

**Figure 4-3.
Memory Estimate**

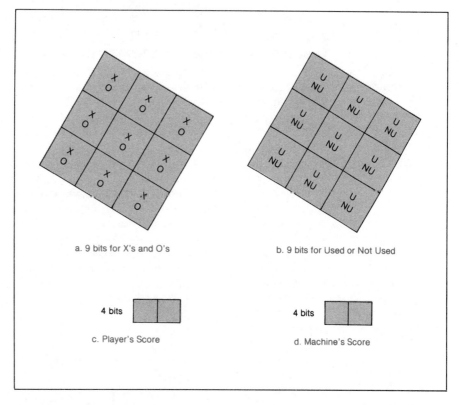

a. 9 bits for X's and O's

b. 9 bits for Used or Not Used

4 bits

c. Player's Score

4 bits

d. Machine's Score

Input/Output Units

The system input and output requirements determine the input and output circuits that must be used to interface with the processor chip.

A careful review of the system behaviour usually reveals what types of input and output circuits are needed. In the game example, as shown in *Figure 4-3*, X lights (9 of them) and O lights (9 of them) are needed as outputs. Inputs required are a power-on switch, a new games switch, and a set of switches, perhaps in a calculator-like keyboard, to allow the player to input his next move. This information must be connected (interfaced) to the microprocessor or microcomputer so that the player and computer can communicate with each other. More complicated systems usually require more complicated input and output circuits. Carefully evaluating the description of what the system must do should pin-point the selection of the right units.

One of the most often needed interfacing units connects the microprocessor to a keyboard and a CRT monitor.

One of the principle means of an input/output interface to humans is a typewriter or a keyboard and TV terminal. Most microprocessors will have family units that match the microprocessor and provide an easy interface to such units. In addition, some microprocessor families will have low-cost terminals for the input of numbers, letters, and symbols in ASC II code built into printed circuit board assemblies with the microprocessor and interface circuits.

Once the right microprocessor or microcomputer is selected for the job and the memory and input and output requirements are summarized, interconnection of the units begins. Fortunately, the components are designed so they can be connected rather directly to each other in fairly obvious ways. Let's examine some of these in more detail.

HOW DO WE CONNECT THE SYSTEM COMPONENTS TOGETHER?

The microprocessor signal lines are address lines, data lines, timing and control lines, clock lines and power lines.

The microprocessor signal lines *(Figure 4-4)* must be connected to the external components properly if the system is to work correctly as desired. Most processors have:

1) Address lines – the digital code that appears on these lines defines the location of instructions or data to be used next by the microprocessor or microcomputer.
2) Data lines – the instruction and data codes are sent to and from the processor on these signal lines.
3) Timing and Control lines – all the timing and control lines sent to and from the processor for the external functional blocks are included. The interrupt signals also are included.
4) Clock lines – for many processors the clock signals (the system's master timing signals) are formed externally and sent to the processor. Other processors and many microcomputers have circuits that generate these clock signals internally.
5) Power lines – obviously, electrical energy must be provided to the microprocessor and the other functional units in order for them to be able to work properly.

Figure 4-4.
Processor Signals

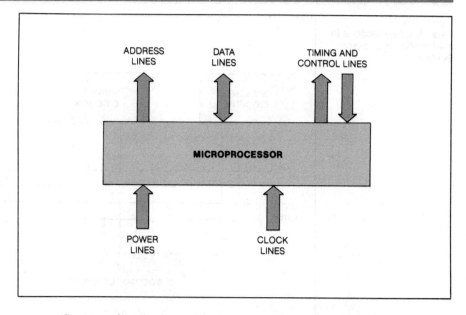

Separate distribution networks are usually used for the clock signals and the power lines. All the functional blocks use power and most of them must be timed by the clock signals. If the clock signals are generated externally from the microprocessor, they are usually formed by an integrated circuit built especially for that purpose. Special wiring layout may be required at times to make sure the clock pulse edges have good clean rise and fall waveforms. If they do not, circuits can be gated at the wrong time and cause system errors.

Data Line Connections

The system data bus interfaces to the units it connects to through a three-state device. The three-state device isolates the system unit from the bus unless the system unit wants to send or receive data on the bus.

As shown in *Figure 4-5*, the data lines in a system go to many integrated circuits from the microprocessor. Some circuits may be input, others output, and others memory blocks. All units have their data lines connected in order as shown in *Figure 4-5*. All the least significant bit lines (d_0) are connected together; all of the next least significant bit lines (d_1) are connected together; and so on. Such connections can be made directly only if all devices have the three-state output feature. Recall this was mentioned before *(Figure 3-28)*. It is shown in more detail in *Figure 4-6*. *Figure 4-6a* shows the output of a latch that is feeding bits onto the data lines. There is an output enable gate that was described in Chapter 3 between the Q flip-flop output and the data lines (called the data bus). If the output enable line is a 0, the output enable gate is inactive and the Q output of the flip-flop is disconnected from the data lines as shown in *Figure 4-6b*. The data line looks like it is not connected to anything. It sees an open-circuit to the Q output of the flip-flop. If the output enable is a 1, the output enable gate is active and acts as short circuit from the Q output to the data line as shown in *Figure 4-6c*. If Q is a 1, this is fed to the data line. If it is a 0, this is fed to the data line.

**Figure 4-5.
Data Line Connections in
a 4-Bit Microprocessor
System**

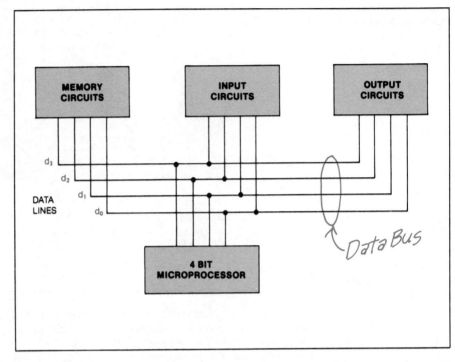

**Figure 4-6.
Operation of Three-State
Output Circuits**

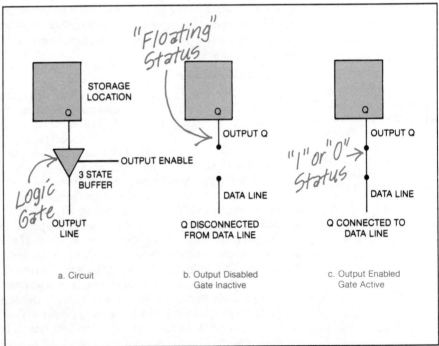

If the three-state device did not act as a buffer, large short circuit currents could flow.

When the signal level is coming from the output of an MOS inverter, the usefulness of the three-state output option can be seen by looking at what a signal of a 0 or a 1 level means in terms of electrical power connected to the line. In *Figure 4-7a*, the bottom transistor of the inverter is OFF and the load transistor is feeding the data line. Thus, the V_{DD} supply will be connected to the line through the load transistor. Remember, it is really acting as a resistor. In *Figure 4-7b*, the bottom transistor of the inverter is ON and the data line is switched to the V_{ss} voltage (usually zero volts or ground). Now suppose that the two outputs of *Figure 4-7* are connected to the data line without a three-state output-enable gate. The V_{DD} power supply would be connected to the V_{ss} power supply through the MOS load transistor resistor as shown in *Figure 4-8*. A large current would flow, possibly damaging the output elements in each device. Certainly, it would not be possible to tell just which signal was appearing on the line, a 0 or a 1.

**Figure 4-7.
MOS Circuit Output
Conditions**

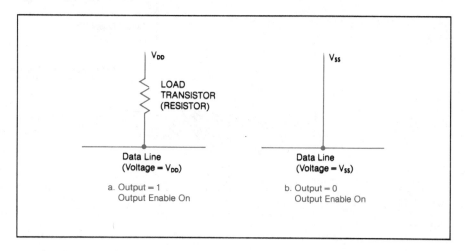

**Figure 4-8.
Effect of Placing a 0 and
1 on Same Data Line**

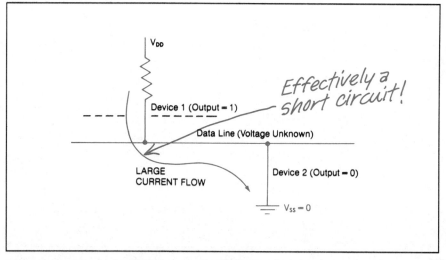

Any number of system units with three-state outputs may be hung on a data line, so long as the timing is correct so that only one device is outputting at a time.

By using the 3-state feature on both devices as shown in *Figure 4-9*, they can share the same wire without any of these problems; assuming, of course, that the output enable signals to the gates are timed correctly. Many devices can share the same line, the only requirement is that just one output-enable signal is ON at any given time. The device, whose output enable is ON, would send its 0 or 1 on the line; all other outputs would be in their open-circuit case. The device to send information on the line is selected by controlling the output-enable signals.

**Figure 4-9.
Use of Output Enables
on Three-State Devices
to Control Access to
Data Line**

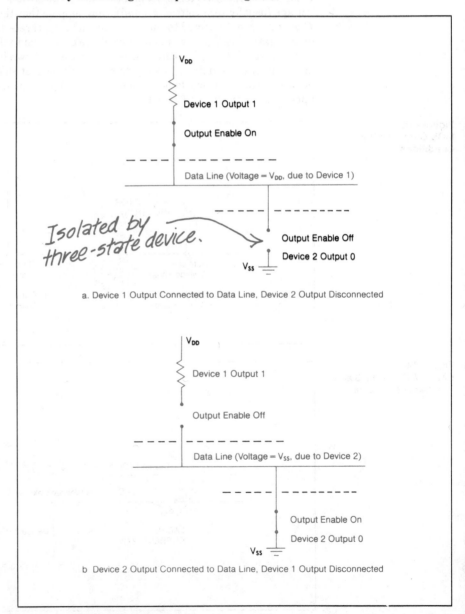

a. Device 1 Output Connected to Data Line, Device 2 Output Disconnected

b Device 2 Output Connected to Data Line, Device 1 Output Disconnected

When several devices are sharing the same set of lines and all the lines form a common group of signals, the group of lines is referred to as a bus. In diagrams in this book these are shown as a broad arrow. The data bus provides the signal flow path for all data and instruction codes between the microprocessor and the other functional blocks in the system. Similarly, the set of lines that carry the address code is called the address bus.

Address Bus Connections

The microprocessor simultaneously addresses inputs, outputs and memory locations by sending address signals on the address bus. It is important that the microprocessor outputs have sufficient address current output to drive all of the devices.

The connection of the address lines in most microcomputers is very simple as shown in *Figure 4-10*. The microprocessor develops the address signals and these are sent to the address input pins of the other functional blocks. There are only two considerations that may be involved in making these connections:

1) Processor Current Capability – Can the processor address line output circuit provide enough current to supply the input requirements of all the devices connected to it?
2) Address Decoding – Can the decoders inside the memory and input and output circuits handle the address decoding or do they need some help from outside decoder circuits?

Let's examine these in more detail.

**Figure 4-10.
Connection of Address
Lines in Microcomputers**

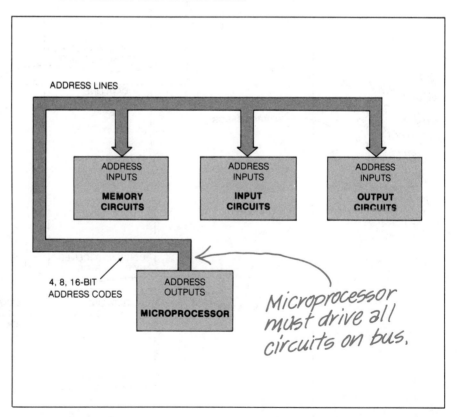

Processor Current Capability

Current flow is from the microprocessor through the address bus to the device input for a 1 state, and is to the micro-processor from the device and bus for a 0 state.

Microprocessor output circuits providing the 0 or 1 level on the address line have the ability to supply current to a line or to receive current from a line. The maximum or minimum limits of this current are specified by the manufacturer on a data sheet. The address inputs of memory and input/output functional blocks have to be supplied a certain level of current in the 0 input case and another level of current in the 1 input case. These currents are similarly specified by the manufacturer on data sheets. In addition, supplying or receiving current depends on the level of the output.

Look at *Figure 4-11*. When the processor output is in the 1 state, current will flow from the processor to the input device and will have to be supplied by the processor. When the processor output is in the 0 state, the current will flow from the input device to the processor and the processor will have to be able to receive this level of current without damaging its output circuit. The processor, in receiving this current, is said to be "sinking" current.

**Figure 4-11.
Current Loading of
Processor Data and
Address Lines**

The microprocessor may either be a source of current ("1" state) or a current sink ("0" state)

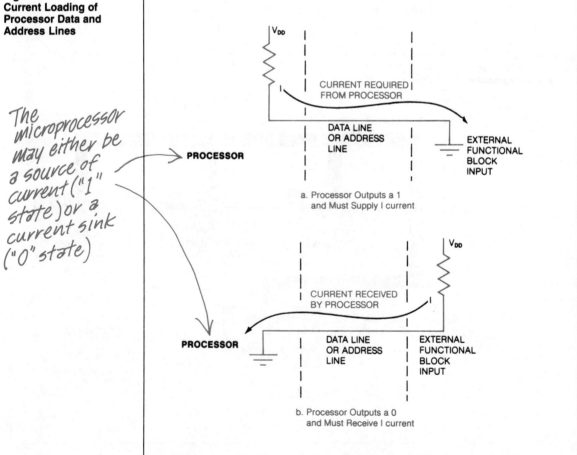

a. Processor Outputs a 1 and Must Supply I current

b. Processor Outputs a 0 and Must Receive I current

If the microprocessor cannot handle the total current requirements, a buffer-driver is used to meet the complete current demands of the system units connected to the address bus.

If each address line feeds a certain N number of inputs, then the total current the processor must supply when its output is in the 1 state is N times the individual input current. Similarly for sinking current, the total current the processor output must "sink" when it is in the 0 state is N times the current flowing out of the input of a memory or the input/output functional blocks. If the processor cannot handle these total currents, a buffer driver integrated circuit must be used. It will take the current levels of the processor output circuits and boost them to the levels required by all the external inputs.

There is another feature of the inputs of memory and input/output functional blocks that affects the currents required by the inputs. Each input acts as a capacitor. A capacitor itself is a storage element as discussed previously. Its voltage can change only if its charge changes. Its charge can change only if current flows to or from the capacitor. *Figure 4-12a* shows a capacitor, representing an input, connected to a data or address line. *Figure 4-12b* shows that the voltage across the capacitor needs a certain amount of time, Δt, to change a certain amount ΔV. The amount of current required to cause the change of ΔV in Δt is given in *Figure 4-12a*,

$$I_c = C \frac{\Delta V}{\Delta t}.$$

**Figure 4-12.
Effects of Line
Capacitance on
Processor Current I**

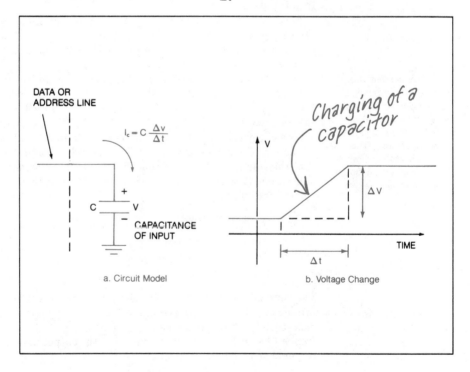

a. Circuit Model

b. Voltage Change

Output Current Required

The equivalent circuit of an address line with input devices on it is a line with a series of capacitors on it. Each capacitor draws a current during charging and gives up a current during discharge.

Without going further into the physics of capacitors, the equation of *Figure 4-12a* can be used to determine if the processor outputs can deliver enough current. Take *Figure 4-13a* as an example. Here the processor's address line output connects to eight address inputs of external functional blocks. I_1, I_2 --- I_8 represents the current that is required by each input. From the manufacturer's data sheet for the functional blocks, I_1 is 0.01 milliamperes (flowing into the input) when the address line is a 1 level and it is -1 milliampere when the line level is a 0. The minus sign means the current is flowing opposite to the direction of the arrow in *Figure 4-13a*. In other words, the output is sinking the current. In electronic circuits, the currents tend to be much smaller than an ampere, the standard unit of current. Therefore, a unit – milliamperes – is used that is 1/1,000th of an ampere (0.001 amperes). The currents, I_{C1}, I_{C2} --- I_{C8} of *Figure 4-13a* are required to change the voltage on the input capacitors from the 0 level to the 1 level (or 1 level to 0 level) in a time, Δt. From the data sheet specifications, the input capacitor is 10 picofarads. Again, electronic capacitors are much smaller than the farad, the standard unit of capacitance, therefore microfarads (1×10^{-6} farads) or picofarads (1×10^{-12} farads) are used.

Figure 4-13a shows how to simplify the problem. All of the input currents can be represented by one value, I_{INPUT}. All the individual capacitors can be combined into one 80pF ($8 \times 10pF$) capacitor, and all charging currents can be combined into one value, I_c, as shown in *Figure 4-13b*.

The driver current that must be supplied during the charging or discharging of the equivalent capacitance is a function of the capacitance, the magnitude of the voltage change, and the amount of time allowed for the change.

First, let's determine what charging current the processor output must supply to change the input capacitor voltage. As shown in *Figure 4-13d*, let's assume that the output is at a 0 level of 0.4 volt and it is to be changed to the 1 level voltage of 2.4 volts or a $\Delta V = 2V$. So that input circuits will react correctly and the microprocessor can run at full speed, this voltage change must occur in 0.0000001 seconds. Again, this is much smaller than the standard unit of a second. Therefore, microsecond (1×10^{-6} sec) or nanosecond (1×10^{-9} sec) are used as time units. Δt then is 100 nanoseconds. Solving the equation,

$$I_C = 80 \text{ picofarads} \times \frac{2 \text{ volts}}{100 \text{ nanoseconds}}$$

gives $\quad I_c = \dfrac{80 \times 10^{-12} \text{ farads} \times 2 \text{ volts}}{100 \times 10^{-9} \text{ seconds}} = 0.8 \times 2 \times 10^{-3} \text{ amperes}$

or $\quad I_c = 1.6 \text{ milliamperes.}$

The microprocessor must supply 1.6 mA (milliamperes) to change the voltage on the address line from the 0 level to the 1 level in 100 nanoseconds. The same amount of current is required to change the level from a 1 to a 0. The only difference is that the output must sink the current rather than supply it. *(Figure 4-13c)*

**Figure 4-13.
Current Requirements
for a Line with 8 Inputs**

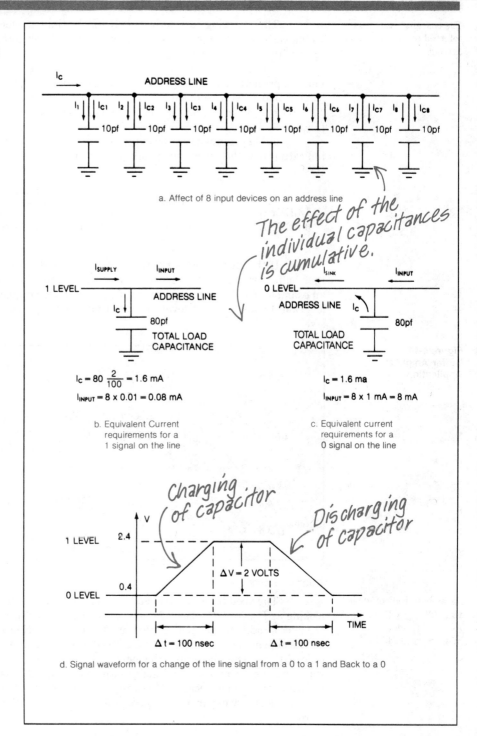

a. Affect of 8 input devices on an address line

The effect of the individual capacitances is cumulative.

$I_C = 80 \dfrac{2}{100} = 1.6 \text{ mA}$

$I_{INPUT} = 8 \times 0.01 = 0.08 \text{ mA}$

b. Equivalent Current
requirements for a
1 signal on the line

$I_C = 1.6 \text{ ma}$

$I_{INPUT} = 8 \times 1 \text{ mA} = 8 \text{ mA}$

c. Equivalent current
requirements for a
0 signal on the line

Charging of capacitor

Discharging of capacitor

$\Delta V = 2$ VOLTS

$\Delta t = 100$ nsec

$\Delta t = 100$ nsec

d. Signal waveform for a change of the line signal from a 0 to a 1 and Back to a 0

The charging current is referred to as a transient current.

This charging current lasts only for the time Δt. Once the capacitor voltage level has changed, I_c is no longer required. Therefore, it is referred to as a "transient" current.

Input current, on the other hand, is a "steady-state" current. It must be present at all times. When the output is a 1 level, the amount of current that must be suppled is $I_{INPUT} = 8 \times 0.01$ mA or 0.08 mA *(Figure 4-13b)*. With a 0 level, the output must sink $I_{INPUT} = 8 \times 1$ mA or 8 mA *(Figure 4-13c)*.

Table I summarizes the output requirements. The minus sign indicating that the output must sink the current.

	I_c	I_{INPUT}	Processor Current
1 LEVEL	1.6 mA	0.08 mA	1.68 mA
0 LEVEL	− 1.6 mA	−8 mA	−9.6 mA

If the microprocessor output cannot supply the required current then buffer drivers must be added to boost the current. *Figure 4-14* shows an example. The I_{INPUT} requirements of the buffer are now 0.05 mA for the 1 level and 1.6 mA for the 0 level but the output can supply 30-40 mA at each level.

**Figure 4-14.
Buffer Amplifier
Application**

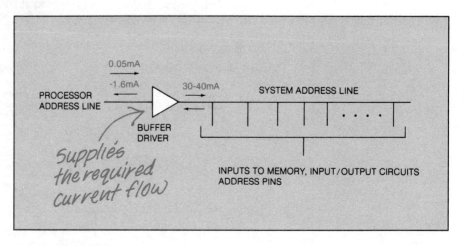

Address Decoding

An address code of 10 bits wide ($2^{10} = 1,024$) is required to address a memory of 1,024 locations.

The need for additional address decoding units is best described by looking at *Figure 4-15*. Each of the blocks being fed by the address bus from the microprocessor is a memory that has 1024 words × N bits. N can be 4, 8, 16 bits depending on the system used. To address the 1024 words, an address code of 10 bits must be sent to the memory because $2^{10} = 1,024$. However, suppose the microprocessor normally outputs a 16-bit address code such that 65,536 words could be located. How are the decoding circuits expanded to allow for memory expansion? *Figure 4-15* expands the 1024 words to 8,192 words.

**Figure 4-15.
Basic Address Decoding
Example, 8192 Location
Memory**

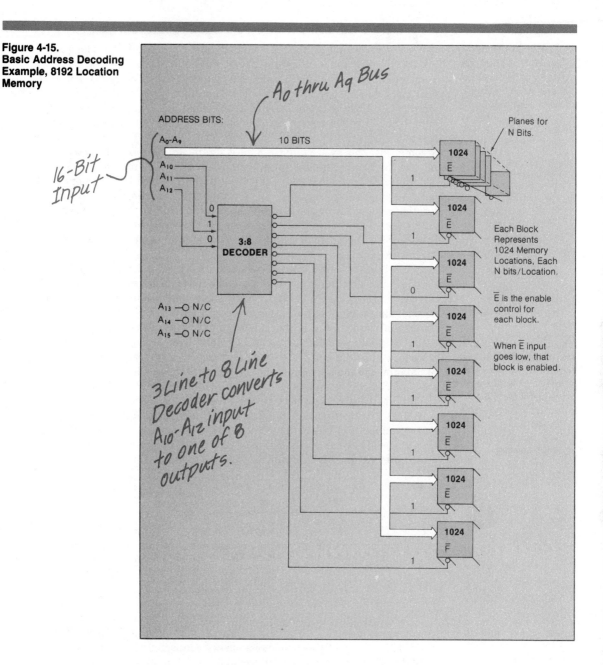

Expanded memory is achieved by utilizing additional decoders to select the particular 1024 block of memory required.

To accomplish this, additional decoder circuits must be added and another input to the memory must be used. The E signal shown on each memory block of *Figure 4-15* is called a memory enable. When E is a 0 level, that memory block is active or enabled. Therefore, each of the eight 1024 word × N bit blocks can be enabled at selected times by controlling the $\overline{\text{E}}$ signal. The third block down is being enabled in *Figure 4-15* because its $\overline{\text{E}}$ signal is a 0 level. All others are a 1 level. The 3-line to 8-line decoder accomplishes this by sensing the 3 most significant bits (A_{10}, A_{11}, & A_{12}) beyond the 10 bits (A_0 through A_9) being fed to the 1024 memory blocks. Therefore, the code on A_{10}, A_{11}, and A_{12} is deciding which 1024 memory block is active and the code on the 10 bits (A_0 thru A_9) is deciding the word location required from the 1024 that are active. Thus, as the 8 blocks are each selected and the individual locations of the active 1024 are selected, 8,192 words of program or data can be written into memory or read out of memory as needed.

The 3-to 8-line decoder is a standard integrated circuit. Additional decoders and/or different decoders would have to be added to expand the memory to the full 65,536 words. But by using simple memory circuits and decoders in the right combination, any size memory can be built, up to the number of words that can be decided on by the microprocessor address code.

The number and organization of individual packages required for a particular word using bits of memory storage will depend on the word and bit organization of the individual memory packages used to make up the total memory.

Figure 4-16 details further the 1024 blocks of *Figure 4-15*. Each word location of memory must have as many bits of storage as the number of data lines in the microprocessor. *Figure 4-16* shows 4 bits, which would be the N of *Figure 4-15*, with one bit coming from each 1024 block. Therefore, the integrated circuit memory package has 1024 word locations of 1 bit each. It is said to organized "1024 by 1." If the integrated circuit package had contained 1024 bits but had 256 word locations, each with 4 bits stored, then it would have an organization of "256 × 4." The number of integrated circuit memory packages organized $W_I × B_I$ to make a total memory of $W_M × B_N$ is:

$$\text{No. of Memory Packages} = \frac{W_M × B_N.}{W_I × B_I}$$

If the 8,192 word memory of *Figure 4-15* is to store 4 bits and is built using memory circuit packages organized 1024 × 1, then the number of packages used is:

$$\frac{8,192}{1,024} × \frac{4}{1} = 32$$

Each individual package would have the 10 bits of the address code connected to it as well as the data-in and the data-out line for each bit. The E signal shown in *Figure 4-15* now is shown connected to $\overline{\text{CE}}$ on each package. This signal is called "chip enable" or "chip select." When the $\overline{\text{E}}$ line is active, each $\overline{\text{CE}}$ activates a 1024 × 1 memory package. Therefore, all four stored bits are activated at the same address so they are written or read at the same time.

Figure 4-16.
1024 Location Memory, 4
Bits/Location

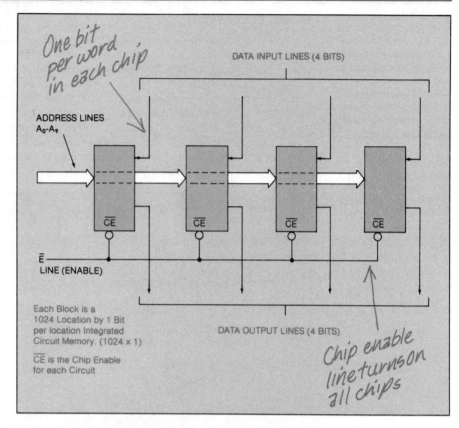

One bit per word in each chip

ADDRESS LINES
A_0-A_9

DATA INPUT LINES (4 BITS)

$\overline{CE}$ $\overline{CE}$ $\overline{CE}$ $\overline{CE}$

$\overline{E}$
LINE (ENABLE)

Each Block is a
1024 Location by 1 Bit
per location Integrated
Circuit Memory. (1024 x 1)

$\overline{CE}$ is the Chip Enable
for each Circuit

DATA OUTPUT LINES (4 BITS)

Chip enable line turns on all chips

All the discussion has been with respect to random access memory, RAM. The RAM shown can be used for program storage or data storage. However, the same decoding principles apply for read-only memory, ROM. Of course, the data-in lines and write signals would not be needed.

Additional decoding circuits can be used in like fashion for an increased number of input or output units beyond that selected by the 10-bit address bus from the microprocessor. These extra decoder circuits enable the additional input/output units with an enable signal just like the memory blocks were enabled. The address lines must be distributed to the additional input or output functional blocks and the data input and output lines gated onto the data bus using circuits previously discussed. Of course, all memory and input/output circuits will be timed and controlled by signals from the microprocessor.

Timing and Control Line Connections

The microprocessor generates control signals for the orderly control of external components.

The microprocessor must generate signals that tell the memory and input/output devices when they are to be turned on and whether they are being read from or written into; otherwise, the system operation would not be orderly. The microprocessor controls the operation of the external components with the following basic types of signals:

Memory Enable Signal

The microprocessor controls the operation of the memory by sending it an address signal on the address bus, ordering it to either read or write, and sending it an enabling signal that allows it to function.

Once the microprocessor knows that a memory operation is to be performed and that the address signals are on the address lines, it must turn on the memory and tell it to read or write. Some microprocessors send out both signals as shown in *Figure 4-17.* A memory enable control signal to turn on the memory and a read/write signal to tell the memory if it is to read or write. Both enable the memory so it carries out the operation in the desired way. The memory enable, no matter how it is provided, must last long enough for the read or write operation to be completed by the memory. These signals must be understood and connected to the memory block correctly if the memory is to behave properly.

**Figure 4-17.
Memory Control**

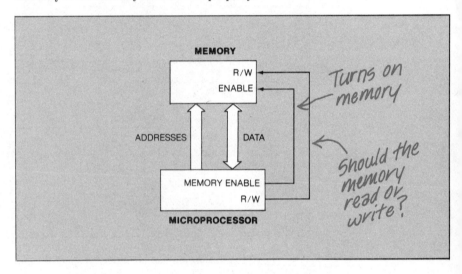

Input/Output Enable Signal

Input/output units of a computer system can be controlled just like memory — with an address, read or write signal and an enable signal.

Some microprocessors are able to treat the input/output devices as a system separate from the memory. In such a case shown in *Figure 4-18,* the microprocessors will send out an I/O enable signal that serves the same purpose for the input/output devices that the memory enable serves for the memory devices. If such an I/O enable signal is used, the read/write signal generated by the microprocessor is used to indicate whether the I/O is sending to the microprocessor or is receiving from the microprocessor. It is also possible for the microprocessor to provide two separate control signals, an I/O read and an I/O write. These signals can be used to turn on the input/output block without turning on the memory blocks. This allows the input/output units to share the same address codes as certain of the memories. Microprocessors that do not support a separate input/output block assume these devices are assigned memory locations, that is, they are treated just as if they were a part of memory. This approach is called memory-mapped I/O, since a certain number of memory locations are assigned to the input and output devices of the system and reserved for their use.

**Figure 4-18.
I/O Control**

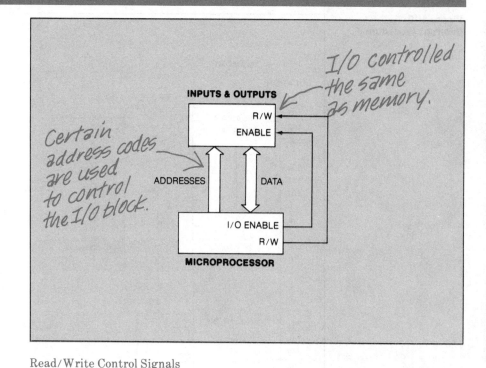

Read/Write Control Signals

The microprocessor provides a signal telling the external peripheral units to send information (read) or receive the information on the data lines (write).

This signal tells the external functional blocks whether they are to send information to the processor (read operation) or receive information from the processor (write operation). Normally, the signal is in the READ state. It only enters the WRITE state for a brief time, during which the microprocessor places data on the data lines. The WRITE state remains long enough for the memory or input/output units to receive the data and to complete the write operation. Microprocessors that provide memory read and memory write control signals instead of the memory enable signal provide a timing signal that can be used with these signals to generate the needed Read/Write control.

Interrupt Signals

An interrupt signal directs the microprocessor to stop what it is doing and handle what caused the interrupt.

All of the timing and control signals discussed so far are ones that come from the microprocessor to control external units. There is one control that is sent to the processor by the external units in order to control the microprocessor. This is the interrupt signal. It does just what it says. It interrupts the microprocessor from what it is doing and causes it to do something indicated by the interrupt signal. This is similar to the way a traffic control policeman is interrupted to get him to handle some emergency, such as a burglary. The policeman responds and tends to the burglary but once he has taken care of it, he returns to his normal job of traffic control. Similarly, when the microprocessor receives the interrupt signal, it finishes whatever instruction it is doing at the time of the interrupt and then responds to the interrupt. This is shown in *Figure 4-19*.

**Figure 4-19.
Interrupt Procedure**

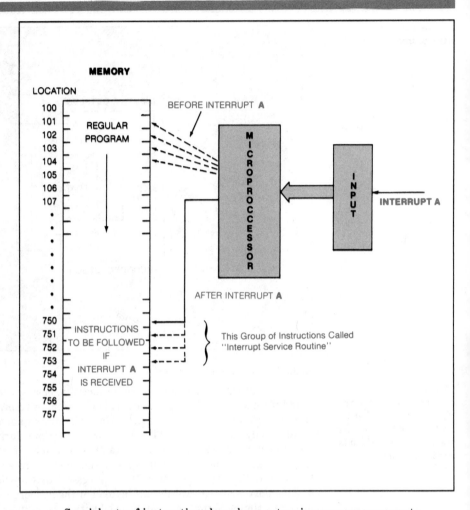

The microprocessor is programmed to respond to an interrupt by going through a specific routine. This involves stopping whatever it was doing in the main program, performing a series of steps and returning to the main program.

Special sets of instructions have been set up in program memory to tell the microprocessor what to do in case a certain interrupt is received. When the interrupt is received, the microprocessor switches and begins following the special instructions until the interrupt requirements are completed. It then switches back to what it was doing before the interrupt. The circuits required to make sure the microprocessor goes to the right sequence of instructions to handle the interrupt varies from microprocessor to microprocessor. The details of these circuits will become clearer when specific examples are discussed in later chapters. For now, it is enough to know that the interrupt signal exists and that without it, information cannot be sent or received from input or output units until the microprocessor says it is ready. With the interrupt signal, in most cases, the microprocessor can be made to receive or send information whenever desired.

Power Connections

All system units will require power. Many early microprocessors made with MOS technology require three power supplies, e.g., $+12V$, $-12V$, $+5V$. Later designs need only a $+5V$ supply and a ground connection. As mentioned previously, when these connections are made through printed wiring on a board, special layouts are required to make sure the conductors are low resistance for the current they carry. Otherwise, errors will occur due to noise signals.

The interconnection phase is now complete. All the address, data, timing and control, interrupts and power lines have now been interconnected between all the system units. What remains is to tell the system what to do. This is done by entering the proper sequence of instructions into program memory. The sequence of instructions – the program – must be written in terms of the instruction set available for the particular microprocessor used.

While generating the program may not be as straightforward as connecting the system together, certainly it is something anyone can do with a little practice. It is difficult knowing where to start, but after a little experience, people catch on quickly. To see what's involved, lets start with the instruction set.

WHAT TYPE OF INSTRUCTIONS ARE THERE?

Most children are used to following instructions. "Wash your face." "Comb your hair." "Eat your lunch." They hear the instructions *(sense)*, understand what the instruction is *(decide)*, and do what is required *(act)*. They understand the language used for the instruction. There is no conversion required.

The same is not true for computers. The language of the digital electronic circuits inside the computer is one composed of the 1 and 0 codes that represent the numbers, letters, symbols, commands used by humans to give instructions to the computer. There is a conversion necessary. A conversion from the human language to the digital codes that the machine understands.

Microprocessors follow instructions in a digital code called machine code.

Any instruction that is to be given to the computer must be in the digital code of the machine so it can *sense* it, *decide* which instruction it is, and *act* to execute the instruction. Therefore, the digital code that the machine understands is called machine code. Instructions for the computer can be programmed directly in the code understood by the machine. If this is done, then the program is being written in machine language, and is called a machine language program. (See *Figure 4-20.*)

**Figure 4-20.
Conversions of High-
Level Language and
Assembly Language
Programs into Machine
Language Programs the
Computer Can
Understand**

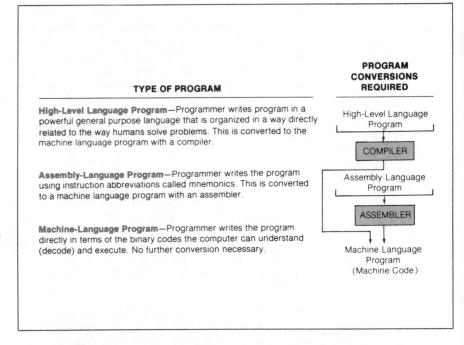

TYPE OF PROGRAM	PROGRAM CONVERSIONS REQUIRED

High-Level Language Program—Programmer writes program in a powerful general purpose language that is organized in a way directly related to the way humans solve problems. This is converted to the machine language program with a compiler.

Assembly-Language Program—Programmer writes the program using instruction abbreviations called mnemonics. This is converted to a machine language program with an assembler.

Machine-Language Program—Programmer writes the program directly in terms of the binary codes the computer can understand (decode) and execute. No further conversion necessary.

High-Level Language Program

COMPILER

Assembly-Language Program

ASSEMBLER

Machine Language Program
(Machine Code)

A computer using a program called an assembler converts an assembly language program into machine language.

The programmer writes the program using assembly language instructions. What the instruction does in assembly language is identified by an abbreviation called a mnemonic.

High-level programming has been developed to make programming easier for humans. The compiler is a program that converts a high-level language program to machine language.

This presents a problem. If the conversion is made by humans, it becomes a tedious, detailed, slow task to get the codes down correctly, and even much more difficult to correct if an error has been made. Computers are good at making such conversions without error. Therefore, the task is usually delegated to the computer. However, a program has to be written to tell the computer what to do. The program that the computer follows is called an Assembler.

Converting to machine code is thus moved one step closer to the human language input. Humans can make their instruction choice by selecting a mnemonic that is an abbreviation of what the instruction does. This programming with mnemonic instructions is called *assembly language programming* because, after the sequence is written, it is fed into the assembler program which makes the conversion to machine code and arranges it into memory in proper order.

Such mnemonic codes are still not like the normal language that humans speak; therefore, additional thrusts have been made to be able to write programs in a language closer to the human language. Such programming is called *higher-level language programming*. Another type of computer program is required to convert from the high-level language statements to the machine code. It is called a compiler. It is more involved now because the conversion is much more difficult. The easier the programming is made by bringing the language closer to the human language, the more complex the computer program needed to convert to machine language statements in machine code. But once that conversion program is available, it can be used over and over again as necessary.

Microprocessor Instruction Set

By using a basic set of assembly language instructions the micro-computer system can perform almost any desired function.

The microprocessor instruction set has its instructions stated in mnemonic assembly-language format, and it is understood that a conversion is required to arrive at the necessary machine code. The instructions that the microprocessor executes are very basic operations as shown in *Figure 4-21*. By using these simple operations in the right combination, the microcomputer system can be made to behave in almost any way desired. These simple instructions will perform very accurate and complicated mathematical operations or act as a very sophisticated communications control center, depending on how they are combined into a total program. Lets look at what basic operations are available. As shown in *Figure 4-21*, a subset of the instructions will do arithmetic – add, subtract, absolute value, negation, multiply, divide. Other subsets provide instructions to move data, to shift data, to perform logical operations, to compare data, and to change program paths (branch) either directly or after a decision is made.

Of all of these types of instructions, the simplest group is the data movement instructions.

**Figure 4-21.
General Types of
Microprocessor
Instructions**

ARITHMETIC	LOGICAL	COMPARISON
Adds	AND	
Subtracts	OR	
Absolute Value	NOT	**BRANCH**
Negation	Exclusive-OR	Unconditional
Multiply		Conditional
Divide	**DATA MOVEMENT**	Subroutine
Shifts	**OR TRANSFER**	
	Move	
	Load	
	Store	

Data Movement Instructions

Data movement instructions are the programmer's way of using the machine codes for relocating data from one functional unit within the microprocessor system to another.

In the past discussions, there have been numerous times when reference was made to moving or transferring digital codes from one location to another. The data movement or transfer instructions are for this purpose. They provide for moving the digital codes from one part of the microcomputer system to another. Here are some examples:

1) Move data from memory to a register inside the microprocessor to prepare for additional operations.
2) Move data from a microprocessor register to memory or to an output.
3) Move program constants from program memory to initialize microprocessor registers.
4) Initialize data memory locations or output unit registers with constant values.
5) Move data from inputs to a register inside the microprocessor.

Basically, these instructions take a digital code from one register or memory location and put it in another register or memory location.

Mnemonics

Most microprocessors support all of these types of data movement operations. Some processors may call these operations load or store. Other processors simply call these operations "movement instructions." Regardless of what the microprocessor manufacturer calls the instructions a shorthand is required so that the full name of movement or load or store does not need to be written everytime they are listed in a program sequence. Here is where the mnemonics come in. These abbreviations are very short (at most three or four letters long) and they usually are relatively obvious abbreviations of the operation, such as: MOV for movement instructions; LD for the LOAD operation; ST for the store operation. Others are SWP for swap and XCHG for exchange. There will be one for each instruction.

Operands

The mnemonic instructions include not only the operation to be performed but what is to be operated on — the operand.

It must be understood that to make these instructions complete, more information is included with the mnemonic to indicate which number, register, or memory location contents are to be "operated on" by the operation called for by the instruction.

For example:

MOV R1, R2

means move the contents of register R1 to register R2. R1 and R2 are called "operands" of the instruction. MOV is the data movement operation. Such instructions are also diagrammed with symbols to describe what the instruction means.

For example:

MOV R1, R2

is summarized by

(R1) $\longrightarrow$ (R2).

The parenthesis means the contents; therefore, the instruction reads: Take the contents of R1 and move these contents to register R2.

There is a significant difference between the address of a memory location and the contents of that memory location.

Remember the parenthesis notation and its meaning. It is very important because careful separation must be made by the microprocessor user between the contents of a memory word and the address. The microcomputer system goes to an address to locate the place of storage. What is contained in that place of storage is the contents. In the MOV R1, R2 instruction, register R1 may be at a storage location (address) identified by the 16-bit code 0000 0101 0000 0001, but the contents of register R1 to be used for the move operation might be the decimal number 32 represented by the binary code 0010 0000.

Assemblying The Instructions

The assembly language program, after conversion by an assembler, is placed in proper order and stored in program memory.

Refer to *Figure 4-22*. When the instruction sequence is written using the language of mnemonics (the abbreviations) the person is programming in assembly language. The assembly language abbreviations for a given processor are easy to learn and are in a form for writing programs. As shown in *Figure 4-22*, before the program is complete, the program statements must be converted to machine code and stored in the proper order in the program memory of the microcomputer system. They must be assembled by the assembler.

This can be done by hand. Each instruction has a machine code listing that corresponds to the mnemonics. The corresponding machine code is recorded at each step in the program, as shown in *Figure 4-22*. Obviously, it is much more convenient to have the program conversion done with the assembler so that the listing is done automatically.

**Figure 4-22.
Microprocessor Program
Languages**

ASSEMBLY-LANGUAGE PROGRAM	MACHINE-LANGUAGE PROGRAM	MEANING OF INSTRUCTION
CMA	0010 1111	Complement A Register
MOV B, A	0100 0111	Move Contents of B Register to A Register
INR A	0011 1100	Increment Contents of A Register

Arithmetic Instructions and Number Codes

The microprocessor typically offers addition and subtraction as the basic arithmetic operations. Some processors will offer multiplication, division, negation (change sign), and absolute value as well. Others offer adding or subtracting by one — increment and decrement.

The mnemonics for most of these instructions again are rather obvious.

1) A or AD or ADD for addition
2) S or SU or SB for subtraction
3) MPY for multiply
4) DIV for divide
5) INC or INR for increment
6) DEC or DCR for decrement
7) NEG for change sign
8) ABS for absolute value

Binary Numbers And Decimal Equivalents

In arithmetic operations, numbers (data) are used as operands. A microprocessor that acts on data N bits at a time has the capability of distinguishing between 2^N different numbers. If all the numbers are positive they will range from 0 up to $2^N - 1$. Therefore, an 8-bit code can represent 256 positive numbers from 0 to 255.

Binary digital codes may be converted to the decimal equivalent by summing the weighted values of each "1" in the binary number.

The method for converting from the binary digital codes to the corresponding decimal numbers is shown in *Figure 4-23*. If the least significant binary code signal (d_0) is a 1, a 1 is added to the decimal equivalent number, starting at zero. If d_0 is 0, nothing is added to the decimal sum. If the next binary digit (d_1) is a 1, 2 is added to the decimal sum; if d_1 is 0, nothing is added to the sum. Similarly, if d_2 is 1, 4 is added to the decimal sum, and so on. In general, if d_N is 1, 2^N is added to the sum. This procedure, called an algorithm in computer terminology, can be summarized as:

Start with the decimal number zero and add 2^j for each binary bit d_j that is a 1.

An algorithm means a procedure for a solution. It is an important word in microprocessor jargon and will be used repeatedly throughout this book.

**Figure 4-23.
Conversion of a Binary
Number to its Decimal
Equivalent**

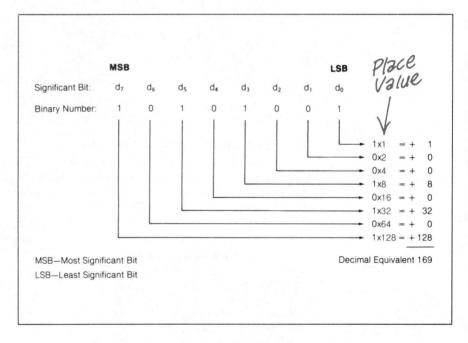

MSB—Most Significant Bit
LSB—Least Significant Bit

Decimal Equivalent 169

Negative Numbers

Negative numbers may be expressed in an 8-bit binary code by assigning the d_7 position as a sign bit. When d_7 is a 1, the number is negative, otherwise it is positive. The other seven binary digits have their usual value.

When a microprocessor performs arithmetic operations, it must allow for the possibility that numbers will be negative. The algorithm of *Figure 4-23* provided all positive numbers. The 256 binary codes could have represented any 256 different numbers. Another algorithm is shown in *Figure 4-24*. It is a two's complement decimal equivalent. *Figure 4-24* illustrates how an 8-bit code can represent positive numbers from 0 to + 127 and negative numbers from -1 to -128. A change has been made in the definition of d_7. Instead of adding + 128 when d_7 = 1, as in *Figure 4-23*, it now means that the number is negative and -128 is added to the decimal sum. Therefore, the positive numbers from 0 to + 127 result when d_7 = 0 and the negative numbers from -1 to -128 result when d_7 = 1. In this case d_7 is no longer a significant bit for the decimal equivalent. It is what is called a "sign bit." It also becomes a convenient check to determine if a number is positive or negative (d_7 = 0 means positive, d_7 = 1 means negative).

**Figure 4-24.
Positive and Negative
Numbers with 8-Bit Code**

8 BIT BINARY CODE	DECIMAL EQUIVALENT OF MAGNITUDE CODE	DECIMAL EQUIVALENT OF TWO'S COMPLEMENT CODE
0000 0000	0	+ 0
0000 0001	1	+ 1
0000 0010	2	+ 2
.	.	.
.	.	.
.	.	.
0111 1111	127	+ 127
1 000 0000	128	− 128
1 000 0001	129	− 127
1 000 0010	130	− 126
.	.	.
.	.	.
.	.	.
1111 0001	241	− 15
1111 0010	242	− 14
.	.	.
.	.	.
1111 1111	255	− 1

In the microprocessor, subtraction of two numbers is performed by adding the first number to the two's complement of the second number.

Figure 4-25 shows how these negative numbers (the two's complement) are used directly for adding negative numbers or subtracting positive numbers. As mentioned previously, subtraction is performed in microprocessors by taking the two's complement of a number and adding it to another number (which is the one it is to be subtracted from). Since the negative numbers are already in two's complement form they are used directly in adding a negative number to a positive number or in subtracting a positive number from another positive number *(Figure 4-25)*.

**Figure 4-25.
Subtraction Using Two's
Complement Addition**

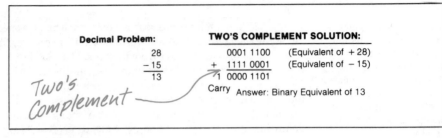

Decimal Problem:		TWO'S COMPLEMENT SOLUTION:	
	28	0001 1100	(Equivalent of +28)
	−15	+ 1111 0001	(Equivalent of −15)
	13	1 0000 1101	
		Carry	Answer: Binary Equivalent of 13

Two's Complement →

Binary-Coded-Decimal Code-BCD

Binary Coded Decimal (BCD) codes are used in some microprocessor systems·rather than straight binary codes. They are most useful for doing decimal arithmetic.

Microprocessor systems also use other forms of number codes. One of these is *Binary-Coded-Decimal* or BCD code. This code is most useful for doing decimal arithmetic with a binary arithmetic unit. In this code, as shown in *Figure 4-26*, the 8-bit code is grouped into two groups of 4 bits each. Each 4-bit group represents a decimal number from 0 to 9 depending on its code *(Figure 4-26a)*. The two groups side-by-side represent decimal numbers from 0 to 99 *(Figure 4-26b)*.

**Figure 4-26.
Binary Addition of BCD
Coded Numbers**

BCD Code	Decimal Equivalent	8-Bit BCD Coded Number	Decimal Equivalent
0000	0	0000 0000	0
0001	1	0000 0001	1
0010	2	.	.
0011	3	.	.
0100	4	.	.
0101	5	0001 0000	10
0110	6	0001 0001	11
0111	7	.	.
1000	8	.	.
1001	9	.	.
		1001 1000	98
		1001 1001	99

a. BCD Code to Decimal
Conversion

b. Range of BCD codes with 8 bits

This is illegal because 1001,(9), is the highest allowed number in BCD. →

Decimal Addition Problem	Binary Addition of BCD Codes	Effect of Decimal Adjust Instruction*
45	0100 0101	0111 1110
+ 39	+ 0011 1001	+ 0000 0110
84	0111 1110	1000 0100
	Illegal Code	BCD Equivalent of 84

*The DAA operation adds 0110 to illegal codes or incorrect decimal results
to produce the correct decimal result in BCD code.

c. Decimal Addition

When adding certain numbers together that are BCD coded, an illegal total may result — a number greater than 1001 is illegal. To offset this, an adjustment code is added to the illegal code.

Now, when adding in this fashion, the microprocessor must make sure that the addition results in the proper code of 0000 through 1001 (binary equivalents of the decimal digits 0 through 9) for each 4-bit group. This is accomplished by the processor by making an adjustment in the code. *Figure 4-26c* illustrates this. The BCD codes for the numbers 45 and 39 are being added. The result is an illegal code in one of the 4-bit group positions. To get back the legal code the microprocessor must do an additional step and add an adjustment code of 0110 to the 4-bit group that has the illegal code. Any carrys resulting from this addition in the 4-bit group must be added to the next-most-significant decimal-digit 4-bit group.

Many microprocessors have a DAA instruction to do this adjustment.

Microprocessors can be instructed to do an adjustment like this with an instruction called a decimal adjust, often using the mnemonic DAA. The DAA not only checks for the illegal codes but it also makes any other adjustments automatically to get the correct decimal result. Therefore, following a binary addition instruction with a decimal adjust instruction performs the BCD code addition. The result is 4-bit groups that are binary equivalents of the decimal digits.

Hexadecimal Codes

Another very useful code is the hexadecimal code. It groups the binary code into 4-bit groups and identifies the groups with a single number or letter.

Another code that is very useful is the hexadecimal code (for a hexadecimal number system). It also groups the code in 4-bit groups and replaces the 4-bit group with a single digit symbol. *Figure 4-27* shows this code. The digits, 0 through F, are the single-digit symbols for the 16 possible 4-bit groups. Thus, this code is sometimes referred to as base 16 code and numbers represented in this code are often shown as 0200_{16}. The small subscript 16 indicating hexadecimal representation. By using the hexadecimal digits, an 8-bit binary code can be summarized with just two symbols. For example, the binary code:

1010 0011

can be written simply with the hexadecimal equivalent:

A3

Similarly, the address code:

1111 1101 0010 1110

can be simplified with the corresponding hexadecimal number:

FD2E.

**Figure 4-27.
Hexadecimal (Base 16)
Digits and Binary
Equivalents**

Binary Code	Hexadecimal Digit	Binary Code	Hexadecimal Digit
0000	0	1000	8
0001	1	1001	9
0010	2	1010	A
0011	3	1011	B
0100	4	1100	C
0101	5	1101	D
0110	6	1110	E
0111	7	1111	F

Hexadecimal has a base of 16. It is widely used because it readily lends itself to a shorthand way of writing binary numbers.

If a code is written in the shorthand hexadecimal form, how does one find the decimal equivalent? As shown in *Figure 4-28*, a method is used that is similar to the approach used in converting a binary code to its decimal equivalent. Multiply the least significant hexadecimal digit (d_0) by 1, the next digit (d_1) by 16, the next digit (d_2) by 16^2 (256) and the next digit (d_3) by 16^3 (4096). Then FD2E would be represented as a decimal number = $(15 \times 4096 + 13 \times 256 + 2 \times 16 + 14 \times 1)$ or 64,814. Throughout this book the hexadecimal code will be used, since it greatly simplifies the writing of binary signal patterns. It will always be a simple matter to convert the hex code to binary form by just replacing each hex digit by its binary equivalent. Thus, to convert the hex number 8B to an 8-bit binary code, the 8 is replaced with 1000 and the B with 1011 to get:

$$8B_{16} = 10001011_2$$

The subscripts 16 and 2 are used to denote which base was used for the code — 16 for hexadecimal, 2 for binary.

**Figure 4-28.
Conversion of
Hexadecimal Number to
Decimal Equivalent**

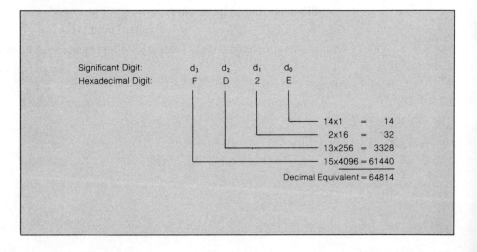

Status Bits — Zero and Sign

Special status bits are used to store important information about the results of an operation for future reference.

After arithmetic operations such as subtraction or addition, some condition of the overall result of the operation is stored to be able to keep track of the result. For example, if the result is zero, this may be important, so processors save that fact in a flip-flop called the zero flip-flop. By referring to the contents of the zero flip-flop with later instructions, a check can be made to see if the results of a given operation was zero or not. Additional actions by the microprocessor are then keyed to this fact. Similarly, by saving the sign bit of a number code in a sign flip-flop, later checks can be made to see if the result of an operation was positive or negative. These are two examples of what are called *status bits*. Processors contain a register, often called the status register, that is made up of these individual sign, zero, and other condition flip-flops. Some processors call these bits the condition code and others call them the status. They serve to save the nature of the result of an operation for later reference by the microprocessor.

Status Bits — Carry and Borrow

An addition may result in a carry condition, or a subtraction may result in a borrow situation. This extra bit is stored in a carry status bit.

Another such status or condition bit that has already been encountered is the carry condition as the result of an addition problem. When two N-bit numbers are added and a carry out results from the bit sum as shown in *Figure 4-29*, this fact is saved in a flip-flop in the status register called the carry status bit. Similarly, if in subtracting two numbers a borrow is needed, that fact is also saved in the carry status bit. The carry and borrow status are passed on to higher-order digit positions in addition or subtraction. Many processors provide add-with-a-carry and subtract-with-a-borrow instructions. This makes it easier to handle the carries and borrows in problems using multiple 8-bit groups (multi-byte problems).

**Figure 4-29.
Carry Status Bit**

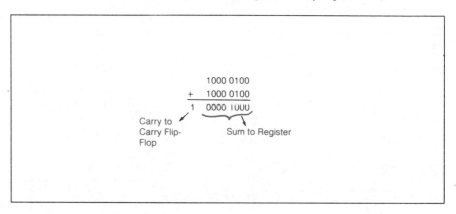

Status Bit — Overflow

If a computation results in an overflow, an overflow status bit is set.

Another status bit that some processors provide is called an overflow status bit. When using the two's complement code for binary numbers, a given N-bit number can only express numbers within a certain range. *Figure 4-24* showed how an 8-bit code represented numbers from -128 to +127. The sum of +100 and +100 = +200 cannot be represented properly by the code. Similarly, subtracting 100 from -100 results in -200 which cannot be represented properly by the code. The situation is much like trying to put 2 gallons of water in a one gallon container. The water overflows the container and spills out over the surrounding area after 1 gallon has been poured and pouring continues. Similarly, if the result of an arithmetic operation is beyond the range of the two's complement code, an overflow results, and this fact is stored by setting an overflow flip-flop in the status register to a 1. In the next instruction the overflow flip-flop can be checked to see if an overflow has occurred. If it has, action is taken to correct the situation.

Some processors use other status bits. Carry, zero, sign and overflow are the ones that are used the most.

Shift Instructions

Shifting a positive binary number one bit to the right and inserting a zero in the MSB position divides the number by 2. A 1 is inserted for a negative two's complement number.

Shifting is a microprocessor operation that is often considered to be a type of arithmetic operation. In Chapter 3, it was shown that shifting a number to the right in a register is the same as performing a divide-by-2 operation. *Figure 4-30* carries this a step further to show the end bits inserted during the shifting. To divide a positive binary number by 2, a 0 is shifted into the vacated most-significant-bit position (d_7). To divide a negative two's complement number by 2, a 1 is shifted into the vacated leftmost position.

**Figure 4-30.
Effect of Right Shift on
Binary Numbers**

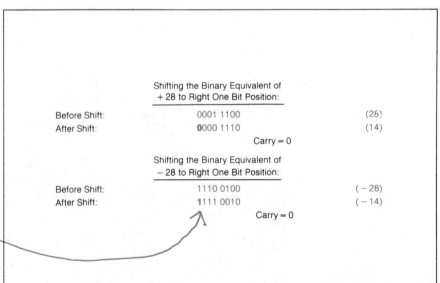

Shifting the Binary Equivalent of
+ 28 to Right One Bit Position:

Before Shift:	0001 1100	(26)
After Shift:	0000 1110	(14)
	Carry = 0	

Shifting the Binary Equivalent of
− 28 to Right One Bit Position:

Before Shift:	1110 0100	(− 28)
After Shift:	1111 0010	(− 14)
	Carry = 0	

This bit must remain a "1" because it signifies this is a negative number.

Shift Right—Logical, Arithmetic, Circulate

Different microprocessors may provide arithmetic, logical or circulating shift to the right or left.

Usually, there are 2 or 3 different shift operations to choose from, depending on the microprocessor. *Figure 4-31* diagrams shifting right for 3 of them — logical, arithmetic and circulate. A logical shift right is one that shifts the least-significant bit into the carry flip-flop and shifts a 0 in from the left. This would be used for dividing an unsigned binary number by 2 or for examining the least-significant bit of a number.

**Figure 4-31.
Microprocessor Shift-Right Operations**

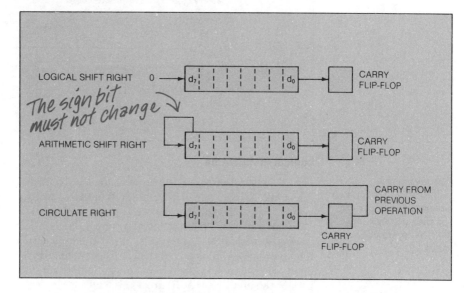

An arithmetic shift right is one that shifts the least-significant bit into the carry flip-flop and shifts the sign bit (d_7) into the next bit (d_6) to the right. The sign bit is unchanged. This shift operation will divide a signed (positive or negative) two's complement number by 2.

A right circulate operation sends the carry flip-flop value into the left side of the number and shifts the least-significant bit into the carry flip-flop. This operation is useful when a shift is performed on a multiple-byte group of binary digits.

Shift Left — Logical, Circulate

The shift left operation multiplies a number by two.

When a binary number is shifted to the left, the number is being multiplied by 2. *Figure 4-32* details these shifts. Most microprocessors have at least 2 of these. The logical shift-left instruction shifts the leftmost bit into the carry flip-flop and shifts a 0 into the vacated least-significant-bit position. This instruction is useful for multiplying a number by 2 or for examining the value of most significant binary bit (d_7).

A left circulate does the opposite operation to the right circulate. The value in the carry flip-flop is shifted into the vacated least-significant-bit position. The bit being shifted out of the most-significant position is stored in the carry flip-flop. This operation is useful for performing a shift left on multiple groups of 8-bit codes (multiple-byte group of binary bits).

**Figure 4-32.
Microprocessor Shift-
Left Operations**

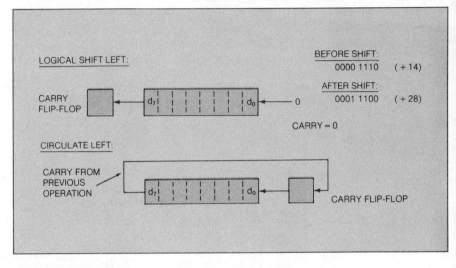

Logical Instructions

The microprocessor is capable, when appropriately programmed, of performing the same logic functions as separate logic gates.

Microprocessors usually offer the basic logical operations of OR, AND, and NOT on a bit-by-bit basis. What this means, as shown in *Figure 4-33*, is that each logical operation is performed as if the input were fed into a 2-input gate, each bit position at a time. Like the OR gate operation discussed in Chapter 3, the result bit (C) at a bit location is a 1 if either of the input bits (A, B) is a 1. In the NOT operation, the result (C) is a 1 if the input bit (A) is a 0. In the AND operation the result bit (C) is a 1 only if both of the input bits (A, B) are a 1. Usually the logical operation called exclusive-OR, often denoted by the abbreviation or mnemonic XOR, is also provided. This is a logical gate that has not been mentioned before, but it is very useful for comparisons. *Figure 4-33* can be used as its truth table. The XOR bit position result bit (C) is a 1 only if the 2 input bits are different (A = 1 and B = 0 or A = 0 and B = 1). Otherwise, when the inputs are the same the result bit is a 0.

**Figure 4-33.
Microprocessor Logical
Operations**

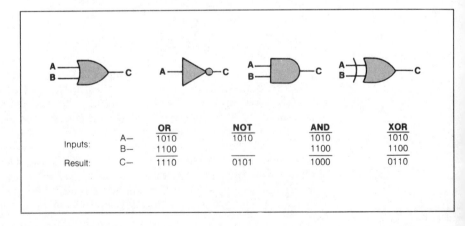

Use Of The NOT Function

The NOT logic function, which is an inverter, may be used to generate the two's complement of a number.

A simple use of the NOT operation is to create the two's complement of a binary number. One way of finding the two's complement of a number is to invert all of its bits and add one to the number. This is detailed in *Figure 4-34*. Thus, the two's complement of the binary number 0010 1001 0101 1010 is 1101 0110 1010 0101 (the NOT of the number) plus 1 or 1101 0110 1010 0110. Recall that in *Figure 3-37* the adder had inverters on the inputs. These inverters provided the NOT function to provide the two's complement addition for the subtraction of numbers.

**Figure 4-34.
Use of NOT Operation to
Form Two's Complement
of a Binary Number**

Binary Number A:	0010	1001	0101	1010
Complement (NOT) of A:	1101	0110	1010	0101
Add 1:	0000	0000	0000	0001
Result is Two's Complement of A:	1101	0110	1010	0110

Use Of The OR Function

Particular bits in a number may be set to a 1 by ORing a control code with the original number.

The OR operation is used to set certain bits to 1 without affecting the other bits in the binary code. An example is shown in *Figure 4-35*. A system has 8 lights that can be turned on (output a 1) or off (output a 0). They are controlled by an 8-bit binary output code. In *Figure 4-35*, under present conditions, lights 1 through 4 are turned on. In the next step these will be left on, but lights 5 and 8 will be turned on also. An instruction to OR the binary number 0000 1001 with the current on-off code of 1111 0000 results in the output code 1111 1001. This code controls the lights so that the first four lights are left on, lights 5 and 8 are turned on, and lights 6 and 7 are left off.

**Figure 4-35.
Use of OR in Simple
Control Operations**

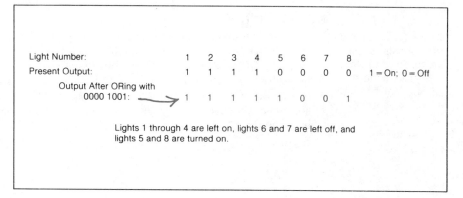

Light Number:	1	2	3	4	5	6	7	8	
Present Output:	1	1	1	1	0	0	0	0	1 = On; 0 = Off
Output After ORing with 0000 1001:	1	1	1	1	1	0	0	1	

Lights 1 through 4 are left on, lights 6 and 7 are left off, and lights 5 and 8 are turned on.

Use Of The AND Function

The AND function may be used to mask out certain bits or to examine a single bit. This is accomplished by ANDing the required masking code with the original code.

The AND operation is used to mask out certain bits of a number. For example, suppose an 8-bit code contains 2 decimal digits, such as the code 1001 0011 representing the decimal number 93 shown in *Figure 4-36a*. Suppose 3 is the only digit of interest. With an instruction to AND the binary code 0000 1111 with 1001 0011, the most-significant four bits will be masked off because in the result they go to 0, and the least four significant bits remain unchanged at 0011. Thus, the 03 has been isolated from the 93. The AND operation also is used to examine a single bit of a binary number. For example *(Figure 4-36b)*, if the least significant bit d_0 is the only bit of interest, it can be examined by the instruction to AND the binary number with 0000 0001. This will zero the first seven bits and leave d_0 unchanged. If d_0 is 0, the zero flip-flop will be set to a 1; if $d_0 = 1$, the zero flip-flop will be cleared to 0. Instructions that refer to the contents of the zero flip-flop later on in the program will verify that d_0 was a 1 or a 0 and react accordingly.

All of these operations have more complicated applications. Later in the book we will look at these in more detail. Generally, they are all based on variations of the examples that have been looked at here.

Figure 4-36.
Use of AND for Masking or Examining Bits

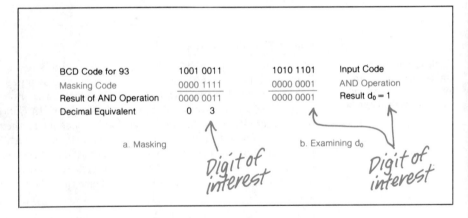

BCD Code for 93	1001 0011		1010 1101	Input Code
Masking Code	0000 1111		0000 0001	AND Operation
Result of AND Operation	0000 0011		0000 0001	Result $d_0 = 1$
Decimal Equivalent	0	3		

a. Masking

Digit of interest

b. Examining d_0

Digit of interest

Use Of XOR For Comparison

The exclusive OR function is used for comparison. By inputting the two codes to be examined bit by bit, the output will be a 1 when any bits are different.

One simple comparison of codes can be accomplished with the exclusive-OR instruction. Referring back to *Figure 4-33*, each bit by bit exclusive-OR result would be 0 if all bits in both codes were the same. If any bit positions are different a 1 will result in that position. All the resulting bits would be latched into a register at the same time and shifted out. If a 1 appears at the output during the shift, the codes were different and action based on this fact is initiated.

Comparison Instructions

Comparison instructions are usually accomplished by subtracting two numbers, which do not change either number. Status bits are set to indicate the result.

Microprocessor instruction sets usually contain comparison instructions because many tests and comparisons must be made on binary codes without changing the codes. These instructions cause the second number in the comparison to be subtracted from the first. The subtraction affects the status or condition code bits but does not change either number involved in the comparison. The results of the comparison can be used later by checking the condition code flip-flops. The most common checks made are to the zero flip-flop to see if the two numbers or codes were the same, and the sign flip-flop to see if the first number were greater than or equal to the second number. By using these comparisons with related instructions called conditional branch instructions, step-by-step sequences of instructions can be written that make very complicated decisions.

Branch Instructions

An instruction that causes the microprocessor to break its normal sequential routine and get its instruction from a new area of memory is called a branch or jump instruction.

Recall that the microprocessor executes the instructions addressed by the program counter. Unless the processor is told to do otherwise, it will continue taking instructions from memory in order, one right after another, because the program counter is normally incremented automatically to the next instruction in sequence. However, sometimes a change is required to a sequence of instructions located somewhere else in memory. A case in point is an interrupt. In such a case, instead of incrementing the program counter to move the instruction address one memory location down from where it was, the program counter is loaded with a new address to cause the next instruction to be taken out of the normal sequence. The instruction that does this is called the branch or jump instruction because the program jumps to a new part of memory to take the next instruction. The result of the jump or branch is to load the program counter with a new value or address. Instructions will then be taken in sequence from that address until another branch or jump instruction is encountered.

Unconditional Branch

The unconditional branch instruction causes the microprocessor to proceed to another instruction location without condition, no ifs, ands or buts.

Figure 4-37 diagrams the sequence of events that happens when a branch instruction occurs. In this case the JUMP mnemonic is used. Let's follow the sequence of events. It starts at **1** with the program counter asking for the next instruction at memory location 500 by placing that address on the address bus. The memory decodes this address and at **2** locates the stored contents at location 500. At **3** it sends the instruction to the instruction register of the microprocessor. The decode and control in the microprocessor decides that the instruction says "JUMP to 1000". At **4** the program counter is loaded with the address 1000. The program counter at 5 jumps the address of the next instruction to 1000 rather than sending the normally incremented next instruction address of 501. At **6** the memory decoder locates memory word 1000 and reads out its contents to the instruction register as the next instruction. As a result of this sequence for

the JUMP instruction the program has departed from its normal
incremented sequence to a new sequence of instructions starting at a new
location. Such a branch or jump instruction is called an unconditional
branch because the instruction is to go directly to another location for the
next instruction. There are no conditions attached to the instruction.

**Figure 4-37.
Effect of a JUMP
Instruction
(Unconditional Branch)**

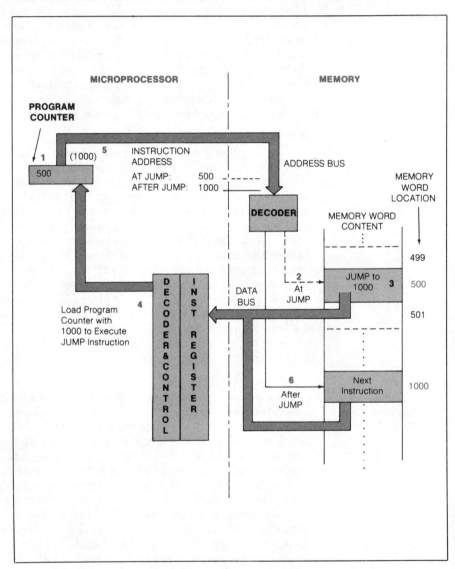

Conditional Branch

In a conditional branch situation, conditions are applied to determine if the program branches to a new location.

Sometimes the jump to the new sequence of instructions should occur only if certain conditions are met. One example that occurs is that the jump to a new sequence should not be done until the present sequence has been executed a certain number of times. *Figure 4-38a* diagrams the events in flow chart form. To help in the use and creating of this type of chart, let's follow it in detail. What the flow chart is saying is this: The rectangle **2** identified by "Loop Sequence of Instructions" are instructions that the microprocessor system will follow to be able to do a task over and over again. An example would be a set of instructions to continue to double a given number. The rectangle **3** is an arithmetic instruction that subtracts 1 from a register value. In this case the register is being used as a counter; therefore, it is named counter. The diamond block **4** is a decision block asking the question, "Is the counter (register) value equal to 0?" This is the operation of the conditional branch. There are 2 paths. If the answer is "No", the microprocessor system is directed along path **5** and will go back to do again the sequence of instructions identified by **2**. If the answer is "Yes", the system moves out of this "loop" of instructions and on into a new sequence of instructions. The block **1** identifies the instructions that are necessary to load the register used as a counter with the initial value of the number of times the system should do the loop sequence. As the flow chart shows, each time the system does the sequence, the counter value is reduced by 1 until it is 0. When it is 0, the loop sequence has been executed the required number of times and the system goes on to do further instructions in the program.

A common program segment that uses a conditional branch instruction is a loop.

Figure 4-38b details portions of what the program steps might look like to instruct the system to perform the loop sequence 8 times. A data movement instruction begins the sequence to set the initial value of the counter to 8. The loop sequence is not detailed but covered by a general notation (it does contain several instruction steps of different types). However, after the loop sequence, the instruction DCR C is the next instruction. This tells the system to reduce the value of the counter by 1. Next is the conditional branch instruction JNZ LOOP. This instruction means Jump on Not Zero to the location labeled LOOP. It is a "branch on not equal to zero." The instruction checks the contents of the counter (zero or not) and sets the zero flip-flop. The zero flip-flop is checked for its value. If it is a 0, the system loops back through the sequence; if it is a 1 (if the register value is zero, the zero flip-flop will be set to a 1), the system does not loop back but goes on to the following instructions in the program. We'll learn more about this later, but note that the sequence of instructions has been labeled with the word LOOP rather than a specific address location. This will make this instruction location easy to reference as it is used in the program.

**Figure 4-38.
Use of Conditional
Branch Instructions**

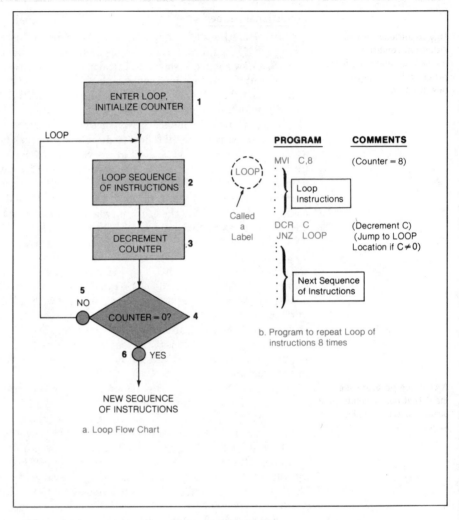

a. Loop Flow Chart

b. Program to repeat Loop of instructions 8 times

There are a great many conditional jump situations possible.

Many other conditional jump instructions are usually available. Some of these make simple checks, such as, "Was the last result positive?", "Was there a carry?", "Was there a borrow?", and so on. Other conditional branch instructions may make more complicated decisions using several of the condition bits stored in a status register, such as the overflow and sign bits which were mentioned previously. Such a variety of conditional branch instructions means that most types of decisions can be written easily in a program.

Linking Back In Subroutines

If a conditional jump
instruction is to return to
the main program at the
place from which it left, a
subroutine jump instruc-
tion is used to provide the
method and information
for the jump instruction to
return to the original
sequence of instructions.

There is one problem that may or may not be apparent with the
jump and branch instructions used thus far. The branch or jump instruction
changed from one sequence of the program to another sequence located in
some other part of memory. There is no way left to get back to the original
sequence of instructions. A branch instruction that provides this link back
to the normal sequence is called a subroutine branch or jump instruction.
The subroutine jump instruction does this by determining the address of
the next instruction after the jump instruction and saves this value
somewhere in the processor or system memory. When the subroutine is
finished and a return to the normal sequence is required, a return
instruction is used that causes the saved value to be reloaded back into the
program counter. The system returns to where it was at the time of the subroutine jump.

In a subroutine jump operation, the address of the
next instruction after the
subroutine call is saved so
that the system may re-
turn to the main program
and continue where it left
off after the subroutine is
completed.

Figure 4-39 diagrams this operation. Everything is the same as
with the JUMP instruction of *Figure 4-37* through step **5** of the sequence,
except that the instruction at location 500 is now "JUMP to subroutine at
1000". Also, at step **5** because of the subroutine jump instruction, the
address of the next instruction in the normal sequence (502) is saved in a
storage register at **6**. At **7** the program counter has directed the system to
the first address of the subroutine sequence, 1000, and the system continues
step-by-step to the end of the subroutine. At **8**, the end of the subroutine,
there is another branch or jump instruction that is decoded and controls the
reloading of the 502 address from the storage register back to the program
counter at **9**. When the 502 address is again placed on the address bus at **10**,
the next instruction is obtained from location 502 at **11** and the system has
returned to the normal sequence it was following before the subroutine
jump instruction.

Let's summarize – a subroutine is a sequence of instructions, a
subprogram, that usually is developed to perform specific tasks that have a
likelihood they will be needed several times in a given program. The first
instruction of the subroutine is located by a branch or jump instruction, and
the subroutine sequence contains an end instruction that returns the
system back to the original point in the normal program sequence where
the subroutine instruction occurred. Arithmetic sequences with large-word-
length numbers, especially multiplication and division, are examples of
subroutines that are prepared and used over and over again in a program
when needed.

4

FUNDAMENTALS OF MICROCOMPUTER SYSTEM OPERATION

**Figure 4-39.
Subroutine Jump
Operation**

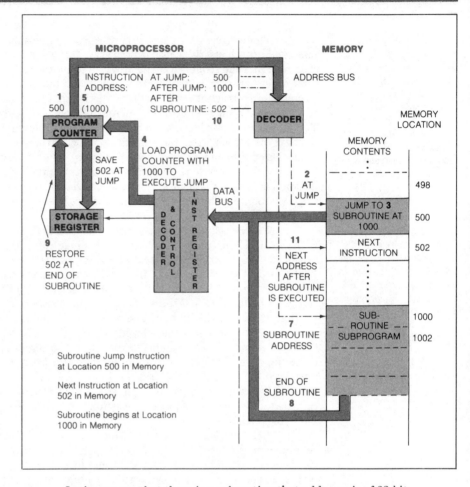

A big advantage of using a subroutine is that it need only appear once in memory, even though a long program sequence may require it many times. Each time in the normal program sequence that the subroutine is required, a subroutine jump instruction is inserted.

Let's suppose that there is a subroutine that adds a pair of 32-bit binary numbers. The normal program sequence is being followed. As it proceeds there is a need to add the 32-bit binary numbers. Instead of the next instruction being the first instruction of an addition sequence, it is a jump instruction to the subroutine. The addition is performed by the subroutine sequence which, after the addition is finished, returns the system to the normal sequence. As the normal program sequence continues another addition of the 32-bit binary numbers is called for. The subroutine jump instruction again takes the system to the same subroutine and, at the end of the subroutine, returns the system to the normal sequence of the program. This happens each time the addition is called for. Instead of writing all the steps of the addition sequence each time it is needed, it is written once and called for by the subroutine jump instrucion. As one can see this requires a lot less program memory. Also, as will be shown later, it allows programs to be organized in a very efficient and easy to understand manner.

HOW IS INFORMATION LOCATED IN A MICROCOMPUTER SYSTEM?

There are several addressing modes which are used for locating information in microprocessors.

Throughout the discussion thus far, program counters have provided addresses for instructions and instructions have provided addresses for other instructions and for data in memory. The question naturally arises, "How do the instructions indicate these addresses?" Such a discussion comes under the general subject of addressing modes. Addressing modes are the allowed ways that are used to locate information in a microprocessor or microcomputer system.

Addressing Modes

The most common addressing modes used by microprocessors are as follows:
a) Immediate Addressing
b) Register Addressing
c) Register Indirect Addressing
d) Indexed Addressing
e) Direct Addressing
f) Relative Addressing

Not all processors use all of these modes, but all processors use most of them. However, before discussing addressing modes, let's cover a subject tied very closely to them – instruction formats.

Instruction Formats

The instruction format is the arrangement of the digital information in the instruction code and the arrangement of the total number of codes in the instruction. Usually the first code contains the op code, which tells which operation is to be performed.

Format is a word that means the general plan or organization of something. It means just that for the instruction. As with numbers, letters, characters and symbols, the instruction comes to the microprocessor in a digital code. The arrangement of the bits in the digital code, the number of codes to be received and in which order, are all part of the organization of the instruction, all part of the format. Look at *Figure 4-40a*. Here is shown an instruction format for an 8-bit microprocessor. Instructions have the possibility of taking three memory locations of a byte (8 bits) each. Some will take only 1, some 2 and some 3. Note that the first byte always contains the "OP CODE." OP CODE is an abbreviation for operations code. It is the digital code that identifies what operation the instruction wants done. It is the portion of the instruction code that corresponds to the mnemonic of MOV for data movement, A for addition, S subtraction, etc. The additional memory bytes are needed to provide the operand or the address of the operand(s). These follow in the sequence shown.

Figure 4-40.
Instruction Formats

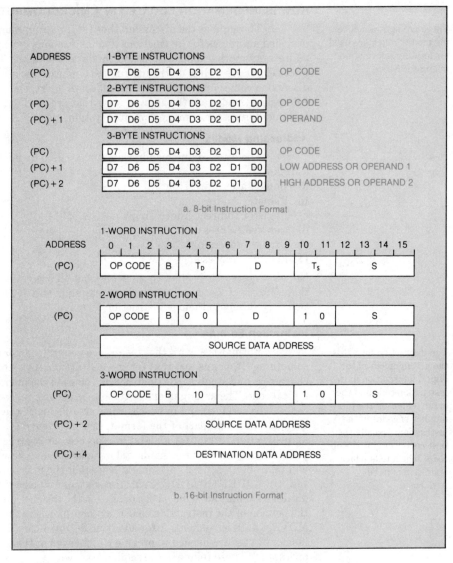

a. 8-bit Instruction Format

b. 16-bit Instruction Format

A 16-bit instruction format is shown in *Figure 4-40b*. Obviously, with 16 bits more information can be contained in a one word instruction. The first 4 bits are used for the OP CODE, B is a bit to tell the microprocessor to use all 16 bits as a word or divide the 16 bits into 8-bit bytes. D is a code identifying the DESTINATION portion of the instruction and S identifies the SOURCE portion. T_D and T_s are bits in the instruction code that identify the kind of addressing mode being used to locate the source and the destination of the instruction. As shown in *Figure 4-40b*, 2 or 3 memory words are required depending on the addressing mode indicated by T_s or T_D.

The instruction format also gives clues as to the number of memory locations needed and the amount of memory required.

Microprocessors may have more than one instruction format for the one word instructions. Its form depends on the type of instruction being used. Instruction formats are not only important to indicate what the instruction code means, but the additional byte or word locations in memory required must be taken into account to determine the amount of memory required to hold the program instructions. The number of memory locations needed by an instruction depends on the addressing mode used. Examining the addressing modes will clarify this. Let's begin with one of the most common modes — immediate addressing.

Immediate Addressing

The operand is the quantity or parameter being acted upon (operated on) by the operation called for in the instruction.

In immediate addressing, the instruction contains the data within the instruction in adjacent memory locations.

The word *operand* has been used previously and was referred to again in *Figure 4-40*. Recall that it is what is to be operated on by the operation called out in the instruction. When adding two numbers together each number is an operand. Both numbers are the data to be used in the addition operation.

The easiest way for the instruction to indicate the data to be used is for the instruction to contain the data as part of the overall instruction. Generally this is done by having the N-bit OP CODE in one memory location and the data to be used as an N-bit number in the next memory location. The 2-byte instruction in *Figure 4-40a* illustrates this. The program counter addresses both the operation code and data. An example is detailed further in *Figure 4-41*. The operation code for an 8-bit microprocessor instruction would be in the memory location addressed by the program counter. This code would be read from memory, the program counter would be incremented, and the data would then be read from the next location in program memory. The number code representing data is part of the program and thus is a constant; it is not changed by program operations. As a result, immediate addressing normally is used for initializing system registers and memory locations to desired values.

**Figure 4-41.
Immediate Addressing**

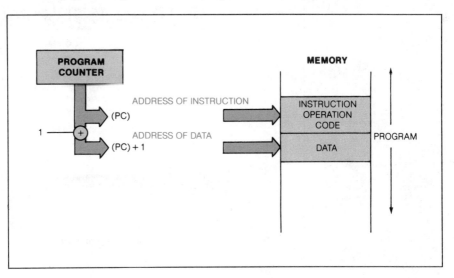

Recall the loop counter that was used for the JUMP instruction example *(Figure 4-38)*. It was initialized to a value of 8 with an instruction using immediate addressing:

$$MVI \quad C, 8$$

The MVI stands for move using immediate addressing; the C identifies the counter register to be initialized; and the 8 is the value to be stored in the C register. The 8-bit op code for MVI C is stored in the first 8-bit byte of the instruction and the binary equivalent of the decimal number 8 is stored in the second 8-bit byte of the instruction. The instruction requires a total of 16 bits – 2 8-bit bytes which take 2 memory locations.

Register Addressing

In register addressing, the instruction designates a particular register or registers where the data involved in the operation is located. This saves computing time, since the operation can take place immediately without further accessing the memory for data address information.

The MVI C, 8 instruction discussed in the last section is an example of another type of addressing: register addressing. The instruction says that the register C is loaded with the constant 8. The instruction has specified the register as one of the data locations involved in the operation. This type of addressing is very often used in microcomputer programming since once the register involved is identified, the operation can take place immediately without having to go to the memory for more data address information.

A more specific example is shown in *Figure 4-42a*. Completely contained in the instruction code is all the information necessary to add register 2 to register 3 and store the results in register 3. The instruction would be executed as soon as it is decoded, since all data locations are in the processor. No additional memory references are required.

**Figure 4-42.
Register Addressing**

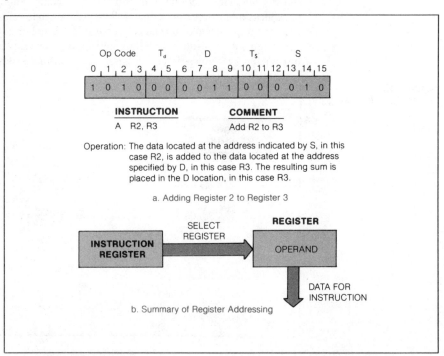

INSTRUCTION   COMMENT

A R2, R3   Add R2 to R3

Operation: The data located at the address indicated by S, in this case R2, is added to the data located at the address specified by D, in this case R3. The resulting sum is placed in the D location, in this case R3.

a. Adding Register 2 to Register 3

b. Summary of Register Addressing

T_s and T_D are bits to indicate the addressing mode. The 00 in each of these bit fields for this format indicates that register addressing is used for both the source and destination. The op code is 1010, identifying the instruction to the microprocessor as an ADD operation.

Register Indirect Addressing

In register indirect addressing, the register does not contain data but contains the address of the data. The address is used to fetch the data from memory.

With this type of addressing, the address of the data in memory is contained in a register on the processor. This is different from register addressing because now the content of the register is the address of the data rather than the data itself. All the instruction need do is indicate which register contains the address to be used. *Figure 4-43* illustrates an example. The instruction from the instruction register is decoded and a register is selected that contains the data address. The data address from the register is sent out to memory to locate the data which is sent back to the microprocessor on the data bus. While time must be taken to read memory to fetch the data or to write the data into its memory location, the instruction coding can be very simple.

Generally, for an N-bit processor, the N-bit instruction op code contains all the information needed: what operation is to be performed, and which register holds the data address. In an application where it is required to access from memory a group of data in some sequence, the indirect addressing approach is very useful. The same instruction is used but the register value is incremented by one to address the next memory location. Easy changes can be made to the data address by loading new values or doing some arithmetic operation on the register containing the address.

**Figure 4-43.
Register Indirect
Addressing**

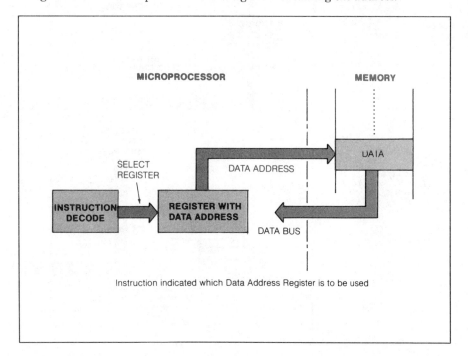

Indexed Addressing

In indexed addressing, the data address exists in two forms — a base address found in an index register and an offset value. During execution, these two values are added to give the final data address.

A variation on indirect addressing that some processors use is indexed addressing shown in *Figure 4-44*. In this addressing mode the operand or data address is in two locations. There is a base value in a register called the index register. There is also an offset value in the instruction code. When the instruction is executed, the offset value is added to the index register value to determine the final data address. With this procedure the address can be modified by operating on the contents of the index register. Groups of data spaced in some regular manner throughout memory can be accessed by using the proper value in the instruction. With this type of addressing, the instruction must contain two code groups. The first is the instruction operation code group to indicate the operation and that indexed addressing is being used. The second group of bits represents the address offset that is to be added to the contents of the index register to form the full data address. Because the program memory is read twice (once for the op code, once for the offset) and RAM once for the data, this instruction addressing approach takes longer than register indirect addressing. Register indirect addressing only requires that program memory be read to get the instruction code (one operation) and then RAM to get the data.

**Figure 4-44.
Indexed Addressing**

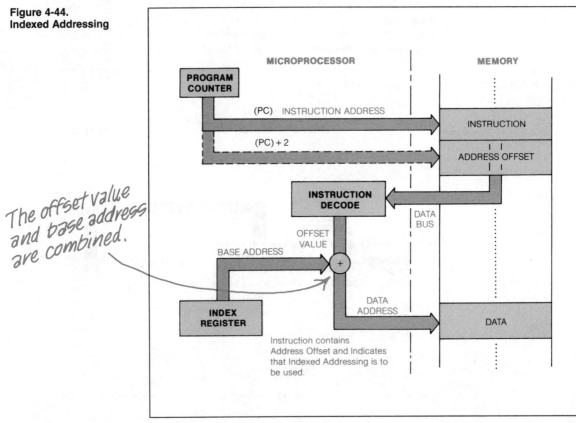

Direct Addressing

In direct addressing, the data address is contained right in the instruction, usually occupying the two memory locations directly following the instruction op code.

Refer back to *Figure 4-40.* In the 3-byte instruction format for the 8-bit processor and in the 2-word and 3-word format for the 16-bit microprocessor, the byte or word after the op code contains a data address rather than data. The address for the data is contained right in the instruction as a byte or word in program memory. Unlike the 2-byte instruction for immediate addressing *(Figure 4-41)* where the second byte contained the data itself, now the second byte (or maybe the third, too) contains the address of the data. This is direct addressing (also sometimes called symbolic addressing). Direct addressing is often used when a microprocessor register is not available for use in storing data.

Direct addressing is relatively slow because of the time required accessing memory.

As shown in *Figure 4-45,* the program counter addresses program memory to get the first part of the instruction which contain the op code and a code that says that direct addressing is being used. This directs the program counter to be incremented so that program memory can be read again to get the data address or addresses. RAM is then read to get the data. This type of addressing is a very slow approach to locating data, requiring possibly four memory operations to get the data location. It is usually used only when register addressing is not possible, or when a single data variable, such as a program counter or control word, is used only once in awhile.

**Figure 4-45.
Direct Addressing**

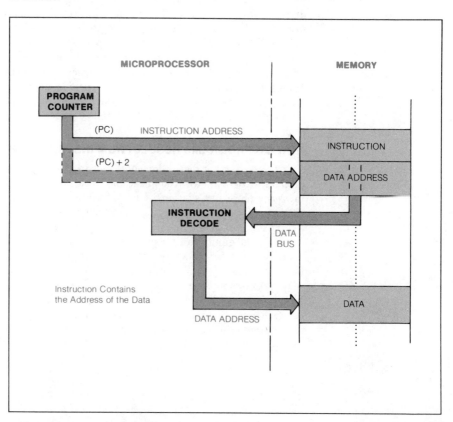

Relative Addressing

In relative addressing, like indexed addressing, the instruction contains an off-set number to be added to the base address to determine the actual address in memory. The base address in this case is located in the program counter.

All of the addressing modes looked at so far have been ways of locating data to be used by the instruction being executed. Sometimes instructions themselves are addressed in the program and these must be located. Branch and jump instructions are prime examples. A type of addressing that is often used in branch operations to specify where the next instruction is located (the instruction to be branched to) is relative addressing. This has some similarities to indexed addressing in that the instruction contains an offset number to be added to a base address to determine the total address to be used. The difference is that the base address is the value in the program counter. The sequence of relative addressing is as follows: The program counter addresses the next instruction and the instruction containing the op code is read. The microprocessor decodes the instruction and finds that program-counter relative addressing is being used. The program counter is incremented and the next location in program memory is read. This is the binary number representing the address offset. The offset value is added to contents of the program counter and the result placed in the program counter. The new program counter value is the address of the next instruction branched to by the branch instruction. The advantage of locating the next instruction branch address in this fashion is that it is faster than direct addressing. The disadvantage is that the offset value is limited. For example, as discussed previously, an 8-bit signed (two's complement) offset value is limited to from -128 to $+127$. As a result, a jump or offset from the present program counter value is limited to the same value. If the next instruction branch address is not in this range, the slower direct or some other addressing approach would have to be used. In fact, people writing programs for microprocessors or microcomputer systems are constantly faced with this problem — which addressing procedure is best for each instruction in the program.

HOW DO PROGRAMS RESULT FROM INSTRUCTIONS

As further discussion continues in this book, the emphasis will be directed to help answer the question, "How do you use a microprocessor or microcomputer in a system?" Obviously, the use of instructions and how they are combined to make a system solve a particular problem by following a program is of prime importance.

The game plan for programming should be clear. Break the overflow chart for the system into many simple flow charts, even down to the instruction level of operation if necessary. Write the instruction sequences or subprograms to implement the elementary operations and combine these to build back to an overall program. Each subprogram should be verified as it is written. If the system is fairly simple, the actual system hardware might be used; otherwise, some type of system development hardware will have to be used. In like fashion, the complete program should be verified to make sure that all subprograms are connected together (linked) into one harmonious overall system program.

WHAT HAVE WE LEARNED?

- The first step in building any system is to completely summarize the operation of the system in tabular or flow chart form.
- From the system flow chart decide what microprocessor or single-chip microcomputer and other components will be needed to build the system.
- Choose the best microprocessor for a system by looking at its bit length, speed, instruction set, and timing features, to see if they will be suitable for the task at hand.
- Connect the components together, using the timing and control signals from the processor to control the operation of the other components.
- Microprocessors provide basic instructions to move data, perform arithmetic, logical, comparison, and branching operations. When these instructions are familiar and are combined correctly the microprocessor can perform very complicated decisions and solve complex programs.
- Develop a program with the same organized, systematic, detailed approach used for other projects. Break the program into many simple understandable tasks.
- Write and verify the subprograms for each of these tasks and combine them into the required overall program.

WHAT'S NEXT?

In this chapter we have covered a lot of the general terminology and considerations involved in interconnecting and operating microprocessors and microcomputers. In order to make this information meaningful, we need to go through an example design problem using a typical microprocessor. In the next chapter we will do just that, using an imaginary microprocessor and a simple design problem that will illustrate the concepts and fundamentals we have discussed thus far.

To aid in understanding the design problem make sure that you work the microprocessor exercise that follows.

MICROPROCESSOR EXERCISE

This exercise is designed to illustrate the operation of microprocessors and the interaction of microprocessors and memory. You are to provide the action for the microprocessor, incrementing the program counter, fetching the next instruction, interpreting and executing that instruction, and reading and writing into data memory and microprocessor registers when needed. As each instruction is executed, enter the results in the processor registers and any memory locations into which data has been written. The Microprocessor Exercise Work Sheet will provide a convenient way to summarize the effects of each instruction on all the microprocessor registers. Assume A & B registers and memory locations can hold only a single decimal digit.

PROGRAM MEMORY

Address Contents

100   Instruction: Clear Carry flip-flop (CY) to zero.

101   Instruction: Place 5 in the B register.

102   Instruction: Place 204 in Data Address Register 1 (DAR 1).

103   Instruction: Place 214 in Data Address Register 2 (DAR 2).

104   Instruction: Place 224 in Data Address Register 3 (DAR 3).

105   Instruction: Move data addressed by DAR 1 to A register.

106   Instruction: Add carry and data addressed by DAR 2 to data in
                     A register; Place the sum in the A register. Set the
                     Carry flip-flop with any carry generated.

107   Instruction: Move data from A register to data location
                     addressed by contents of DAR 3.

108   Instruction: Decrement all DARs and B register. If B register
                     contains zero, set the EQ flip-flop.

109   Instruction: If EQ = 1, Stop; If EQ = 0, put 105 in the Program Counter.

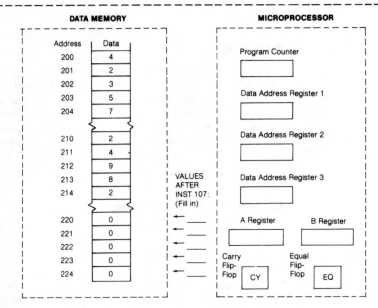

Questions:

1. What does the program stored in memory locations 100 through 109 do?
2. Does a Read Memory operation affect the contents of the location?
3. Does a Memory Write Operation affect the content of the location?
4. Why are three separate Data Address Registers used?

MICROPROCESSOR EXERCISE WORK SHEET

STEP	PROGRAM COUNTER	DATA ADDRESS REGISTER 1	DATA ADDRESS REGISTER 2	DATA ADDRESS REGISTER 3	B REGISTER	A REGISTER	EQ CY FLIP-FLOPS
1	100	0	0	0	0	0	0 0
2							
3							
4							
5							
6							
7							
8							
9							
10							
11							
12							
13							
14							
15							
16							
17							
18							
19							
20							
21							
22							
23							
24							
25							
26							
27							
28							
29							
30							
31							
32							
33							
34							
35							

Fill in the Program Counter Value for the next instruction. Then fill in the register contents as they would appear after the execution.

PROBLEM SOLUTION
WHENEVER AN ACTION CHANGES A NUMBER THAT NUMBER IS MADE BOLD

MICROPROCESSOR EXERCISE WORK SHEET

STEP	PROGRAM COUNTER	DATA ADDRESS REGISTER 1	DATA ADDRESS REGISTER 2	DATA ADDRESS REGISTER 3	B REGISTER	A REGISTER	EQ C FLIP FLOP
1	100	0	0	0	0	0	0 0
2	101	0	0	0	**5**	0	00
3	102	**204**	0	0	5	0	00
4	103	204	**214**	0	5	0	00
5	104	204	214	**224**	5	0	00
6	105	204	214	224	5	**7**	00
7	106	204	214	224	5	**9**	00
8	107	204	214	224	5	9	00
9	108	**203**	**213**	**223**	**4**	9	00
10	109	203	213	223	4	9	00
11	105	203	213	223	4	**5**	00
12	106	203	213	223	4	**3**	**01**
13	107	203	213	223	4	3	01
14	108	**202**	**212**	**222**	**3**	3	01
15	109	202	212	222	3	3	01
16	105	202	212	222	3	**3**	01
17	106	202	212	222	3	**3**	**01**
18	107	202	212	222	3	3	01
19	108	**201**	**211**	**221**	**2**	3	01
20	109	201	211	221	2	3	01
21	105	201	211	221	2	**2**	01
22	106	201	211	221	2	**7**	**00**
23	107	201	211	221	2	7	00
24	108	**200**	**210**	**220**	**1**	7	00
25	109	200	210	220	1	7	00
26	105	200	210	220	1	**4**	00
27	106	200	210	220	1	**6**	00
28	107	200	210	220	1	6	00
29	108	**199**	**209**	**219**	**0**	6	**10**
30	109	199	209	219	0	6	10

Numbers stored in memory locations 220 thru 224: 67339

Answers:

1. 5 digit decimal addition:

    42357
    +24982
    ———
    67339

2. No   3. Yes

4. There are three areas of memory being referenced to locate data.

A System
Application with SAM

ABOUT THIS CHAPTER

In previous chapters we have seen what microprocessors and microcomputers are and generally how they are used. We are ready to start looking at some specific applications of these devices. In this chapter we will go through the application of a microprocessor to a specific problem. To simplify the discussion, we'll use a fictitious microprocessor with limited capabilities that has a small instruction set and a four-bit data bus.

WHAT FEATURES ARE FOUND IN A TYPICAL MICROPROCESSOR?

This question has been answered in general terms in the last chapter. How specific features are used to solve problems will now be discussed. While the processor being used does not exist, it illustrates most of the basic features of microprocessors presently available.

Internal Features

The internal functional blocks of the microprocessor determine its general features when the microprocessor is connected to memory and input and output units.

First, one must understand the internal architecture of the microprocessor in terms of the functional building blocks it contains. This internal structure of functional blocks is used for addressing, internal data storage, arithmetic and logical operations, and timing. The way the functional blocks work together when they are connected to memory or input and output units determines the features of the microprocessor and its instruction set. In fact, the instruction set can be understood best only in terms of these internal features.

A microprocessor with a very simple internal structure, as shown in *Figure 5-1*, will be used for this example. Of course, the detailed circuits that would be required to implement such a structure would be very complicated. Fortunately, the microprocessor user does not have to concern himself with the detailed circuits, but only the overall functions provided by the blocks that contain the circuits.

In the case of the microprocessor of *Figure 5-1*, which is named SAM (Simplified Architecture Microprocessor), many of the internal registers are the same as those found in integrated-circuit microprocessors. For example, all processors must have a program counter, an instruction register, and an accumulator, and SAM is no exception. SAM has a 12-bit program counter and a 12-bit address bus that enables SAM to address any of 4096 (2^{12}) memory locations. When an instruction addressed by the Program Counter is received, the instruction register (IR) provides 4 bits of storage for the instruction operation code (OP code) and a 12-bit address register (DAR) holds any direct data addresses contained in the instruction. All information is received from memory by the 4-bit data bus coming into SAM.

**Figure 5-1.
SAM Internal Structure**

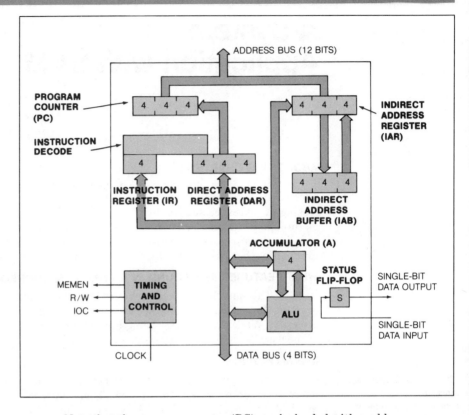

Note that the program counter (PC) can be loaded with a address contained in the direct-address register (DAR) portion of the instruction register. This enables the processor to jump or branch from one part of memory to another to obtain its next instruction. The accumulator register (A) can be loaded with a value obtained from a memory location or by a value which may be a constant contained in the instruction. It can send data to and receive results from the arithmetic logic unit (ALU). The contents of the accumulator can be stored in memory. Since SAM is a 4-bit processor, the accumulator register provides 4 bits of storage.

In addition to the basic registers (PC, IR, and A), there is an indirect-address register (IAR) which can be used to quickly indicate the location of data in memory for a given instruction. This register can be initialized to some value by an instruction and later used to locate data whenever it is needed in the problem. There is an indirect-address buffer register (IAB) that can be used to save data addresses that are not currently being used for later transfer to the IAR register. There is a single status flip-flop used to summarize the results of arithmetic and logic operations. The combination of registers, ALU, timing and control functions in SAM is not nearly as extensive as one might find in an actual IC microprocessor. However, even with this simple internal structure, SAM has just about all the features that any problem might require.

Instruction Set

SAM has a limited instruction set of 16 instructions.

To simplify the discussion, SAM is limited to the 16 instructions shown in Figure 5-2. This is because the 4-bit operation code that SAM receives can only distinguish 16 different instruction codes. Most IC microprocessors have an 8-bit or 16-bit instruction code to provide a much more expanded instruction set. For the intended applications of SAM, a 4-bit op code is entirely adequate.

**Figure 5-2.
SAM Instruction Set**

INSTRUCTION	MNEMONIC (Abbreviation)	OPERATION	AFFECT ON STATUS
Arithmetic:			
Addition	ADD	A ← A + M	Status = Carry
Subtraction	SUB	A ← A − M	Status = Borrow
Decrement	DEC	M ← M − 1	Status = 1 if M = 0
Rotate Left	ROL		Status = left bit rotated out of A
Logical:			
AND	AND	A ← A AND M	Status = 1 if A = 0 after operation
OR	OR	A ← A OR M	Status = 1 if A = 0 after operation
Data Movement:			
Accumulator-to-Memory	TAM	M ← A	None
Memory-to-Accumulator	TMA	A ← M	None
Constant-to-Accumulator	LDA n	A ← n	None
Input Bit to Status	IN	S ← Single Data Input Value	Status = Value of Input Signal
Output Bit From Status	OUT	Single Data Output ← S	None
Branching:			
Jump	JMP loc	PC ← loc	None
Conditional Branch	BS loc	PC ← loc If S = 1	None
Indirect Address:			
Initialize IAR	LDX value	IAR ← Value	None
Decrement IAR	DEX	IAR ← IAR-1	None
Exchange IAR & IAB Contents	XCHG	IAR ←→ IAB	None

0 ≤ n ≤ 15: loc is an address value (12 bits); value is an address containing 12 Bits. M indicates the memory data at the location indicated by the contents of the IAR.

The instruction set consists of five data movement operations, six arithmetic-logical operations, two branch instructions, one operation to load an address code into the indirect-address register, one instruction that decrements the contents of the indirect-address register, and one instruction that exchanges the contents of the IAR and IAB registers.

Data Movement Instructions

These instructions are used to move data from the accumulator to memory (named TAM mnemonic), move data from memory to the accumulator (named TMA), to input or output a binary signal (to or from the status flip-flop) on the serial input and output lines (named IN and OUT), and to initialize the accumulator data to a given value (with the LDA instruction).

Since addressing data is contained within the instruction, the LDA movement instructions are immediate addressing, rather than the indirect addressing used by other instructions.

The LDA instruction uses immediate addressing, since the data is contained in the instruction. The sequence of steps is shown in *Figure 5-3*. The other data transfers use the contents of the indirect-address register to specify the location of the data in memory involved in the transfer. The sequence of steps is shown in *Figure 5-4*. Thus, the effect of each of these instructions can be summarized as follows:

TAM	The contents of A are sent to the memory location specified by the address code in the IAR register.
TMA	The contents of the memory location specified by the contents of the IAR register are sent to A.
LDA n	The value n (0 through 15) is sent to the A register in binary form (0000 through 1111).
IN	The bit selected by the contents of the IAR register is sent to the status flip-flop.
OUT	The contents of the status flip-flop is sent out to the external flip-flop selected by the address code in the IAR register.

Indirect-Address Register Control Instructions

A load (LDX) and a decrement (DEX) instruction are used to control the indirect-address register; either to set it to a value or to change it one step at a time.

There are two instructions that can be used to control the indirect-address register. The LDX instruction is used to initialize the contents of the IAR to some desired address-code value. The DEX instruction is used to decrement the contents of the IAR. By using the LDX instruction, the IAR address code can be set to some desired starting value and then the DEX instruction is used to go through successive locations in data memory. The LDX instruction uses immediate addressing, i.e., the address code (12 bits) is contained in program memory along with the instruction code. *Figure 5-5* shows the steps to initialize the IAR to contain the address code for location 100_{16} (256 in base 10), when the program contains the following instruction:

LDX 100

**Figure 5-3.
Effect of the LDA 8
Instruction**

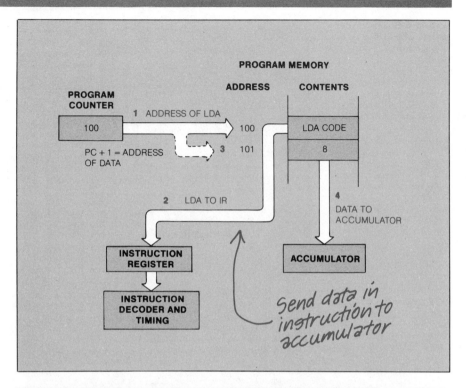

**Figure 5-4.
Indirect Addressing
Example — the TMA
Instruction**

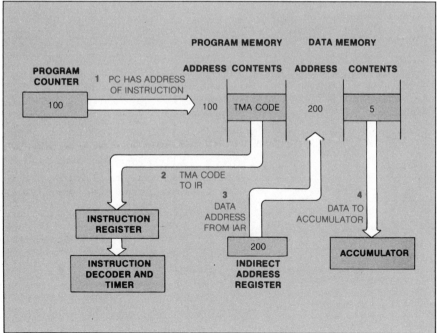

**Figure 5-5.
Effect of a LDX
Instruction**

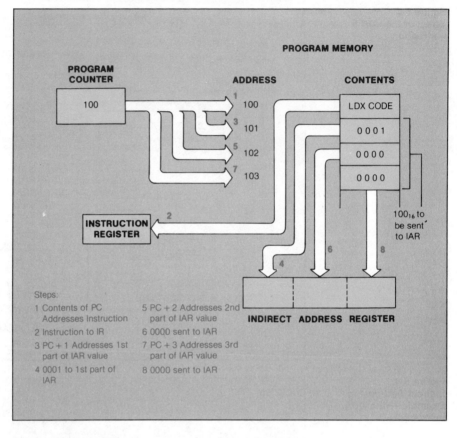

PROGRAM MEMORY

Steps:
1 Contents of PC
  Addresses Instruction
2 Instruction to IR
3 PC + 1 Addresses 1st
  part of IAR value
4 0001 to 1st part of
  IAR

5 PC + 2 Addresses 2nd
  part of IAR value
6 0000 sent to IAR
7 PC + 3 Addresses 3rd
  part of IAR value
8 0000 sent to IAR

Arithmetic Instructions

SAM can do basic
addition, subtraction
and shifting.

      The basic arithmetic operations are addition (ADD), subtraction
(SUB), decrementing (DEC), and shifting left − called rotation left (ROL).
These are performed on the memory location indicated by the address in the
indirect-address register and on the accumulator (in the case of ADD and
SUB). ADD, SUB, DEC and ROL operations are defined to be:

ADD   Add the contents of the memory location specified by
the address in IAR to the contents of the accumulator.
Place the sum in the accumulator. A carry sets the
status flip-flop (S = 1).

SUB   Subtract the contents of the memory location specified
by the address in IAR from the contents of the
accumulator and place the difference in the
accumulator. A borrow sets the status flip-flop (S = 1).

DEC   Decrement the contents of the memory location
specified by the address in IAR. A zero result sets the
status flip-flop. The results of the operation are stored
in the same memory location.

The ROL rotate left instruction is best explained with a diagram *(Figure 5-6)*. The contents of the accumulator are shifted left one position; the vacated right-most bit is filled with the value of the status flip-flop. Then, the status flip-flop is set to the value of the bit shifted out of the left end of the A register. Thus, if the status flip-flop contains a 0 before the ROL operation and the A register contains a 1001 before the operation, the ROL will change the contents of the A register to 0010 and the contents of the status flip-flop to a 1.

**Figure 5-6.
The Rotate Left
Operation**

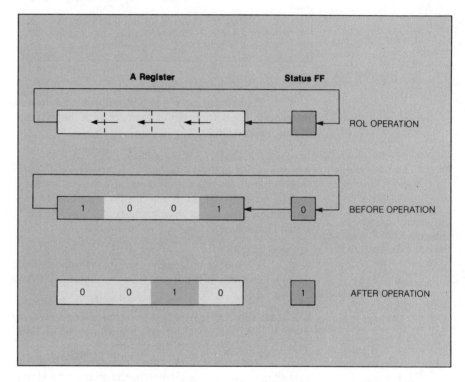

Logical Instructions

SAM's instruction set contain OR and AND instructions for logic operations. AND is used to clear a bit to 0, OR for setting a bit to 1.

The basic logical functions of OR and AND are provided by the instruction set. These operations are performed bit-by-bit on the contents of the accumulator and the contents of the memory location specified by the IAR register. The result is sent to the accumulator. The status flip-flop is set to 1 if the result is a 0, i.e., all bits of all results are 0's. This is reviewed in *Figure 5-7*.

The AND operation is usually used for selectively clearing a bit to 0 and the OR operation is usually used for selectively setting a bit to a 1.

Figure 5-7.
SAM Logical Instructions

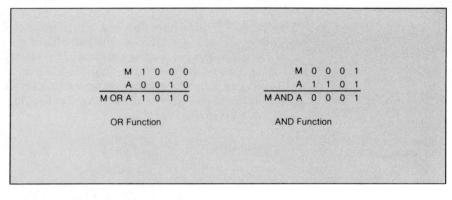

```
        M   1  0  0  0              M   0  0  0  1
        A   0  0  1  0              A   1  1  0  1
     M OR A  1  0  1  0          M AND A  0  0  0  1

        OR Function                 AND Function
```

Jump and Branch Instructions

The instruction set of SAM supports an unconditional jump to an instruction in another part of memory with the JMP instruction. The form of this instruction is:

JMP location

Program branches can be either unconditional by using a jump instruction (JMP location) or conditional by using a branch instruction (BS location, if the status flip-flop is a 1).

where location is the address to be jumped to, *that is, the address of the next instruction to be executed.* This address value is loaded into the program counter to cause the jump to occur. For example, to cause the next instruction to be taken from memory location 100, the following instruction would be used:

JMP 100.

A conditional branch instruction is also available (BS) which will make a jump only if the status flip-flop contains a 1. Thus, the instruction:

BS 100

will cause the next instruction to be taken from memory address 100 if S = 1. Such a conditional jump or branch is needed if decision making is to be built into a microcomputer system.

More detail is contained in *Figure 5-8.* The address part of the branch instruction is contained in the memory locations right after the instruction operation code. The processor reads the instruction code to determine that the instruction is a branch, either JMP or BS. Then the next three memory locations will be read and the information sent to the memory address portion (DAR) of the instruction register. Once the complete address to be jumped to is in the DAR, the program counter is loaded directly with this address code if the instruction is JMP; or if the instruction is BS, loaded only if S = 1.

Of course, SAM's sixteen instructions are a very limited instruction set for a microprocessor. However, they are the basic ones that are found in all microprocessors, and they are more than sufficient to solve many problems that will be encountered.

Figure 5-8.
Operation of Branch
Instructions

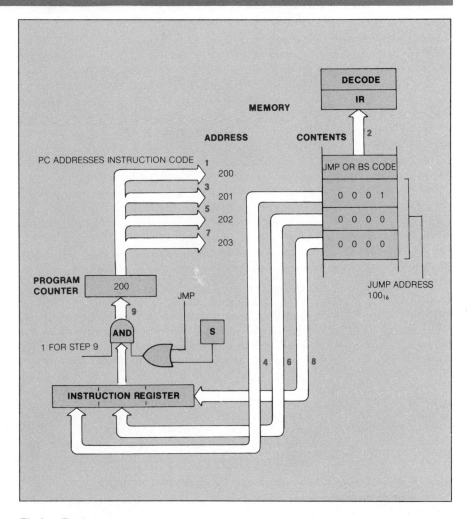

Timing Features

The last area that needs to be examined is how SAM tells the external world what is going on and how the external world communicates with SAM.

Memory Read Operation

When performing a memory read operation, SAM sends a memory enable signal and a read/write signal concurrently to the memory circuits.

A timing diagram for a memory READ is shown in *Figure 5-9.* When memory is to be read, SAM outputs a memory enable signal (MEMEN = 1) to turn on the memory circuits. It also sends out a signal on the read/write (R/W = 1) line to indicate that a read operation is being performed. To assure correct timing, the addresses are sent to memory at the same time MEMEN = 1.

Figure 5-9.
Memory Read Operation
Timing

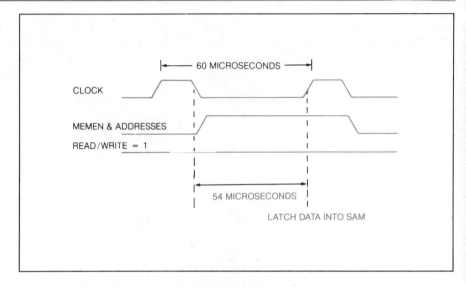

SAM inputs the data from memory on the leading edge of the clock pulse. Thus, the memory must respond with correct data within the time between the trailing edge of one clock pulse and the leading edge of the next clock pulse. In *Figure 5-9* this is approximately 54 microseconds, which is more than enough time for semiconductor memory devices.

Memory Write Operation

The memory must be able to store (receive data) within the MEMEN time frame.

When memory is to be stored (receive data from the processor), the address, data, and memory enable signals are sent to memory at the same time as shown in *Figure 5-10*. The read/write signal goes low (R/W = 0) to indicate a write operation. In the write case the memory must be able to store the information within the MEMEN time, which is 60 microsecond.

Figure 5-10.
Memory Write Operation
Timing

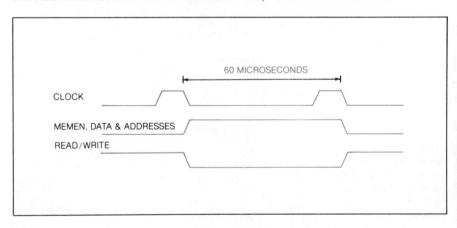

SAM has instructions that control an input data device just as if it were a memory location. This is called a memory-mapped input. Single bit input can also be controlled.

Input Operations

Figure 5-11 shows an input data device that is treated as if it were a memory location. It is called a memory-mapped input. A 4-bit register is assigned a memory address and an address decoder is designed to generate an enable control signal in response to the correct address, R/W = 1, and MEMEN = 1. The input device places its data on the data bus when SAM wants the data read from the memory address for the input device.

Figure 5-11.
Memory-Mapped Input
Control Circuits

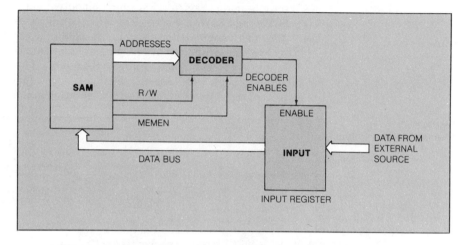

The SAM microprocessor also supports an input port through its IN instruction as shown in *Figure 5-12*. When this instruction is executed, the address in the IAR is sent out on the address lines, the input/output control (IOC) signal is generated and the read/write signal is maintained at a 1. To provide the single-bit input that this instruction expects, the address is decoded and the input signal from a selected flip-flop is gated onto the single-bit data line of SAM. The single bit is sent to the status flip-flop inside SAM. After the IN instruction, S will contain the same binary value that the selected input flip-flop had stored. This special-purpose input scheme is useful in testing single-bit digital signals throughout the system and in setting up serial data transfers from other systems.

Figure 5-12.
Single-Bit Input Port
Control

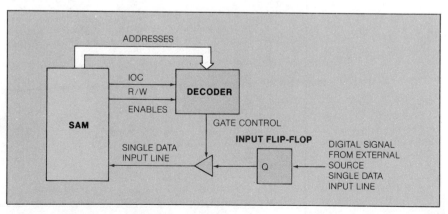

Output Operations

Outputs can also be controlled by SAM either as memory mapped outputs or as single bit outputs.

As in the case of the input operations, SAM supports memory-mapped outputs and single-bit outputs *(Figures 5-13* and *5-14)*. Just as in the input operation, a 4-bit register is used as if it were a memory location. However, now it receives signals from SAM and stores outputs. A decoder that detects the address and the memory write conditions (MEMEN = 1, R/W = 0) outputs a control signal that latches the data on the data bus from SAM into the output register. For single-bit outputs, the output control signals (IOC and R/W) are used along with the addresses to provide a control signal that latches the data into the output flip-flop. The data comes out from the status flip-flop onto SAM's single-bit data output line.

By using the timing features of SAM properly (as illustrated in *Figures 5-9* through *5-14)*, memory and input/output functional blocks can be connected to SAM to form a smoothly operating system.

**Figure 5-13.
Memory-Mapped Output
Control**

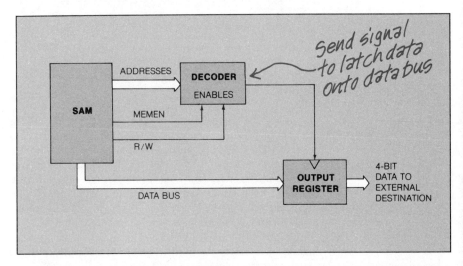

**Figure 5-14.
Single-Bit Output Port
Control**

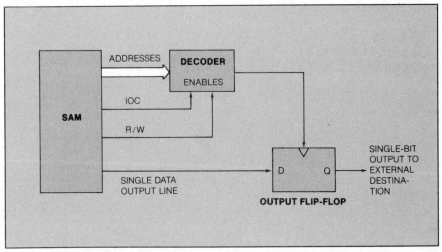

WHAT CAN BE BUILT WITH SUCH A MICROPROCESSOR?

To demonstrate that a simple microprocessor like SAM can solve complex problems, a 32-bit binary number will be converted to its BCD equivalent.

The hardware features and instruction set of SAM are complete enough to satisfy the needs of many applications. To illustrate the power of this simple microprocessor, let's go through the solution of an example problem. Let's assume that SAM is required to receive a total of 32 binary data bits, one at a time (that is, serially) on the single-bit input line. It must then convert this 32-bit binary number to its decimal equivalent consisting of 10 binary-coded-decimal (BCD) 4-bit groups. The codes for these ten digits are then to be displayed using seven-segment LED display devices. In other words, part of SAM's job is to convert numerical information in the binary number system to its decimal equivalent and display the resulting 10-digit decimal number.

Properties of BCD Numbers

To understand the details of this problem a review of the BCD code would be useful. The BCD code is simply the binary equivalent of the decimal numbers 0 through 9 as shown in *Figure 5-15*. Any code other than the ones listed (such as the binary equivalent of 15 which is 1111) is illegal and must be corrected. One way in which such an illegal code could be generated is illustrated in *Figure 5-16*. Here a two-decimal-digit number is shifted to the left one bit position. Such a left shift should multiply the number by two. If the BCD number is 04 with a code of 0000 0100 as shown in *Figure 5-16a*, this is exactly what happens. This 04 code, when shifted left, becomes 0000 1000, the code for 08 (2 x 04). The answer is correct and contains only legal BCD codes.

**Figure 5-15.
BCD Code for Decimal
Numbers**

Decimal Digit	BCD Code
0	0000
1	0001
2	0010
3	0011
4	0100
5	0101
6	0110
7	0111
8	1000
9	1001

**Figure 5-16.
Effect of Left Shift on
BCD Coded Numbers**

	BEFORE LEFT SHIFT	AFTER LEFT SHIFT	
a. 2 × 4 = 8	0 0 0 0 0 1 0 0	0 0 0 0 1 0 0 0	Correct
b. 2 × 5 = 10	0 0 0 0 0 1 0 1	0 0 0 0 1 0 1 0	Incorrect (0A)
	+ 0 0 0 0 0 0 1 1		
	0 0 0 0 1 0 0 0	0 0 0 1 0 0 0 0	Correct (10)
c. 2 × 8 = 16	0 0 0 0 1 0 0 0	0 0 0 1 0 0 0 0	Incorrect (10 ≠ 16)
	+ 0 0 0 0 0 0 1 1		
	0 0 0 0 1 0 1 1	0 0 0 1 0 1 1 0	Correct (16)

When performing the binary to BCD conversion, illegal codes are encountered because only codes for digits 1 through 9 are legal. An algorithm must contain the correction to eliminate illegal codes.

Look at *Figure 5-16b*. The BCD number is now 05 with a code of 0000 0101. When this is shifted left the result is 0000 1010, which contains the illegal code 1010. The answer should have been 0001 0000 for 10 (5 × 2 = 10). The correct answer would have been obtained if a 0011 had been added to the 0101 prior to the shift. Then the resultant code 0000 1000 shifted left would have given the correct code for the answer 0001 0000.

Similarly, if the BCD code has been 0000 1000 (for 08) prior to the shift, as shown in *Figure 5-16c*, the shift left would yield 0001 0000, which is a legal BCD code but, unfortunately, it is the wrong answer. Twice 8 is 16, not 10. Thus, the result should have been the BCD code 0001 0110. Again, this result could have been obtained if prior to the shift the number 0011 had been added to the 0000 1000 to give 0000 1011. Shifting this left yields 0001 0110 (BCD for 16) which is correct. *Apparently, if the BCD code for a digit is 0100 or less (4 or less) the code will be correct after a left shift. However, if the code is 0101 or greater (5 or greater), 0011 must be added to that digit code prior to the shift in order for SAM to provide the correct code after the shift.* Recall the definition for an algorithm that was discussed previously. This simple rule is an algorithm. In this conversion it must be used whenever a BCD coded number is shifted left one bit position.

Binary-to-BCD Conversion

To convert 32 binary to BCD, 40 bits of memory storage are required to hold the binary number 32 in BCD code, plus 32 bits to initialize the binary number. The complete conversion will be processed in 18 4-bit groups.

The procedure for performing a binary-to-BCD conversion is stated simply in flow chart form in *Figure 5-17*. If the binary number to be converted is 32 bits, a shift counter must be initialized to a value of 32. It will take a 10-digit decimal number to hold the decimal equivalent of the largest binary number. Since each decimal digit is represented by a 4-bit group, then 40 bits of storage are required to hold the decimal number in BCD code. As shown in *Figure 5-18a*, the 40 BCD bits along with 32 bits to hold the binary number forms a 72-bit "number" in the system memory.

The 4-bit SAM microprocessor must handle such a 72-bit group as 18 4-bit groups, 10 BCD digit groups and 8 binary number groups. Given this data in memory in 18 successive 4-bit memory locations, the conversion procedure for 32 bits is as follows:

1) Input the binary number and store in the 32-bit binary number locations.
2) Clear the BCD digit groups to 0000.
3) Set the binary bit counter to 32.
4) Repeat the following sequence of operations 32 times:
   A) Add 0011 to any BCD code greater than 0100 (BCD coded 4-bit groups only)
   B) Shift the 72-bit combined BCD-Binary number to the left one bit position.
   C) Decrement the counter.

**Figure 5-17.
Binary to BCD
Conversion Flow Chart**

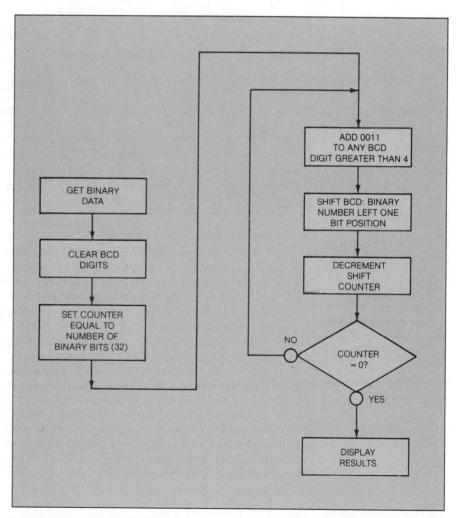

After the 32nd shift, the BCD equivalent of the original binary number is contained in the 10 BCD digit storage locations. This information can then be displayed using readily available display devices. An example of the conversion is shown in *Figure 5-18b* using 4-bits.

**Figure 5-18.
4-Bit Binary to BCD
Conversion**

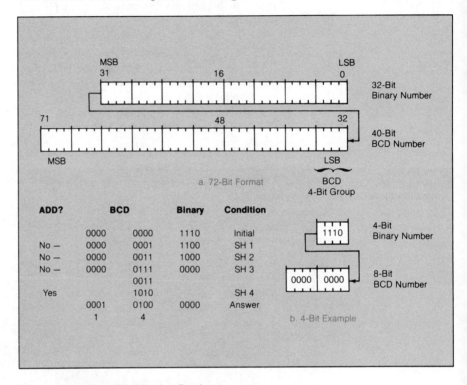

Seven-Segment LED Display Devices

The decimal numbers will be displayed using 7-segment LED (Light Emitting Diode) displays. Amplifiers and a BCD decoder are required separately or may be self contained within the display.

The seven-segment Light-Emitting-Diode (LED) display device shown in *Figure 5-19* is commonly used to display decimal numbers. When a specific current is passed through one of these diode segments, it emits light. By turning on the appropriate light-emitting diode segments, any of the decimal numbers can be displayed. For example, turning on all the LED segments except the ones on the left side of the display unit will show the number 3. The display units can be purchased as individual devices or as an array. A BCD-to-seven-segment decoder must be used to convert the BCD-code signals (4 lines) to the seven-segment display signals. As shown in *Figure 5-20a*, these signals must be amplified with driver amplifiers to provide the energy necessary to turn on the LED lights. Alternatively, single units are available for purchase containing the BCD-code decoder, the drivers, the LED seven-segment display, and even a storage register to hold or remember the BCD code being displayed. One such self-contained unit is the TIL311. To use such a device, the BCD code to be displayed is latched into the TIL311 4-bit register and the device does the rest, displaying the decimal number for the code stored inside the device.

**Figure 5-19.
Seven Segment LED
Displays**

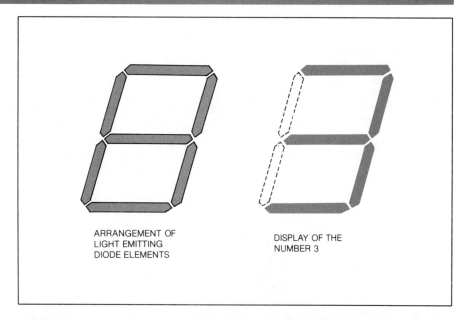

ARRANGEMENT OF
LIGHT EMITTING
DIODE ELEMENTS

DISPLAY OF THE
NUMBER 3

**Figure 5-20.
LED Display Circuit
Requirements**

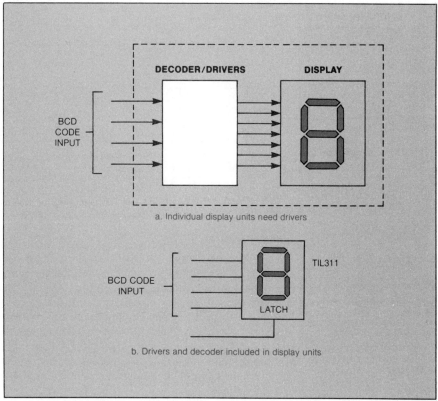

a. Individual display units need drivers

b. Drivers and decoder included in display units

Basic Serial Data Transmission

Systems receiving asynchronous serial data transmission must monitor the signal lines for start or stop bits and sample the line at a time interval based on the transmission data rate. The rate at which data is sent is called the Baud rate.

One of the tasks the microprocessor is to perform in the example problem is to receive the binary number from some device one bit at a time until the full 32-bit binary number has been received and stored in the appropriate portion of memory. Many different formats are used for sending data. One common format for serial data is shown in *Figure 5-21.* 8 bits are sent at a time beginning with a start bit and ending with one or two stop bits. The system receiving such a signal must monitor the signal line to determine when the start bit occurs. It then must determine the center of the start bit interval, and check for the value of the 8 data bits by checking the input line at the appropriate intervals. Finally, a stop bit must be detected, after which the data transmission is over for that 8-bit group. The interval times involved in this type of reception depend on how many 8-bit groups (bytes) are sent per second. 10 bits are sent for each 8-bit data byte. Thus, if 15 such bytes are sent per second, the bits would be arriving at the rate of 150 bits/second. Each bit interval is 0.0067 seconds (6.67 milliseconds). This rate is referred to as 150 Baud in computer terminology. Each 8-bit data group is received in this way. Four such 8-bit data groups would be used to send the entire 32-bit binary number to the SAM conversion system.

Figure 5-21.
**Serial Data Transmission
— Not Synchronized**

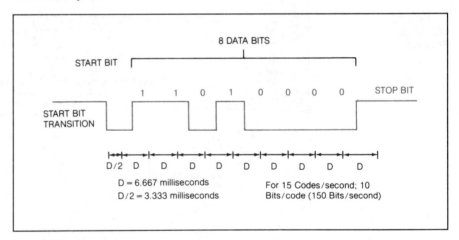

Summary of Tasks

The basic computer functions of sense, decide and act are being performed by SAM in doing the conversion.

Taken individually, the three tasks that our system is to perform are relatively simple. The processor must input the serial data and send it to the microcomputer memory. It must determine when all 32 bits have been received and then convert this binary number to its decimal equivalent. It must then display the decimal numbers and wait for the next binary number to be received. The total system is simply implementing the basic operations of sense (received the input binary number), decide (decide what its decimal equivalent is), and act (output the result to the display devices). SAM, with the additional appropriate hardware devices, will do these tasks according to instructions contained in a program.

HOW IS THE PROGRAM DEVELOPED?

The program is developed for the microcomputer by breaking the programming effort down into simpler subprograms. Each subprogram will handle a specific task that the microcomputer is to perform. In the case of the number converter, the program for SAM will consist of three subprograms:

Programs are developed by breaking the overall task into simple subprogram tasks. Input, conversion, and output are the subprograms for this task.

1) Input Subprogram – This subprogram will handle the task of receiving the serial data and storing it in memory.

2) Conversion Subprogram – This subprogram will handle the task of converting the binary number to its decimal equivalent.

3) Output Subprogram – This subprogram will output the decimal codes to the display devices.

The overall program will start out with the input subprogram. After this task is complete the conversion subprogram will be used, followed by the output subprogram. Then the processor will jump back to the input subprogram to await new data. Thus, the overall programming effort can be broken down into subprograms that are directly related to the operations required of the system.

The Input Subprogram

The Input Subprogram shown in *Figure 5-22* must perform the following operations:

1) It must determine when the start bit transition occurs. This can be done by continually checking the serial data line for a zero. Once a zero is detected, the processor can go to the next input operation.

The input subprogram determines when the transmission starts, inputs a byte of data, and verifies the transmission.

2) It must determine the mid-point of the start bit. It can do this by checking for a zero 3.333 milliseconds (for a 150 Baud signal) after it has detected the start bit transition. If the input line still has a zero on it at this time, the subprogram can start looking for data bits. If not, the subprogram will have to return to the first task of checking for a start bit transition.

3) Once the start bit has been verified, the program will input a data bit once every 6.667 milliseconds until 8 data bits have been received and stored in memory.

4) After 8 bits have been received, the program must wait 6.667 milliseconds to see if the input is a 1. If it is, the transmission terminates properly, and a byte has been received. If the input is a zero, the transmission is incorrect and the program must request a retransmission of the same byte.

Steps 1) through 4) are repeated until all four bytes of binary data have been received. The Conversion Subprogram then will be used.

**Figure 5-22.
Input Subprogram Flow
Chart**

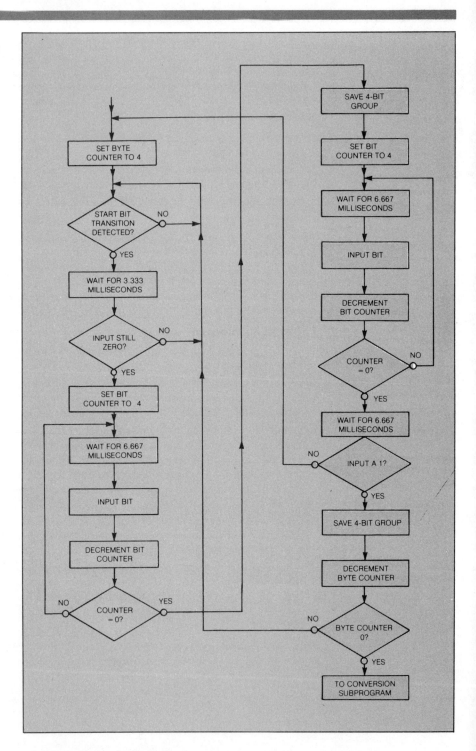

Timer Instruction Sequences

Timer instruction sequences are required to find the center of the start bit and the interval between data bits.

The basic recurring operation that the input subprogram must provide is that of a timer. First, it must provide 3.333 millisecond time intervals to find the center of the start bit. Second, it must be able to time 6.667 milliseconds to determine the interval between data bits. A program sequence, discussed previously, that provides such a timing operation consists essentially of a counter and a program loop that will continue decrementing the counter until the counter is zero. *Figure 5-23* shows such a sequence for the SAM system. By computing the time it takes to perform the loop operations from data sheet specifications, the total loop time of 420 microseconds is determined. The time that is consumed in setting up the loop counter value and the location of the counter in memory is 420 microseconds. This value is subtracted from the 3333 or 6667 before division by 420. Dividing 3333 minus 420 microseconds, the time desired, by the loop time of 420 microseconds determines the value to initially place in the counter. Therefore the counter should be initialized to 7. Similarly, to time an interval of 6667 microseconds, the counter would be initialized to 15.

Figure 5-23.
Interval Timer Flow Chart and Program Sequence

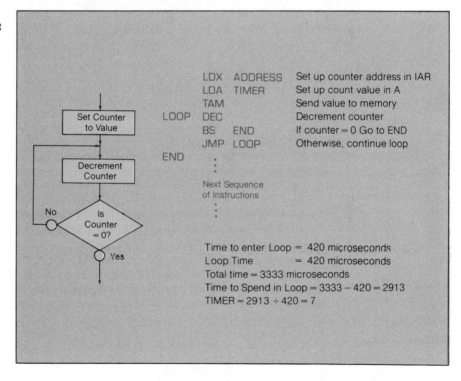

UNDERSTANDING MICROPROCESSORS

179

Accumulation of Data Bits

The input subprogram must keep track of the bits as they come in, store 4-bit groups in the proper locations, and determine when all 4 bytes (32 bits) have been received.

Another basic operation of the input subprogram is to store the 4-bit groups as they are accumulated. To do this the program must keep track of how many bits have been received. After 4 bits have been received, the program must store the completed 4-bit group in memory. Assuming successive memory locations are to be used for these groups as they are received, the program must also keep track of the next memory location to be used to store the next group of 4 bits. The program also must keep track of the 8-bit bytes as they are stored to know when 4 bytes have been received. Thus, a byte counter must be initialized to 4 at the beginning of the input subprogram, and a bit counter must be initialized to 4 after each 4-bit group has been sent to its memory location.

The Flow Chart

Each of these basic tasks can be identified in the overall input subprogram flow chart of *Figure 5-22*. A byte counter is first initialized to 4 and the program starts looking for a start-bit transition from high to low. Once this transition occurs, the program times 3.333 milliseconds and checks the start bit again. If it is still 0, the program inputs a bit once every 6.667 milliseconds, until 4 bits are in the accumulator. This information is sent to memory to the location for the least significant 4 bits (assuming information is coming in least-significant bit first). Again, the program inputs bits every 6.667 milliseconds until the next 4 bits are in the accumulator. This information is sent to the next 4-bit memory location. Since 8 bits have been received, the byte counter is decremented and the procedure is repeated until all 4 bytes have been received and stored in memory. After this step the work assigned to the input subprogram is completed and the microcomputer can go on to the conversion subprogram.

Instruction Sequences for Flow Chart Operations

Much of the input subprogram flow chart can be implemented rather directly with SAM's instructions. The timer operations have already been examined *(Figure 5-23)* and the sequence of instructions for interval timing can be used to implement these operations in the flow chart. Initial values must be placed in the counters. This is accomplished easily by loading the accumulator with the desired constant value with an LDA instruction, loading the IAR address register with the desired counter location address in memory with the instruction LDX, and sending the counter value to this address with the instruction TAM. The sequence is shown in *Figure 5-24*. As long as the IAR contents remain unchanged, the DEC instruction can be used to directly decrement the count value in this memory location.

Figure 5-24.
Initialization of a Counter
Value in Memory

```
LDA    VALUE      Set up counter value in A
LDX    ADDRESS    Set up counter address in IAR
TAM               Transfer counter value to its memory location
```

The XCHG instruction interchanges the contents of two registers. It is used in the input subprogram to save an address in a side register while another address is used in the main register.

SAM detects what is on the serial input line when given an IN instruction. The bit value is stored in the S flip-flop and is shifted into the accumulator with an ROL instruction. Four such shifts would accumulate an entire 4-bit group. Storing the 4-bit group requires keeping track of the last memory location used. Refer to *Figure 5-25*. By using the LDX instruction, the IAR can be initialized to the address of the last four-bit group location in memory (*Figure 5-27* shows this to be the least-significant binary group.) XCHG can be used to save this in the indirect address buffer register (IAB) until it is needed again. When the binary memory storage address is needed again, another XCHG will restore this value back to the IAR. The XCHG operation provides a means of saving an address that is referred to from time-to-time while a counter address is used in the IAR register in the meantime.

Figure 5-25.
Use of XCHG Instruction
to Maintain Two
Addresses

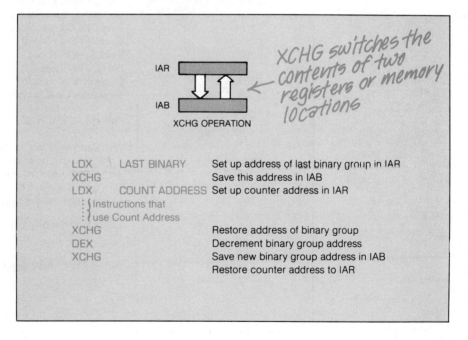

XCHG switches the contents of two registers or memory locations

```
LDX    LAST BINARY      Set up address of last binary group in IAR
XCHG                    Save this address in IAB
LDX    COUNT ADDRESS    Set up counter address in IAR
  �runstructions that
  ⌡use Count Address
XCHG                    Restore address of binary group
DEX                     Decrement binary group address
XCHG                    Save new binary group address in IAB
                        Restore counter address to IAR
```

The complete input subprogram is shown in *Figure 5-26* written in terms of the basic instruction sequences for each flow chart block. The entire program is written in easy-to-understand mnemonic form using symbols (labels) such as P1, P2, etc. for locations of instructions in memory. *Figure 5-27* details the assignment of memory locations. The symbol START is used to denote the address of the most-significant BCD digit. 10 locations away in order (START + 9) is the address of the least-significant BCD digit. START + A_{16} (START + 10, the 11th location) is the address of the most-significant 4-bit group of the binary number, so that START + 11_{16} (the 18th location) is the address of the least-significant 4-bit group of the binary number. The locations START + 12_{16} through START + 15_{16} are reserved for the 6.667-millisecond counter value, the bit counter, the 3.333-millisecond counter value, and the byte counter, respectively. By setting up the memory in this way, most of the locations can be accessed in order (sequentially) by simply decrementing the contents of the IAR for each new location.

**Figure 5-26a.
First Half of Input
Subprogram**

Label	INST	Operand	Comments
INPUT	LDX	START + 11_{16}	Set address for least significant binary group in IAR
	XCHG		Save in IAB
	LDX	START + 15_{16}	Set up Byte Counter address in IAR
	LDA	4	Set up Byte Counter value in A
	TAM		Save Byte Counter in memory
P1	IN		Check for Start Bit = 0
	BS	P1	If not, keep checking
	LDA	7	Set up timer value in A
	DEX		Decrement address to point to timer storage
	TAM		Send timer value to memory
P2	DEC		
	BS	P3	Perform 3.333 millisecond interval timing
	JMP	P2	
P3	IN		Check to see if Start Bit still 0
	BS	P1	If not, check for new Start Bit
	LDA	4	Set up Bit Counter value in A
	DEX		Change address to that of Bit Counter
	TAM		Save counter value in memory
LP	DEX		
	LDA	15	Set up 6.667 millisecond timer value
	TAM		
P4	DEC		
	BS	P5	Perform 6.667 millisecond timing
	JMP	P4	

**Figure 5-26b.
Last Half of Input
Subprogram**

Label	INST	Operand	Comments
P5	IN		Input data bit to S flip-flop
	ROL		Rotate into accumulator
	LDX	START+13$_{16}$	Get Bit Counter address into IAR
	DEC		Decrement Counter
	BS	P6	If 4 bits inputted, go to save operation
	JMP	LP	If not, go to 6.667 millisecond timer for next bit
P6	XCHG		Restore current binary group address
	TAM		Send 4-bit binary group to memory
	DEX		Set up address for next 4-bit group
	XCHG		Save Address in IAB
	LDX	START+13$_{16}$	Set up Bit Counter address in IAR
	LDA	4	Set up Bit Counter value in A
	TAM		Save Bit Counter in memory
LPA	DEX		
	LDA	15	
	TAM		Same operations as in LP to P6
P4A	DEC		
	BS	P5A	
	JMP	P4A	
P5A	IN		
	ROL		
	LDX	START+13$_{16}$	
	DEC		
	BS	P6A	
	JMP	LPA	
P6A	XCHG		
	TAM		
	DEX		
	XCHG		
	LDX	START+12$_{16}$	
	LDA	15	Set up address for 6.667 millisecond counter
	TAM		and repeat sequence to implement 6.667
PS	DEC		millisecond timer.
	BS	PSA	
	JMP	PS	
PSA	IN		Check for Stop Bit
	BS	P7	If 1 continue
	JMP	INPUT	If not, start over
P7	LDX	START+15$_{16}$	Get address of Byte Counter in IAR
	DEC		Decrement Counter
	BS	CONVERT	If Byte Counter = 0, go to conversion subprogram
	JMP	P1	If not, wait for receipt of next byte.

Figure 5-27.
RAM Memory Assign-
ments (Assuming START
= 200₁₆) for Programs

Program Label (Hexadecimal Numbers)	Hexadecimal (Base 16) Address	Decimal Address	Storage Allocation
START	200	512	1st (Most-Significant) BCD Code
START + 1	201	513	2nd BCD Code
START + 2	202	514	3rd BCD Code
START + 9	209	521	10th BCD Code (Least-Significant Digit)
START + A	20A	522	First (Most-Significant) Binary Group
START + B	20B	523	2nd Binary Group
START + 11	211	529	8th (Least-Significant) Binary Group
START + 12	212	530	6.667 millisecond Counter Value
START + 13	213	531	Bit Counter Value
START + 14	214	532	3.333 millisecond Counter Value
START + 15	215	533	Byte Counter Value
START + 16	216	534	0011
START + 17	217	535	0101

Development of the Conversion Subprogram

The conversion program, following the flow chart, will shift the combined BCD and binary numbers to the left one bit, after 0011 has been added to all BCD digits greater than 0100. This procedure is followed for each bit until all binary bits are shifted.

The flow chart of *Figure 5-17* identifies two basic operations for the conversion subprogram. The fundamental operation is the shifting of the combined BCD and binary numbers (a 72-bit group) to the left one bit position. Prior to the shift, 0011 must be added to all BCD digits greater than 0100. This is the second basic operation. This procedure is repeated until all binary bits have been shifted.

Since the data is already in memory, the subprogram begins with the clearing of the 10 BCD-digit storage locations. The program steps are shown in *Figure 5-28*. The bit counter at START + 13₁₆ is used as a digit counter to keep track of the BCD digits cleared to 0. It is initialized to a value of 10 in the first three instructions. The counter address is saved in IAB with the XCHG instruction. Now the IAR can be loaded with the address of the least-significant BCD digit, START + 9. Next, the accumulator is cleared to 0 with the LDA 0 instruction; then a TAM sends the 0 in the A register to the location directed by IAR. One is subtracted (decremented) from IAR with the DEX instruction, and the XCHG brings in the counter address so the counter can be decremented with DEC. A second XCHG restores the BCD digit address before the digit counter is checked by the BS instruction for zero. Recall from the instruction set *(Figure 5-2)* that when a DEC instruction is carried out by SAM, the status

FF is set equal to 1 if the memory location value equals 0. If the digit counter has not been decremented to zero, this loop sequence will be repeated. If the loop counter is zero all 10 BCD digits have been cleared to 0 and the conversion procedure will be entered.

**Figure 5-28.
Subprogram to Clear
BCD Digits**

```
              LDX       START + 13₁₆      Set up counter address in IAR
              LDA       10                Set up counter value of 10 in A
              TAM                         Send 10 to Memory
              XCHG                        Save counter address in IAB
              LDX       START + 9         Set up BCD address (LS Digit) in IAR
              LDA       0                 Clear A
       LOOP   TAM                         Send 0 to BCD location
              DEX                         Decrement BCD address
              XCHG                        Get counter address; save BCD address
              DEC                         Decrement counter
              XCHG                        Set up BCD address in IAR; save counter address
              BS        CORR              If counter = 0 go to BCD digit correction prog.
              JMP       LOOP              If not, repeat loop
```

BCD Digit Corrections

As shown in *Figure 5-17*, prior to entering the BCD correction procedure the counters and data to be used by the program must be initialized. This is done by using several times the same sequence of instructions that was used in *Figure 5-24* – LDA n to set up the counter value, LDX to set up the counter address, and TAM to send this value to the counter memory location. Thus, as shown in *Figure 5-29*, 0011 is sent to START + 16 to save the correction code; 0101 is sent to START + 17 to save the BCD reference value; and 32 is sent to START + 14_{16} and START + 15_{16} to save the shiftcounter value (an 8-bit number).

To determine if a BCD code must be corrected, It is examined to see if it is 4 or less by subtracting 5(0101) from it. If a borrow flip-flop is set to 1, no correction is needed. The code was 4 or less.

With these values in memory, the basic BCD correction scheme would be to bring the BCD code from memory and subtract 0101 from it. A borrow would set the S flip-flop indicating the memory digit was 4 or less (no correction needed). If S = 0 after the subtraction, 0011 must be added to the BCD digit code and the result is stored in the digit location in memory. This process is repeated until all 10 BCD digits have been corrected. The program to accomplish this activity, along with the initializations required by the entire conversion program, is shown in *Figure 5-29*. The first nine instructions store the constants 0011, 0101, and 32 as discussed. The next four instructions, starting with the label BEGIN, set up the Bit Counter used as a BCD digit counter to 10 and start the address for data at the least-significant BCD digit (START + 9).

**Figure 5-29.
BCD Digit Pre-Shift
Correction Subprogram**

CORR	LDA	3	Set up 0011 in A
	LDX	START + 16$_{16}$	Set up memory address for 0011 storage
	TAM		Send 0011 to memory
	LDA	5	Set up 0101 in A
	LDX	START + 17$_{16}$	Set up memory address for 0101 storage
	TAM		Send 0101 to memory
	LDA	2	Set up shift counter to 32 (2 in 14, 0 in 15)
	LDX	START + 14$_{16}$	Set up address of higher part of shift count
	TAM		Send 32 out to 8-bit counter location
BEGIN	LDA	10	Set up BCD digit counter value of 10 in A
	LDX	START + 13$_{16}$	Set up counter address in IAR
	TAM		Send 10 to Memory
	LDX	START + 9	Set up address for least significant BCD Digit
LOOP1	TMA		Get BCD digit to A
	XCHG		Save BCD digit address;
	LDX	START + 17$_{16}$	Set up address for 0101 location in IAR
	SUB		Subtract 0101 from BCD digit code
	BS	DIGOK	If borrow, BCD ≤ 5; Digit OK
	XCHG		Otherwise, must add 0011 to digit, restore BCD address
	TMA		Get digit to A
	XCHG		Save digit address in IAB
	DEX		Get 0011 address in IAR
	ADD		Add 0011 to BCD digit
	XCHG		Restore digit address to IAR
	TAM		Send corrected digit to memory
	XCHG		Save digit address in IAB
DIGOK	LDX	START + 13$_{16}$	Get BCD counter address in IAR
	DEC		Decrement counter
	BS	SHIFT	If counter = 0, go to shift sequence.
	XCHG		Restore digit address
	DEX		Move digit address back to next digit
	JMP	LOOP1	Go back through loop to correct next digit

Starting with the label LOOP 1, the rest of the program is a loop of instructions which, when repeated 10 times, will examine and modify BCD digits as needed. The addressed digit is brought into the accumulator and 0101 is subtracted from it (first four instructions of the loop). The BS instruction is used to branch around the correction sequence if there was a borrow ((A) = BCD digit less than 5) to the instruction labelled DIGOK.

If there was no borrow, the digit address is returned from the IAB with the XCHG instruction and again the digit is sent to the accumulator with the TMA. The digit address is again saved with XCHG, but this instruction also restores the address for the location storing 0101 into the IAR. A DEX decrements the address down to the 0011 correction code The digit address is restored with the XCHG and the corrected digit sent to memory (TAM) and the digit address once again saved in IAB.

The last 6 instructions (beginning with DIGOK) decrement the digit counter, decrement the digit address, and return to the beginning of the loop of instructions if the digit counter has not been decremented to zero. The loop is completed when the counter goes to 0.

Shift-Left Operation

Each sequence is a subroutine in itself and is performed best by programming it into a loop.

At this point in the program, the microprocessor will branch to the shift subprogram sequence of instruction shown in *Figure 5-30a*. The first part of this subprogram contains instructions to load the IAR data address register with the address of the least-significant 4-bit group of the binary number (START + 11_{16}) since the 72 bits of data (10 BCD digits and 8 Binary 4-bit groups) are to be shifted left or up through memory as shown in *Figure 5-30b*. The entire shift requires performing the following sequence of instructions 18 times:

TMA   Send 4-bit group to accumulator A
ROL   Rotate 4-bit group Left, using S to save bit rotated out of group. S also sends to the next most-significant group the bit rotated out of the previous least-significant group.
TAM   Send shifted group back to memory
DEX   Decrement address to move up to the next most-significant group.

Two of these are shown detailed in *Figure 5-30a*. Ideally these four instructions would be programmed in a loop with a loop counter set to 18 as follows:

```
           Count=18
Loop       TMA
           ROL
           TAM
           DEX
           DEC Count
           Branch on Not Zero to Loop
```

Since a simple decrement count could change the value of the data, it is difficult to use a loop structure to implement the shift-left due to SAM's limited capability.

However, with SAM's limited status information, this cannot be done very easily. S is saving the bit rotated out of the previous 4-bit group to be rotated into the next 4-bit group. But the decrement count operation would affect and possibly change this value, so the loop structure cannot be set up easily. As a result, a lot more memory locations (17 × 4 instructions extra) are used to implement the 18 repeated operations. Six instructions could be substituted if a loop structure could be used.

After the 18th rotation, the 8-bit shift counter is decremented and when it has been decremented to zero, the processor would go to the output subprogram. Otherwise, the program would branch back to the point labelled BEGIN — the beginning of the conversion program.

Figure 5-30.
Shift-Left Operation

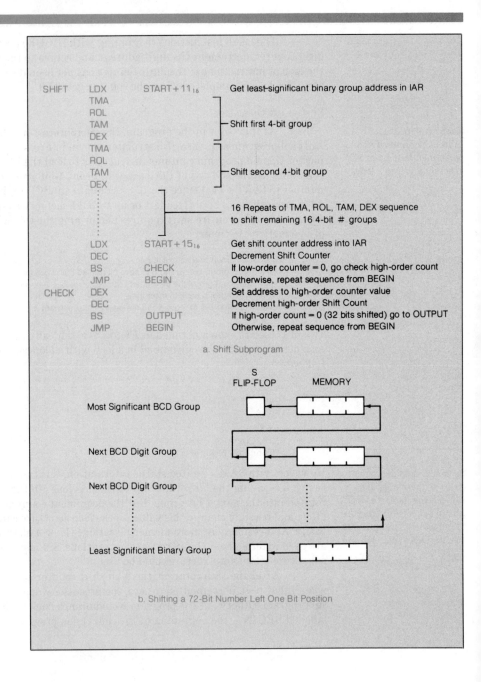

```
SHIFT    LDX    START + 11₁₆    Get least-significant binary group address in IAR
         TMA
         ROL                    Shift first 4-bit group
         TAM
         DEX
         TMA
         ROL                    Shift second 4-bit group
         TAM
         DEX
                                16 Repeats of TMA, ROL, TAM, DEX sequence
                                to shift remaining 16 4-bit # groups

         LDX    START + 15₁₆    Get shift counter address into IAR
         DEC                    Decrement Shift Counter
         BS     CHECK           If low-order counter = 0, go check high-order count
         JMP    BEGIN           Otherwise, repeat sequence from BEGIN
CHECK    DEX                    Set address to high-order counter value
         DEC                    Decrement high-order Shift Count
         BS     OUTPUT          If high-order count = 0 (32 bits shifted) go to OUTPUT
         JMP    BEGIN           Otherwise, repeat sequence from BEGIN
```

a. Shift Subprogram

S
FLIP-FLOP   MEMORY

Most Significant BCD Group

Next BCD Digit Group

Next BCD Digit Group

Least Significant Binary Group

b. Shifting a 72-Bit Number Left One Bit Position

Development of the Output Subprogram

The Output Subprogram shown in *Figure 5-31* is the simplest program to write. All that is required is to send the 10 BCD digits out to the 10 LED display register units. Again, the following loop structure would be very advantageous:

```
        Count=10
        LDX      LEDLSB      Set up address for LSB LED
        XCHG                 Save address in IAB
        LDX      START+9     Set up address for least-significant BCD digit
Loop    TMA                  Get BCD digit to Accumulator
        DEX                  Decrement BCD address
        XCHG                 Swap BCD and LED addresses
        TAM                  Send Accumulator to LED
        DEX                  Decrement LED address
        XCHG                 Swap BCD and LED addresses
        Decrement Count      Decrement Loop Counter
        Branch to Loop if Count≠0
```

The output subprogram consists of sending the BCD digits to the LED display register units. Again, because of SAM's limited capability ten repeats of the structure are used instead of a loop.

However, the limited addressing capability of SAM precludes this. Thus, again the program is simply 10 repeats of the 6 loop instructions, at a cost of 52 extra memory locations ($6 \times 9 = 54$ minus the last two loop operation instructions).

Once the BCD digits have been outputted, the program will jump back to INPUT to start waiting for new binary information to be received on the single data-input line.

**Figure 5-31.
Output Subprogram**

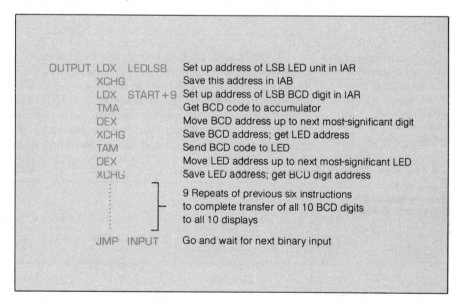

```
OUTPUT LDX  LEDLSB      Set up address of LSB LED unit in IAR
       XCHG             Save this address in IAB
       LDX  START+9     Set up address of LSB BCD digit in IAR
       TMA              Get BCD code to accumulator
       DEX              Move BCD address up to next most-significant digit
       XCHG             Save BCD address; get LED address
       TAM              Send BCD code to LED
       DEX              Move LED address up to next most-significant LED
       XCHG             Save LED address; get BCD digit address

                        9 Repeats of previous six instructions
                        to complete transfer of all 10 BCD digits
                        to all 10 displays

       JMP  INPUT       Go and wait for next binary input
```

Program Requirements

Total memory consists of both program and data memory. The ROM (Program memory) requires 413 4-bit locations, and RAM (data memory) requires 34 4-bit locations.

The total memory required consists of program memory and data memory. *Figure 5-32* shows the total memory locations required for the program. All instructions require one location except LDA n (2 locations required) and LDX, JMP, and BS (4 locations required for each). Thus, the total ROM or program memory requirement is 413 four-bit locations (nibbles). The total RAM data requirement is 34 four-bit locations, the 24 of *Figure 5-27* and the 10 LED locations. For simplicity, the program is assumed to start at hexadecimal location 000_{16} in memory and extends down through the hexadecimal location $19C_{16}$. Arbitrarily RAM can be assigned the 24 addresses from 200_{16} through 217_{16}, and the LED'S the 10 addresses from 300_{16} through 309_{16}

**Figure 5-32.
Program Memory
Requirements of
Problem**

Subprogram	Memory Requirements (Number of 4-Bit Groups)
INPUT	148
CONVERSION	192
OUTPUT	73
Total	413

Address assignments fix the location of data memory and program memory in the memory map, and assign the labels in the program to particular memory addresses.

These address assignments will be important to the hardware design portion of the problem, and they fix the meaning of the labels for the instruction and RAM addresses in the program. Thus, BEGIN has the address 000, START has the address 200, LED LSB has the address 309, and so on. Since the LED devices are assigned the hexadecimal addresses 300_{16} through 309_{16}, they are addressed just like portions of RAM. These assignments (memory map) and chosen conditions of the enable signals are shown in *Figure 5-33*.

**Figure 5-33.
Memory Map and
Subsystem Enables**

Type of Storage	Address Range	Value of 1st 4 Address Bits			
		A_{11}	A_{10}	A_9	A_8
Program (ROM)	000-1FF	0	0	0	0 or 1
Data (RAM)	200-217	0	0	1	0
LED Units	300-309	0	0	1	1

ROM ENABLE = MEMEN $\cdot \overline{A_9}$
RAM ENABLE = MEMEN $\cdot A_9 \cdot \overline{A_8}$
LED ENABLE = MEMEN $\cdot A_9 \cdot A_8$

HOW IS THE SYSTEM BUILT?

Once the program memory and RAM requirements of a system are known, and once the addresses for each portion of the system have been assigned, it is possible to design the system memory (including any input or output devices assigned memory addresses). All that's required is that an appropriate address decoder be provided along with correct connection of the processor memory control signals to appropriate memory and input/output integrated circuits.

Design of the Program Memory

The program instructions occupy addresses 000_{16} through $19C_{16}$ is a total of 413 locations. One programmable read-only memory (PROM) integrated circuit is the SN74S287. This device provides 256 locations 4 bits per location, so that two such circuits would provide adequate storage requirements for the 413 instruction locations of the program that has been developed. The first device would hold the first 256 instruction locations (addresses 000 through $0FF_{16}$), and the second device would provide storage locations with addresses from 100_{16} through $1FF_{16}$.

Figure 5-34 shows the interconnection of the program PROM. Since each device offers 256 locations, an 8-bit address code must be sent to each device to determine which of the 256 locations is being requested by the processor. Thus, address lines A_0 through A_7 would be sent from SAM to the address pins of the two memory circuits. Address lines A_8 through A_{11} would have to be used to distinguish these two circuits from the RAM and LED devices. Both PROM circuits will be turned on when MEMEN is a 1 and when the address bit A_9 has a 0 on it. One of the two PROMS will be selected by the condition of A_8.

RAM will be turned on when MEMEN is 1 and when $A_9 = 1$ and $A_8 = 0$. LED's will be activated when MEMEN is 1 and when A_9 and A_8 are both 1's. Thus, the memory subsystems and output subsystem can be easily distinguished by looking at the address bits A_9 and A_8. Address line outputs A_{10} and A_{11} are available from SAM but since limited memory and output locations are required they are ignored in this problem.

The PROM subsystem is turned on at the appropriate time when a NAND gate recognizes MEMEN = 1 and $A_9 = 0$ and provides one of the chip select lines a low level under these conditions. A_8 is used to distinguish which of the two SN74S298's is to be on at any given time. If A_8 is a 0, the first '278 will be turned on indicating a memory location in the range 000 through $0FF_{16}$; and if A_8 is a 1, the second '287 will be turned on, indicating a memory location in the range 100 through $1FF_{16}$ is requested. The overall PROM memory design, including timing and address decoding, is really very simple as an examination of *Figure 5-34* indicates. The three-state outputs of the SN74S283 provide easy interface to the data bus.

By using address bits and the enable signal as control bits, address codes through logic circuits determine if RAM or the LED displays are being addressed when memory is enabled.

In like fashion, program memory is also controlled by the address code and the enable control signal.

**Figure 5-34.
Connection of SAM to
the Program PROM
Subsystem**

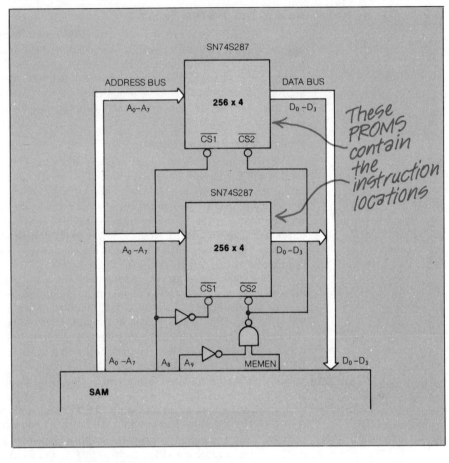

Design of the Data Memory

The data RAM has three-
state output integrated
circuits just like a pro-
gram ROM, to make it
easy to interface to the
bidirectional data bus.

The RAM requirements of 24 storage locations can be satisfied, as shown in *Figure 5-35,* by using two 16 locations, 4 bits per location integrated circuits such as the SN74S189. This device, like the SN74S287, offers three-state outputs so that it can be connected directly to the data bus of the system. It has address pins for A_0 through A_3 to distinguish which of the 16 internal locations is requested. It has 4 data-input lines and 4 data-output lines which can be connected together to serve as a bidirectional data bus. It has a Read/Write control line and single chip-enable line $\overline{CE}$ (The bar over the CE indicates that when the line is a low level the chip-enable is active).

**Figure 5-35.
Organization of
SN74S189 RAM**

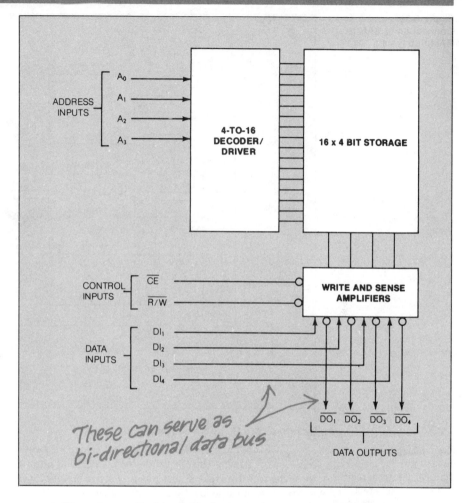

To assure true data out of the RAM, input data should be inverted before being stored. This is due to the way the RAM is designed.

The only peculiarity of this device is that the outputs are the complements of the data stored in the device. To avoid inverting the data from the write operation to the read operation, the input data should be inverted before it is stored in memory. The connections of this device to SAM to form a 32×4 RAM memory are otherwise straightforward, as shown in *Figure 5-36*. The Chip Enable is driven low on the first '189 when A_4 is a zero and when RAM is enabled ($\text{MEMEN} \cdot A_9 \cdot \overline{A_8}$). The chip enable of the second '189 is driven low when A_4 is a 1 and when RAM is enabled. The Read/Write signal generated by SAM is sent to both circuits and only controls the enabled unit. The data bus coming from SAM is inverted to store the complement of the data in the RAM circuits. Then, when the RAM locations are read, the inversion built into the '189 on the output lines brings the data back to what it was when SAM sent it to the RAM. Other than this slight problem caused by the design of the memory circuits, the connections of the RAM subsystem to SAM are again straightforward.

**Figure 5-36.
Connection of SAM to
RAM Subsystem**

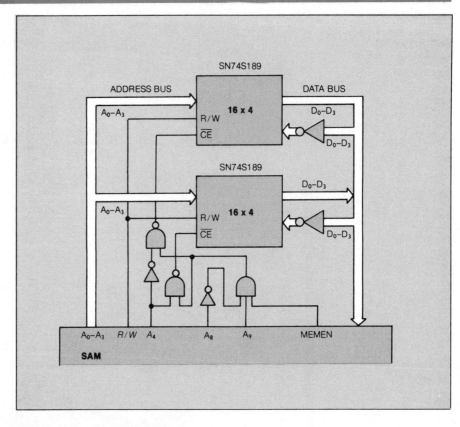

Design of the Output Subsystem

Even though they are addressed just like memory, the LED's internal registers are a bit different. Data can only be written to the registers.

Since each TIL311 LED display device contains an internal register for storing the 4-bit code for the decimal number to be displayed, these devices are treated just like any other memory location except data is not read from these locations; it is only written to these locations. This is shown in *Figure 5-37*. The 4-bit data bus coming from SAM is sent to the data inputs of all 10 TIL311 devices. These represent the memory locations 300_{16} through 309_{16}. An address decoder must be provided to select 1 of the 10 '311's to receive the data when a WRITE signal is received. This decoding can be done directly with a 4-to-16-line decoder such as the SN74154. By sending the address lines A_0 through A_3 to such a decoder, a low level will appear on one of the output lines from 0 to 9 of the decoder, which in turn will latch the data on the data bus into the corresponding TIL311. The decoder has two enables that can be used to further decode addresses, control and time the subsystem. Read/Write is connected to one of these enables to turn on the decoder only when a write operation is being performed by SAM. The other enable is driven low when the LED output enable is active, that is when MEMEN, A_9, and A_8 are all 1 *(Figure 5-33)*. As a result, the decoder, and one of the TIL311's will be activated only when SAM wants to write data to one of the addresses 300_{16} through 309_{16}.

**Figure 5-37.
Connection of SAM to
Output Subsystem**

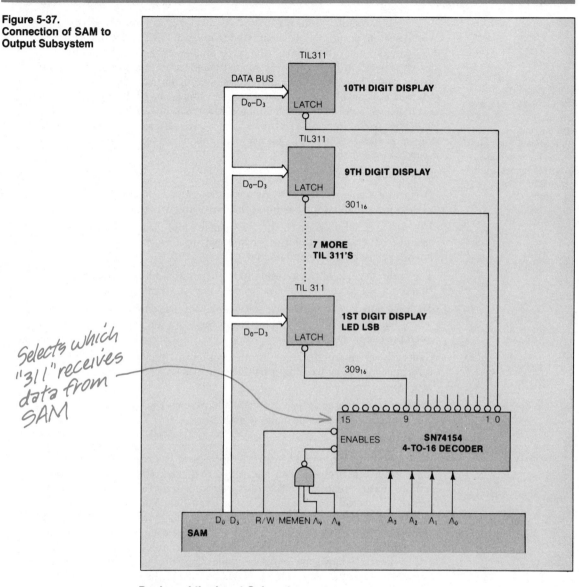

*Selects which
"311" receives
data from
SAM*

Design of the Input Subsystem

Since the system is monitoring only one input line with the single data-input line, there are no address decoding or timing circuits required. Other examples of interconnecting the single-input and single-output data line with circuits controlled by a memory address or receiving or sending data by the data bus under address control were shown *(Figures 5-11, 12, 13, 14)*. If a specific application calls for using these techniques, the programming and interconnection is similar to what has already been shown.

Even a simple micropro-
cessor system can perform
sophisticated tasks that
would otherwise take a
complex non-programmed
digital system to perform.
This is the advantage of
writing system programs
with microprocessor to
sub-system connections
over designing complete
non-programmed digital
systems for each
application.

If the subsystems of *Figure 5-34, 36* and *37* are combined, the
overall system design will be completed *(Figure 5-38)*. The details of the
design of the subsystems have been fairly simple, even though the final
system is performing some fairly sophisticated tasks. A non-microprocessor
system would have been much more complicated, but would not have
required a program to be written. However, this is one of the advantages
that has been pointed out for microprocessors, *it is generally far easier to
write the system program and connect the microprocessor to the appropriate
subsystem elements than it is to design a complete equivalent non-
programmed digital system.*

WHAT HAVE WE LEARNED?

- Designing a microprocessor system requires the development of the
  system program and the design of the hardware structure.
- In order to effectively use the instructions to build the system program,
  the internal features (architecture and instruction set) of the
  microprocessor must be understood.
- The basic concepts of the system input, output and microprocessor
  functions can be understood best by defining an overall system flowchart
- The program development task is broken down into simpler subprograms
  whose basic operations are implemented easily by simple sequences of the
  microprocessor instructions.
- Generally, the more extensive the instruction set, status register
  information, and addressing capability, the easier it is to write the system
  program.
- In order to be able to design the system hardware, the microprocessor
  timing and control signals must be understood.

WHAT'S NEXT?

In this chapter a fictional microprocessor has been applied to a
simple but useful problem. This has served to illustrate how microprocessor
instructions are combined to form subprograms to perform solutions to
parts of the overall problem. These subprograms are combined to complete
the solution of the problem. Similarly, designing memory and input/output
subsystems as separate tasks and combining these complete the design for
the entire system. In the next few chapters, other problems will be solved to
further illustrate how a system is designed. The difference being that real
microprocessors and microcomputers will be used in the problem solutions.

Hopefully the foundation established in this chapter will help to
understand how these real microprocessors with their individual
architectures and instruction sets are used in systems and are programmed
to perform given tasks.

Figure 5-38.
Complete System Wiring

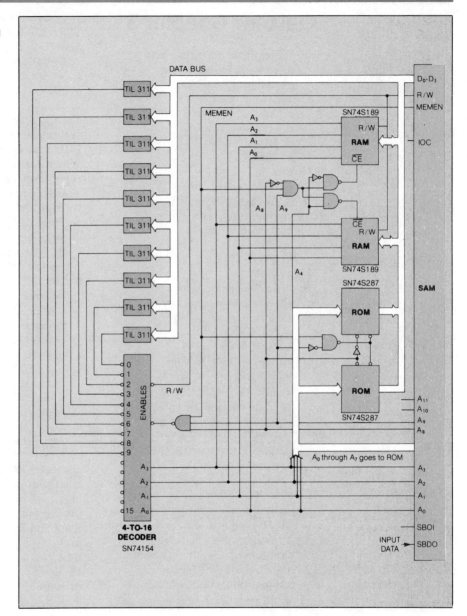

Quiz for Chapter 5

1. Which of the following data
   addressing modes are not
   available in SAM?
   a. Immediate
   b. Register Indirect
   c. Register
   d. Direct
   e. Indexed
   f. d and e above
   g. b through e above
2. SAM has the capability of
   distinguishing how many
   memory locations?
   a. 1024
   b. 2048
   c. 4096
3. A SAM memory write
   operation is indicated by the
   following:
   a. MEMEN = 1
   b. R/W = 0
   c. MEMEN = 1, R/W = 1
   d. MEMEN = 0, R/W = 1
   e. MEMEN = 1, R/W = 0
4. If serial transmission at 1000
   Baud is required, what time
   interval is required after
   detection of the first 1-to-0
   transition before the start
   bit = 0 check is made?
   a. .5 milliseconds
   b. 1 millisecond
   c. 3.33 milliseconds
5. How many 4-bit memory
   locations are required to hold
   the machine code for the
   subprogram of figure 5-28?
   a. 13
   b. 26
   c. 27

6. What value would be used for
   TIMER in the program of
   figure 5-23 to achieve a delay
   of 4.6 milliseconds?
   a. 8
   b. 10
   c. 12
7. The LED's are assigned
   separate addresses from the
   BCD data storage locations.
   Why not use the LED
   registers to provide the data
   storage locations 200_{16}
   through 209_{16}?
   a. The LED's are set up as a
      write-only device and the
      BCD data locations must be
      read as well as written into
   b. The LED register
      information would
      continually change until
      the conversion was
      completed, causing a
      confusing display
   c. The LED's will be storing
      previous BCD numbers
      while a new conversion is
      in progress
   d. All of the above
8. If the LED's had been
   assigned hexadecimal
   addresses 400 through 409,
   what address bit could have
   been used to directly
   distinguish the LED's from
   RAM and ROM?
   a. A_{12}
   b. A_{11}
   c. A_{10}
   d. None of the above

Programming Concepts

ABOUT THIS CHAPTER

In past chapters the importance of the program in developing microprocessor systems has been emphasized. In the SAM application, the basic procedures involved in writing programs were illustrated. Since developing the program is such a basic requirement in all microcomputer applications, these procedures will be examined in more detail in this chapter, starting with basic concepts of program development.

HOW ARE PROGRAMS DEVELOPED?

Program development is similar to most types of design efforts. It starts by describing overall system performance with specifications, subdividing the system and identifying inputs, outputs and subsystem operation. It ends when the individual subsystem tasks are combined into the complete program.

Developing a program is just like developing any other type of design in terms of the sequence of tasks that have to be performed. First, the system performance must be completely described before the design effort can begin. The program is to be built from the instructions of a given microprocessor. Therefore, the system performance description must be precise enough so there will be no problem building the component parts with the available instructions. The task of providing such a description is an interative one which ultimately results in breaking the original system into many elementary functional modules. Each of these elementary functional modules (subprograms) can be converted rather directly into instruction sequences. These subprogram modules can then be interfaced together to form the overall desired system program. The basic procedure is as follows:

1. Write a general description of the desired overall system performance.

2. Identify the overall system inputs, outputs, and general subsystem operations.

3. Describe each subsystem operation, identifying inputs, outputs, and the tasks involved.

4. Continue subdividing system tasks and developing task descriptions until they are defined at the most elementary level.

5. Write the instruction sequences that implement all the elementary subsystem tasks.

6. Combine the individual subsystem task instruction sequences into the desired overall system program.

Program Descriptions

Three key elements of program development are proper system description, dividing the tasks into subsystems with inputs and outputs, and sub-program module programming. Descriptions may be written in paragraph form, or another method is to write a check list in sentence form.

Program development involves three key elements that must be understood. The first element, as mentioned, is that of description, and it includes almost the total procedure because every step in the programming procedure is one of describing. There are a number of ways in which the descriptions can be written. One way is to simply write down the description in paragraph form as was done in the first paragraph of this section to describe the programming development procedure. This offers the most compact method of describing what is to be done. However, descriptions written in this form are often difficult to refer back to later.

An alternative form for a written description is to make a list of the things to be done. This was done above for the program development procedure and since it is a type of check-list it can be referred to easily. The only difficulty with this form is that again complete sentences have to be read and the relationship of one step to another may not be immediately evident.

The flow chart is a program description that is easy to understand, but it does require additional effort.

For this reason, another form of description, the flow chart, can be used that will graphically show the relationship of the steps in the procedure as well as carry the description. To illustrate the use of this form a flow chart for the program development procedure is shown in *Figure 6-1a*. It has the advantage that it presents the overall procedure in a form that's easy to understand and that may be referred to easily. It's only disadvantage is that it takes somewhat more effort and most often a more detailed description and more space to draw the flow chart than is required for the list or paragraph form of descriptions.

Another form of description combines the list and flow chart into one with the best features of both formats.

As a result, a form that combines the list and the flow chart descriptions is illustrated in *Figure 6-1b* alongside the flow chart. This mnemonic form has the readability of the list and the structure of the flow chart. It does not require as much space and certainly somewhat less effort than the flow chart form. It can be the same form as the final main program, and the mnemonics may even be the names of the major subprograms in a system description. Notice, however, that the mnemonics used are really abbreviated sentence structure and not abbreviated words as in the case of instructions. These macro-mnemonics (macro-meaning larger scope) also have a one-to-one correlation to the statements and structure of certain higher-level languages such as BASIC or PASCAL, making it possible to start describing the program for system operations directly in a programming language. In this chapter, both the flow chart form and the mnemonic form of descriptions will be used as much as possible.

**Figure 6-1.
Description of Program
Development Procedure**

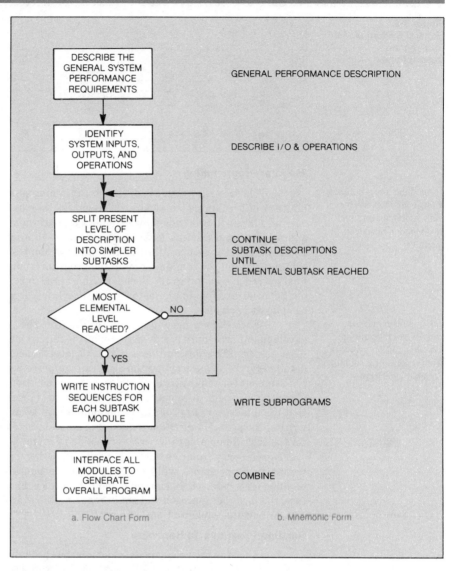

a. Flow Chart Form

b. Mnemonic Form

Subprogram Modules

When describing sub-
systems, inputs, outputs,
and their related opera-
tions are the focus of
consideration.

A second key element in the program development procedure is the
method of thinking of each system and subsystem module as a component
with inputs, outputs, and operations that relate outputs to inputs. This is
described by the general system model shown in *Figure 6-2*. By thinking of
each task and subtask in this way it will be easy to interface modules later
once the subprogram for each module has been written. This approach also
provides an organized approach to analyzing each subsystem task so that
the program requirements for that task can be quickly recognized and
described.

Figure 6-2.
General System Model
for Program
Descriptions

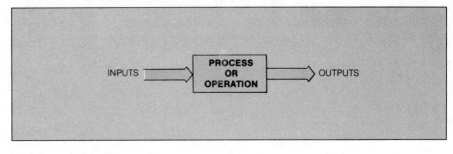

In modular programming
a large complex system
task is divided into self-
contained subprogram
modules.

The modular method
simplifies programming.
The description evolves
from a concept level into a
detailed algorithm.

Modular Programming

The third key element of the programming procedure is the
strategy of breaking a single large system task into many simple subtasks,
each of which will be handled by a simple subprogram module. This modular
approach to programming makes each separate subprogram effort a simple
and manageable problem. It also simplifies program testing of each
subprogram and the combining of all the program modules into the desired
final overall system program. Such a modular programming approach might
not be necessary for simple systems, but it certainly is a necessity for very
complicated systems.

Each elemental subtask that results from the program
development procedure is a description of the requirements that that task
must perform. This description is a concept level description that must be
detailed further by describing the algorithm or procedure that will meet the
requirements of the task and provide a problem solution. Once this
algorithm has been developed, it must be described in sufficient detail so
that the final stages of program development can be completed, that of
writing the actual instruction sequences that will implement the algorithm
for the task. Some programmers will be able to write the instruction
sequence directly from the module description. Others, particularly
beginner programmers, will have to describe the algorithm down to a very
detailed level before they can implement it with a subprogram. In either
case, the modular approach will aid in reducing the overall programming
task into manageable portions.

Relating Programs To Hardware

Thus far the program development has been discussed as if it were
totally independent of the way the system hardware is connected together.
If the system is to complete its task in an efficient manner, the hardware
and software must work in harmony. For example, in order for the
microprocessor to direct the operation of the system components correctly it
must identify the parts properly at the appropriate time and in the right
sequence. It does this with addresses, control signals and timing signals. As
a result, one of the first tasks for the hardware designer is to choose certain
address ranges for program memory and for data memory.

The program designer
must choose certain ad-
dress ranges for program
and data memory and
input/output subsystems.
This is called memory
mapping.

In many cases these are chosen to simplify the hardware circuits required to interpret or decode the addresses coming from the microprocessor. In other cases these addresses are dictated by the processor and the designer has no choice in the matter. For example, in responding to system interrupts in many cases, the location of subprograms or addresses of interrupt subprograms are dictated to be at certain locations. The exact location varies depending on the microprocessor or microcomputer used. Likewise, certain processors limit input/output subsystems (not memory mapped input/output) to certain ranges of addresses. Throughout the system operation, the program must use the correct addresses for the instructions in sequence, for the data to go with these instructions or for the input/output units requires.

When all of these factors have been considered, the designer assigns addresses to the various memory and input/output subsystems. This assignment is called memory mapping, since it maps or relates the devices to the addresses the program must use to locate and interact with those devices. By using these addresses, the program is related directly to the circuits that make up the hardware part of the system. By assuring that control and timing signals occur in the correct sequence and at the correct time and by providing enough drive and decode power, the hardware system can be completed.

An Example

Possibly these concepts are best solidified by a programming example. One simple example is a temperature control system in a house; more specifically – the control of the heating system. To begin, the system performance requirements will be described in paragraph form:

The system is to monitor eight temperature sensors per room area. When a majority of those sensors fall below a preset reference temperature the furnace will be turned on (if it is not already on) and the flow-control valve will be positioned to permit hot air to flow to that room area. This flow will continue until the majority of sensors indicate a temperature above the reference level.

This system can be described in terms of the general system model as shown in *Figure 6-3*. The values of the room and reference level temperatures are inputs from the sensors. The outputs control the valve position for the air flow and turn the furnace on or off. The decide function or process that relates these outputs to the inputs must implement the conditions described above. The flow chart description *(Figure 6-4)* and the corresponding mnemonic description *(Figure 6-5)* can be written rather directly from the paragraph system description. This level of flow chart description is at the algorithm level for all operations except for the sensor sample block. Thus, it would be a simple matter to write most of the instruction sequences directly from this flow chart.

Figure 6-3.
Furnace Control System
Structure

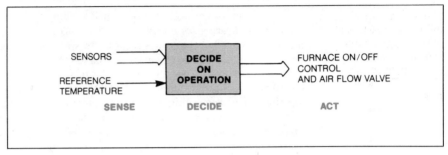

Figure 6-4.
Flow Chart Description
of Furnace Controller

Figure 6-5.
Mnemonic Form of
Description of Furnace
Controller

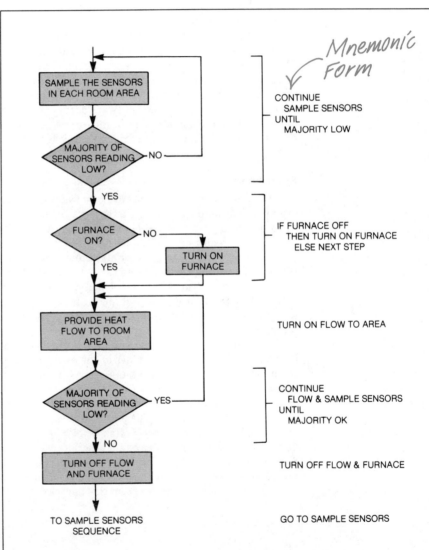

As an example, the furnace-on decision block can be further described in terms of hardware related blocks as shown in the instruction level flow chart of *Figure 6-6b*. The furnace-on decision sequence can be thought of as a decision block, with furnace status as input, furnace control as an output, and a simple decision (if the furnace is not on, turn it on) as the process block.

To illustrate the one-to-one correspondence between instruction and flow chart at this level, the program sequence is shown in *Figure 6-6c*, implemented with the corresponding TMS8080A microprocessor instructions. The other blocks in the flow chart of *Figure 6-4* could be detailed to this level and converted to the corresponding instruction sequences just as easily. Of course, the precise instruction sequence that implements a given flow chart depends on the microprocessor instruction set being used.

Figure 6-6.
Development of Furnace
Check Program Module

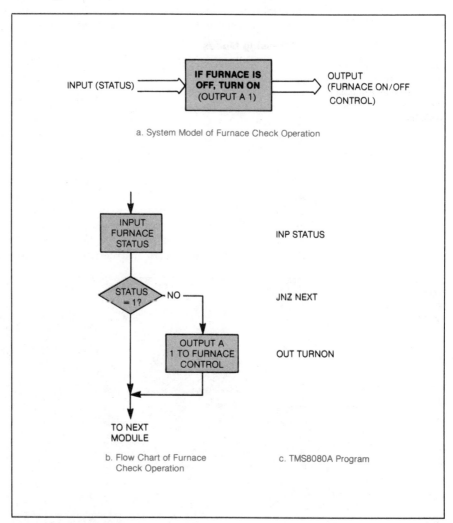

INPUT (STATUS) → IF FURNACE IS OFF, TURN ON (OUTPUT A 1) → OUTPUT (FURNACE ON/OFF CONTROL)

a. System Model of Furnace Check Operation

INPUT FURNACE STATUS — INP STATUS

STATUS = 1? — NO — JNZ NEXT

OUTPUT A 1 TO FURNACE CONTROL — OUT TURNON

TO NEXT MODULE

b. Flow Chart of Furnace Check Operation

c. TMS8080A Program

HOW DO INSTRUCTION SETS DIFFER?

The complexity of a microprocessor's instructon set
is determined largely by
its bit capacity and by its
features.

Each microprocessor family supports its own unique instruction set. However, there are similarities from one instruction set to another. All microprocessors support the instructions used by the fictional SAM microprocessor of the last chapter, but they can support many other instructions as well. Generally, the more bits the processor can handle at one time, the more extensive its instruction set. To illustrate some of the typical differences between processors, three microprocessor instruction sets will be summarized in this section. The 4-bit processors will be represented by the TMS1000 microcomputer instruction set, which is basically an expansion of the SAM architecture and instructions used in the last chapter. The 8-bit processors will be represented by the TMS8080A instruction set, and the 16-bit microprocessors by the instruction set for the TMS9900 family of devices. One of the first features that is of interest in comparing instruction sets is how versatile they are in locating system data, that is, how extensive are the addressing modes they support.

Addressing Modes

Many times the versatility
of a microprocessor can be
determined by examining
the addressing modes
available.

A comparison of the addressing modes available in the three devices is shown in *Figure 6-7*. It shows that the 16-bit unit supports all addressing modes currently used by microprocessors, the 8-bit unit supports all but indexed addressing, and the TMS1000 4-bit unit offers only limited addressing options. As a result, it is much more difficult to write a program using the TMS1000 unit than it is using the TMS9900 unit, not just because it is a 4-bit processor, but simply because with the TMS1000 it is often more awkward to locate needed data. This is a problem that has already been experienced in the SAM example of the last chapter. It must be remembered however, that the TMS1000 is a self-contained microcomputer with included memory and therefore limited to using what memory is available. Not only do the many addressing modes aid in programming but having a more extensive instruction set helps as well. This can be seen by looking at the arithmetic-logic instructions of the three devices.

Figure 6-7.
Comparison of
Microprocessor
Addressing Capability

Addressing Mode	TMS1000	TMS8080A	TMS9900
Immediate	Yes	Yes	Yes
Register	Yes	Yes	Yes
Register Indirect	Yes	Yes	Yes
Data Counter	Yes	No	Yes
Indexed	No	No	Yes
Direct	No	Yes	Yes

The ALU functions available vary with the microprocessor. Generally the more sophisticated microprocessor or micro-computer has instructions that perform an operation directly rather than having to build it from more elementary instructions.

Arithmetic-Logic Instructions

Figure 6-8 compares the arithmetic-logic instructions for the three microprocessors. While all processors have increments, adds, decrements, and subtract, only one processor supports add with carry and subtract with borrow (TMS8080A). Only the 16-bit unit supports all arithmetic and logic operations listed, including absolute value, multiplication, and division. The latter two can be accomplished with one instruction rather than a complete sequence of instructions made up to do the operation. By contrast, the 4-bit unit has a rather limited ALU offering.

**Figure 6-8.
Comparison of
Microprocessor
Arithmetic-Logic
Operations**

Operation	TMS1000	TMS8080A	TMS9900
Addition:			
Incrementing	IMAC,IA,IYC	INR,INX	INC,INCT
Without Carry	AMAAC,Ac†AAC	ADD,ADI,DAD	A,AB,AI
With Carry	—	ADC,ACI	—
Subtraction:			
Decrementing	DMAN,DAN,DYN	DCR,DCX	DEC,DECT
Without Borrow	—	SUB,SUI	S,SB
With Borrow	—	SBB,SBI	—
Negation	—	—	NEG
Absolute Value	—	—	ABS
Multiplication	—	—	MPY
Division	—	—	DIV
OR	—	ORA,ORI	ORI
AND	—	ANA,ANI	ANDI
Exclusive OR	—	XRA,XRI	XOR
NOT	CPAIZ	CMA	INV
Clear	RBIT,CLA	—	CLR
Set	SBIT	—	SETO
Shifts (S) or	—	RLC,RRC	SLA,SRA
Rotates (R)		RAL,RAR	SRC,SRL

†Displacement 6, 8 or 10

Data Movement Instructions

Data movement operations inside the various micro-processors or microcom-puters are pretty similar. Stack operations, however, can be unique.

The devices have somewhat comparable data movement operations as shown in *Figure 6-9.* All provide for moving program constants into registers or memory. All provide single-bit or multiple-bit input and output instructions and all provide for moving data from registers to and from memory. The TMS8080A needs and provides stack control operations, the PUSH and POP instructions. These are about all the data movement options that could be available and all three devices are quite adequate in this area.

Figure 6-9.
Comparison of
Microprocessor Data
Movement Operations

Operation	TMS1000	TMS8080A	TMS9900
Input	TKA	INP	TBIT,STCR
Output	SETR,RSTR TDO,CLO	OUT	SBO,SBZ,LDCR
Memory-Register & Register-Register	TAY,TYA TAM,TMA TMY,TYM TAMZA,TAMIY XMA	MOV,LDA,STA LDAX,STAX LHLD,SHLD SPHL	MOV,MOVB
Constants	TCY,TCMIY LDP,LDX	MVI,LXI	LI,LWPI,LIMI
Stack Operations	—	PUSH,POP, XTHL	—

Comparison And Branch Instructions

The type comparisons and branch instructions vary considerably between microprocessors. Unconditional and conditional branch instructions have the most variability.

The range of comparison and branch operations are summarized in *Figure 6-10*. The TMS1000 is the most limited in this area, offering less than or equal comparisons between the accumulator and memory or a constant, and checks to see if the accumulator, Y register, or memory is not equal to zero. The Branch (BR) checks a status flip-flop which has saved the results of a comparison or a carry resulting from a previous arithmetic operation. One level of conditional branch (subroutine call) is possible depending on the condition of the status flip-flop.

The TMS8080A offers arithmetic comparisons, unconditional branches, an unconditional subroutine jump (call) and conditional branches, subroutine jumps (calls), and subroutine returns. The allowed TMS8080A condition checks include carry, no carry, zero, not zero, plus, minus, odd parity, and even parity.

The TMS9900 offers arithmetic and logical comparisons, the same branch and jump options of the 8080A, as well as additional branch conditions and broader scope subroutine calling procedures. These additional options enable the TMS9900 programmer to implement decision making, subroutine structures, and input/output subprograms more efficiently when compared to what's available with the TMS8080A and especially the TMS1000 device.

Figure 6-10.
Microprocessor
Comparison and
Branch Operations

Operation	TMS1000	TMS8080A	TMS9900
Arithmetic Comparison	ALEM,ALEC	CMP, CPI	C,CB,CI
Logical Comparison	MNEZ,YNEA, YNEC,KNEZ	—	COC,CZC
Unconditional Branch	—	JMP,RET	B,JMP
Unconditional Subroutine Jump	—	CALL	BL,BLWP, RTWP,XOP,X
Conditional Branch	BR,CALL, RETN Conditioned on Status Flip-Flop	Jcond,Ccond Rcond	Jcond

Conditions (TMS8080A):
Z—zero
NZ—not zero
C—carry
NC—no carry
P—plus
M—minus
PO—odd parity
PE—even parity

Conditions (TMS9900):
EQ =
NE ≠
OC Carry
NC No carry
GT >
LT <
OP Odd Parity
NO No Overflow
H   Higher Than
HE Higher or =
LE Lower or =
L   Lower

Summary

Obviously, the microprocessors chosen (the TMS 1000 is really a microcomputer) are examples of three that are used widely. There are many others used also and different variations of instructions result. A complete understanding of the use of an instruction set for a given microprocessor can occur only by designing systems with them. In the remaining chapters of this book, applications of the TMS8080A and one of the TMS9900 family of microprocessors will show how a limited number of these instructions are used to perform system tasks. It is beyond the scope of this book to explain how each instruction is used in detail . It remains for the reader to acquire and study the necessary manufacturer's specifications for any microprocessor or microcomputer chosen to gain the details and insight required for good design.

Here, however, are some general overall comparison statements for 4, 8, and 16-bit microprocessors. Reviewing again *Figures 6-7* thru *6-10* indicates, as one would expect, more capability in the instruction set for the 16-bit over the 8-bit over the 4-bit microprocessor. That does not mean that the 4-bit microprocessor or microcomputer does not have a place in system designs. It does and has. Automotive and appliance controls, electronic games and toys are evidence of that.

The larger bit capacity microprocessors are usually more versatile and more efficient than their smaller cousins, however, smaller units are often adequate for a task so the one used should be chosen carefully for the specific task to be performed.

A 16-bit microprocessor processes four times as much data as does a 4-bit unit in a given instruction. This means that the 16-bit unit will be at least four times more efficient in processing data and other information than the 4-bit unit. Similar advantages exist for the 8-bit over the 4-bit or the 16-bit over the 8-bit. However, many applications do not require the efficiency and power the 16-bit unit instruction set features. They need only the capabilities of an 8-bit unit, or of a 4-bit unit. Or for a given application it may be that one instruction of the 4-bit microprocessor or microcomputer may mean that it performs as well as a 16-bit unit in that application. Whichever unit is chosen for a given task, the programs must be written for the application and stored in the microcomputer memory. Generally these programs are written in a program-oriented language in order to simplify the program development task.

WHAT TYPES OF PROGRAMMING LANGUAGES ARE AVAILABLE?

The programmer develops programs in assembly language or in a high-level language. High-level language programs are converted to machine code by a compiler. Assembly language programs are converted to machine code by an assembler.

As an end result, the program must be in machine code form so it can be interpreted and the operations performed by the microprocessor. However, these machine codes are not meaningful to the programmer. Thus, it is not desirable or even very feasible to write the programs initially in this machine language. Instead, the programs are written in either **assembly language (mnemonic)** form or in a **higher-level language.** The conversion of the higher-level language to the assembly language form is called compiling (see *Figure 4-20*), and the conversion of an assembly language program to machine code form is called assembling.

Assembling can be done fairly easily by the programmer or by a computer program called an Assembler. In either case, the assembly procedure is to look up the machine code that corresponds to each assembly language statement and fill out the complete machine code program. The compiling of a high-level language program into machine code form is somewhat more complicated and generally requires a special purpose compiler computer program to successfully perform the conversion.

Assembly Language Programming

It is much easier for the programmer to write his program using assembly language mnemonics than it is to write it in machine language

The assembly language for a given microprocessor instruction set is simply a list of abbreviations that represent the operations and addressing modes for the processor. Since these abbreviations or mnemonics are meaningful to the programmer it is far easier to write the program in this language than it is to write it directly in machine language. Several examples have already been presented of programs written in this form, including the short sequence of TMS8080A instructions in *Figure 6-6*. To get a better idea of the effort involved in assembly language programming and how that effort is dependent on the instruction set used, an addition example will be considered in this section.

An Addition Example

Assume the problem is to add two 32-bit binary numbers and store the result in place of the second number. It is also assumed that the hardware design has fixed the location of data memory at 8000_{16} through $8FFF_{16}$, and that it has been decided to locate the first 32-bit number in locations 8000_{16} through 8003_{16} and the second 32-bit number (and the sum) in locations 8010_{16} through 8013_{16}. Each location stores an 8-bit byte, so four locations are needed for a 32-bit number.

The algorithm for this addition is the same procedure that would be used if the addition were to be done on paper. The least significant group of bits are added first, with the carry out of the group noted. The next least significant group of bits are added with this input carry. This process is continued until the most significant group of bits and their input carry have been added.

This procedure is shown diagramatically in terms of memory locations in *Figure 6-11* and in flow chart form in *Figure 6-12*. *Figure 6-12* implies a repetitive loop structure, which would best be implemented with a program loop in the case of the 4-bit and 8-bit processors. A program loop would not be necessary in a program written for a 16-bit processor. The TMS8080A program of *Figure 6-12b* that will perform 32-bit binary addition is almost directly related on a one-to-one basis to the flow chart as shown in *Figure 6-12a*. H and D registers are set initially to the address of the least significant bytes of the two numbers, and a loop counter (C register) is initialized to 4 (for the four bytes to be added). The carry is cleared with the XRA A instruction, after which the repetitive loop is entered. If the Exclusive Or function, bit by bit, is performed by the accumulator on itself, the accumulator will be cleared to zero.

The algorithm for this example is the same as if the problem were worked on paper.

Performing an Exclusive-OR function with itself, bit by bit, on the contents of a register results in the register being cleared to zero.

**Figure 6-11.
32-Bit Addition Memory Structure**

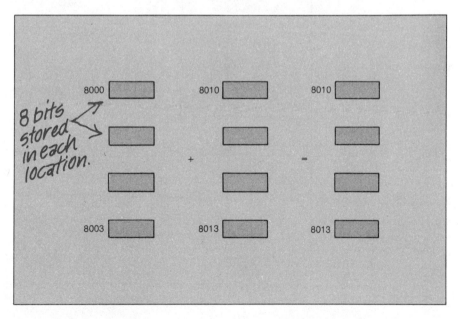

8000

8003

8010

8013

8010

8013

+

=

8 bits stored in each location.

The machine code version of 12 assembly language instructions results in 19 bytes of program memory being required.

Inside the loop, the first byte of the first number is moved into the accumulator with the LDAX D and the first byte of the second number is added to it with the ADC M. The byte sum is sent back to the second number location with the MOV M, A operation. After this, the address registers are decremented to indicate the next least significant bytes and the loop counter is decremented.

If the loop counter has been decremented to zero, the addition is complete; otherwise, the loop is repeated. This program requires 12 assembly language statements. Each of these instructions requires either 1, 2, or 3 bytes of program memory as shown in *Figure 6-12b*. Therefore, the machine code version of this program requires 19 bytes in program memory.

**Figure 6-12.
32-Bit Additional Flow
Chart and Program**

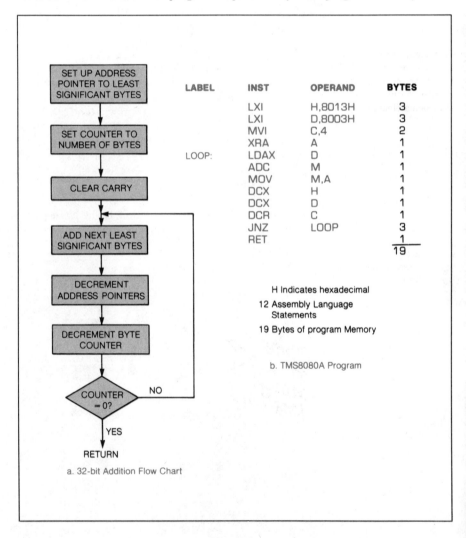

LABEL	INST	OPERAND	BYTES
	LXI	H,8013H	3
	LXI	D,8003H	3
	MVI	C,4	2
	XRA	A	1
LOOP:	LDAX	D	1
	ADC	M	1
	MOV	M,A	1
	DCX	H	1
	DCX	D	1
	DCR	C	1
	JNZ	LOOP	3
	RET		1
			19

H Indicates hexadecimal

12 Assembly Language Statements

19 Bytes of program Memory

b. TMS8080A Program

a. 32-bit Addition Flow Chart

For comparison, the TMS9980 version of a 16-bit binary addition is shown in *Figure 6-13*. The TMS9980 acts like a 16-bit microprocessor, even though it actually operates on data one byte at a time. It processes two bytes per instruction. In this case, the address is set initially by loading a register called the workspace pointer with 8000_{16} with the LWPI >8000 instruction. No loop counter is needed so locations 8002_{16} and 8003_{16} can be added to locations 8012_{16} and 8013_{16} with the A R1, R9 instruction. The JNC S1 checks for a carry to the next 16-bit addition. If there is a carry, 1 is added to the second 16-bit number (most significant 16 bits) located in workspace register R8 with the INC R8 instruction. Then the most significant 16-bit groups are added with the A R0, R8 instruction.

Figure 6-13.
TMS9900 32-Bit Addition
Program

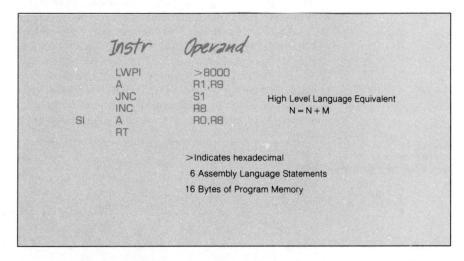

The 16-bit version requires 6 assembly language statements and 16 bytes of memory. Processing more data bits per instruction saves programming time and memory.

This program requires only 6 assembly language statements which is a two-to-one reduction over the requirements for the 8-bit microprocessor program. The 16-bit unit only requires 16 bytes of program memory to store the machine code for the program of *Figure 6-13*. The advantage of processing data 16 bits per instruction is evident even in this simple example — 6 assembly language statements and 3 bytes of memory are saved.

High-Level Languages

Substituting a high level language program for assembly language programming simplifies the program development further. One statement replaces 6 16-bit statements and 12 8-bit statements.

While going to the longer-bit processors can simplify the assembly language programs, using a high-level language to write the programs can simplify this task even further. Examples of such languages include FORTRAN, BASIC, and PASCAL. In each of these languages, the add operation indicated by the assembly language programs of *Figure 6-12* and *Figure 6-13* can be written simply as:

$$N = N + M.$$

Thus a single statement replaces 6 TMS9980 statements or 12 TMS8080A statements.

Unless the microprocessor manufacturer provides the compiler to convert high-level language programs to machine code, the high-level language is not very useful.

It certainly is easier to write the initial program in the high-level language. In order to arrive at the assembly language program, everytime this high-level language statement is encountered the program sequences of *Figure 6-12* or *Figure 6-13* are substituted depending on the microprocessor being used. To make this an efficient approach, the manufacturer must provide the program that will automatically perform these substitutions. This is the compiler program. To program, the programmer writes relatively short high-level language programs, and the compiler converts these to assembly language equivalents. Finally, an assembler program will convert the assembly language program to its machine language equivalent. Of course, if the manufacturer does not provide the high-level-language-to-assembly-language converter, this type of programming approach would not really be feasible.

Further examples of the features of typical high-level language statements are shown in *Figure 6-14*. Examples of arithmetic and decision making formats are shown in *Figure 6-14a*.

All three of the example languages use the same single line statement for multiplication. Their decision statement structures are similar and allow for reasonably complicated arithmetic and logic tests to be made to decide which of two program sequences are to be executed.

**Figure 6-14.
Comparison of High-Level Language Formats**

Language	Multiplication	Decisions
FORTRAN	Z = W°Y	IF (condition) GO TO condition true sequence condition not true sequence
PASCAL	Z = W°Y	IF condition THEN condition true sequence ELSE condition not true sequence
BASIC	Z = W°Y	IF condition THEN condition true sequence condition not true sequence

a. Arithmetic and Decision Making Formats of High-Level Languages

FORTRAN	PASCAL	BASIC
DO 10 I = 1,N Loop Statements 10 CONTINUE	I : = 1 WHILE I< = N DO BEGIN Loop Operations END	FOR N = 1 TO 25 STEP 1 Loop Statements NEXT

b. Loop Structure Formats of High-Level Languages

The loop control statements of *Figure 6-14b* are very similar, allowing the programmer to control quite easily the number of repetitions of the loop and the extent of the loop subprogram. All of these operations would have assembly language equivalents for any given microprocessor. Again, the advantage of the high-level language is that a system subprogram can be described in a short easy-to-understand high-level language program instead of a lengthy assembly-language program.

PROGRAM VERIFICATION

Minimum System

All programs written for various tasks should be verified before they are used in a system. The least desirable is where entering and assembling is done all by hand.

Regardless of the level of the language used to write the system program and subprograms, the programmer must verify the operation of these programs before they can be used to control the microcomputer system. The various options available for program verification are listed in *Figure 6-15.* The most tedious of these options (A) is where the entry of the machine code is made directly into the microcomputer memory and execution is done on the microcomputer. Such an option is available by using microcomputer modules with keyboard entry and LED display. The programmer must hand-assemble the program and then enter the hexadecimal machine codes for the program into the microcomputer.

**Figure 6-15.
Program Verification
Options**

PROGRAM ENTRY FORM	EXECUTION
A. Hexadecimal Machine Code entered into Microcomputer Board	Machine Code program executed on Microcomputer
B. Assembly Language Code entered into Microcomputer	Assembly and Machine Code program executed on Microcomputer
C. High-Level Language Code entered into Microcomputer	Compiling, Assembly, and Execution on Microcomputer
D. Assembly Language Code entered into General Purpose Computer	Assembly by Computer; Simulation of Microcomputer execution by General Purpose Computer or Execution of Machine Code on actual Microcomputer.
E. High-Level Language Code entered into General Purpose Computer	Compiling and Assembly done on General Purpose Computer. Execution simulated on General Purpose Computer or executed on actual Microcomputer.

Assembler System

A second way of verifying is to use a microcomputer software development system; enter the assembly language program in mnemonic form.

A more convenient approach shown in B, using some available microcomputer program development boards or any of the microcomputer development systems, is to enter the assembly language programs into the microcomputer in mnemonic form and let the microcomputer perform the assembly and execution of the program. Some microcomputer development systems also offer the option (C) of entering the desired program in high-level language form and the microcomputer performs the compiling, assembly, and execution of the program. This option offers the most efficient way to develop programs from the standpoint of program development time.

General Purpose Computer

A third way of verifying uses a general purpose computer to simulate the operation of the microcomputer system. The program runs as if it were controlling the actual system.

As shown in D and E, even if a microcomputer is not availabe, many manufacturers provide program development software on general purpose computers that will perform the assembly and compiling operations. Once the machine code has been generated, the general purpose computer will then execute the machine code program just as the microcomputer would. This is called simulating the execution of the program and will verify the program operation. The only problem that may arise from this type of program verification is that the program does not run in the actual environment of the final microcomputer system. Thus, some timing or interrupt problems may not be detected by this approach.

The Choice

The advantage of using a general purpose computer, if one has access to such a machine, is that it allows programs to be developed and verified without having to buy an actual microcomputer. The advantage of using an approach with a microcomputer is that the program verification is on a system that is identical to the final system on which the program is going to be used. Also, developing the program on an actual microcomputer opens up the option of using this microcomputer directly to build the desired system, thus avoiding an extra purchase. Which approach is used ultimately depends on the resources and goals of the programmer.

WHAT ARE SOME TYPICAL PROGRAM REQUIREMENTS?

There are certain types of subprograms that must be developed for all systems. For example, all systems must have some form of input and output subprograms. Usually there is some requirement for arithmetic or logical operations on the system data. Often a decision table or a look-up table procedure is required. To further illustrate the relationship between high-level language programs and the corresponding microprocessor programs some typical examples of these operations will be considered.

Input/Output Subprograms

A single line statement in the high-level BASIC language would satisfy this program that took 6 statements for a 16-bit and 10 statements for a 4 and 8-bit microprocessor.

In Chapter 5 using SAM, BCD codes had to be sent as outputs to 10 LED displays to display 10 decimal digits. The same task will be used as an output subprogram example. The BCD information is located in 10 successive memory locations, and the LEDs occupy 10 successive addresses. The programs for accomplishing this transfer are shown in *Figure 6-16*. There is no difference in the length of the TMS1000 and the TMS8080A assembly-language programs. Each require 10 statements. The TMS1000 program occupies 10 program memory locations while the TMS8080A program requires 17 bytes of program memory. The TMS9980 program can be written in only 6 assembly language statements since no program loop is involved. It requires 16 bytes of program memory. The equivalent BASIC statement is a *single line* statement, which certainly is the most efficient way to summarize the program being written.

**Figure 6-16.
Comparison of Output
Subprograms**

TMS1000 Program		TMS8080A Program		TMS9980 Program	
OUTPUT	LDX 2	OUTPUT:	LXI D,200H	OUTPUT	LI R2,>200
	TCY 0		LXI H,300H		LI R3,>300
LOOP	TMA		MVI C,5		MOV *R2+,*R3+
	TDO	LOOP:	LDAX D		MOV *R2+,*R3+
	SETR		MOV M,A		MOV *R2+,*R3+
	RSTR		INX D		RT
	IYC		INX H		
	YNEC 10		DCR C		
	BR LOOP		JNZ LOOP		
	RETN		RET		
Assembly Language Statements:	10		10		6
Machine Code Memory Locations:	10		17		16

All of these equivalent programs are much shorter than the output program for SAM. This is due to the limited instruction set of SAM compared to the processors of *Figure 6-16*. All of these programs are simply transferring a group of bits from the microcomputer memory to the LEDs arranged to display the 10 digits, continuing this process for successive groups of bits and LEDs until all BCD codes have been transferred. The reader should study the program segments of *Figure 6-16, 17, 18* and *19* again after reading Chapter 7 and 8 to gain further insight into the writing and understanding of microprocessor programs.

**Figure 6-17.
Microprocessor
Multiplication Programs**

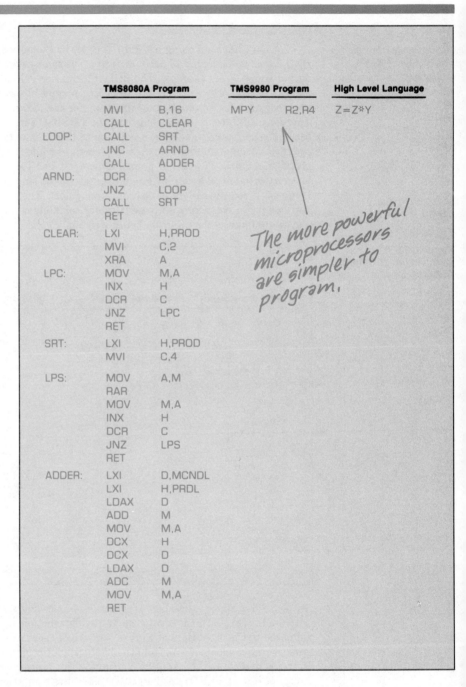

	TMS8080A Program		TMS9980 Program		High Level Language
	MVI	B,16	MPY	R2,R4	Z=Z*Y
	CALL	CLEAR			
LOOP:	CALL	SRT			
	JNC	ARND			
	CALL	ADDER			
ARND:	DCR	B			
	JNZ	LOOP			
	CALL	SRT			
	RET				
CLEAR:	LXI	H,PROD			
	MVI	C,2			
	XRA	A			
LPC:	MOV	M,A			
	INX	H			
	DCR	C			
	JNZ	LPC			
	RET				
SRT:	LXI	H,PROD			
	MVI	C,4			
LPS:	MOV	A,M			
	RAR				
	MOV	M,A			
	INX	H			
	DCR	C			
	JNZ	LPS			
	RET				
ADDER:	LXI	D,MCNDL			
	LXI	H,PRDL			
	LDAX	D			
	ADD	M			
	MOV	M,A			
	DCX	H			
	DCX	D			
	LDAX	D			
	ADC	M			
	MOV	M,A			
	RET				

The more powerful microprocessors are simpler to program.

Arithmetic Operation Subprograms

The program for multiplication is greatly simplified by the powerful instruction set offered by the 16-bit microprocessor. Only one statement is needed compared to 37 for the 8-bit microprocessor.

An example of an arithmetic operation is multiplication. If the system requires the multiplication of one 16-bit binary number by a second 16-bit binary number to yield a 32-bit binary product, the programs would look like those in *Figure 6-17*. The TMS1000 version is not shown, since it is much too long to be clearly understood. Again, the high-level language statement takes only one line. In this case, the TMS9980 assembly language subprogram only takes one line, since this is one of the instructions available on the TMS9900 family devices. By comparison, the TMS8080A multiplication program requires 37 assembly language statements which would require 64 bytes of program memory. The flow chart for the TMS8080A multiplication program is shown in *Figure 6-18* to help the reader understand the program structure. The algorithm is much the same procedure that one would follow if the multiplication were being performed by hand on a sheet of paper. Without going through this program in detail it is easy to see the advantage of the more powerful instruction set offered by the 16-bit microprocessor.

**Figure 6-18.
32-Bit Multiplication Flow Chart (16-Bit X 16-Bit Problem)**

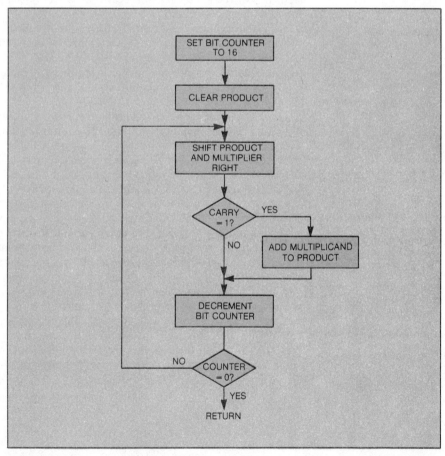

Look-Up Table Procedures

A look-up table containing the start-up addresses for subroutines to service an input or output can be sequenced to a shift register to provide an efficient program structure.

There are many situations that require the microcomputer to refer to a table for a value or address location that is needed for a given operation. One such situation occurs when the program must jump to a subroutine to serve an input or an output or some other need. Assume that a pattern of 1's and 0's are stored in register R1 in a TMS9900 system. A 1 in the least-significant-bit location indicates that the subsystem related to that bit location is to be serviced in a way described by a subprogram located in program memory. Since R1 is 16-bits long it can save the service request status for 16 subsystems. The 16 subsystems would require 16 subprograms located at different places scattered throughout program memory. In order to locate the needed subprogram, an address table is established in memory, starting at the address BASE. The contents of the BASE memory location contains the address of the first instruction of the subprogram which services the system identified by the least-significant-bit of R1 (system 1). The contents of the memory location at BASE + 2 contains the address for the beginning of the subprogram that services the system identified by the next least-significant-bit of R1 (system 2), and so on through the next 14 bits.

A system will be serviced with a subprogram when a 1 appears at the output of R1 when the contents are shifted right. Thus, by rotating the contents of R1 until a 1 is encountered (it may have to be rotated 16 times) the subsystem to be serviced can be determined. By incrementing a counter register from 0 by 2 while this shifting is occurring, the displacement down the address table from BASE is maintained.

The overall program and table structure is shown in *Figure 6-19* for a TMS9900 implementation. First the counter register R2 is cleared with a CLR R2. Then, the repetitive loop is entered with the first operation being to shift the register R1 right. If there is a carry (a 1 shifted out of R1), the most important system requiring service has been identified and the table location is BASE + R2 for the address of the subprogram. If the carry is zero, R2 is incremented by two with the INCT R2 and if it has not been incremented to 20_{16} (decimal 32), the loop will be repeated. Once a 1 in R1 is detected, the next instruction is a subroutine jump (BL) using indexed addressing. As a result the address of the first instruction is located at the contents of R2 plus the BASE address, which is the correct entry through the address table.

Of course, a similar program could be written for the TMS8080A processor, though it would probably be somewhat longer in terms of assembly language statements. A comparable type of program activity in BASIC or FORTRAN would be obtained by using the computed GO TO in which a counter k is incremented until the proper condition is met. This value indicates the subprogram address. The program statement is again a single entry of the form (BASIC format):

ON K GO TO 10, 20, 46, 87

where the numbers are the labels of the statements to be executed next. The instructions at these points could in turn call a subroutine much like the scheme used in *Figure 6-19*.

Of course, there are many other types of program requirements that could be illustrated. They would all tend to illustrate the realtionship between assembly language efficiency and instruction set capability, which is in turn generally related to **microprocessor bit-length. Using higher-level** language programming would allow such programs to be written with ease and overwhelming efficiency.

Figure 6-19.
Table-Look-up Example
TMS9900

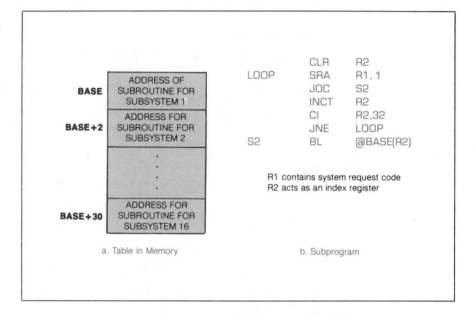

R1 contains system request code
R2 acts as an index register

a. Table in Memory   b. Subprogram

WHAT CAN WE EXPECT IN THE FUTURE IN PROGRAMMING TECHNIQUES?

Developing programs in the high-level language will gain in popularity because it is the easiest method for the programmer, although assembly language will still be very common. This is only possible, however, where high-level language conversion software is provided.

As more and more manufacturers provide high-level language software support, it will become increasingly popular to write the microcomputer programs initially in these high-level languages. While this does not always generate the most efficient code in terms of the amount of memory required for a given program, it is the most efficient approach in terms of initial programming time and the time to test or verify the program. It is simply the path of least resistance and effort in developing programs. In the meantime, assembly language programming will be the most common form of generating microcomputer programs. Small and individual design groups will tend to work with single-board microcomputer development systems, while large design groups will tend to use the complete microcomputer development systems with their higher capability, offering assemblers, floppy-disc memory, and typewriter terminals. A few programmers will make use of the assembler and simulator programs available on general purpose computers through time-sharing companies or private computer installations.

In all cases, the overall procedure will remain essentially as described at the first of this chapter: Describe the overall system operation. Divide the overall task into manageable elementary task descriptions. Write the programs that implements these elementary tasks. Verify the subprograms and then recombine into the overall program and verify it. This will lead to a very successful overall system program development.

WHAT HAVE WE LEARNED?

• Designing programs is very similar to designing hardware systems: the design effort is broken down into manageable functional parts and the designs for each of these parts are completed before combining all the parts into one overall system design.

• The higher the level of programming language used to write the programs the simpler it is to write and verify the programs. However, a much greater amount of software aid is required as support for the product.

• The more bits that are processed at a time and the more extensive the instruction set of a microprocessor, the shorter the assembly language programs.

• Program requirements at any given level can be described in terms of the general system model by defining the module inputs, outputs, and operations.

• Program requirements at any given level can be described in a variety of forms, with the flow chart and macro-mnemonic coding forms being the most directly related to the final program organization.

WHAT'S NEXT?

In the last three chapters the basic concepts involved in the design and programming on microcomputers have been covered. In the rest of the book these concepts will be applied to the design and programming of real microcomputer systems, beginning with 8-bit microprocessors in the next chapter.

Programming Exercise

Write a TMS 8080A subprogram called CONTROL for the furnace Controller example (Flow Chart in *Figure 6-4*) for a system with the following features:

a. An external timer will interrupt the processor causing it to jump to the subroutine CONTROL beginning at location 56 in ROM.

b. There are 10 room areas with 8 sensors each, with each sensor providing an 8-bit temperature code (0 through 255 degrees). The first 8 sensors (area 1) are assigned memory addresses 1000_{16} through 1007_{16}, the next 8 sensors are assigned addresses 1008_{16} through $100F_{16}$, and so on so that the last 8 sensors are assigned the addresses 1048_{16} through $104F_{16}$. The reference temperature 8-bit code is at address 1050_{16}.

c. The furnace on-off control is assigned to output 0. The furnace on-off status is assigned to be input port 0.

d. The 10 area flow controls are assigned output ports 1 through 10 to turn the flow on and output ports 11 through 20 to turn the flow off for a given area.

The CONTROL subprogram must implement the first four blocks of the flow chart of *Figure 6-4*, using the memory assignments above. Assume the hardware automatically turns the furnace and valves off after five minutes.

**Figure 6-20.
Sensor Examination
Interrupt Subprogram**

```
Solution
             ORG   56
CONTROL: PUSH  PSW  ⎫
         PUSH  B    ⎪  Save contents of processor registers in the stack
         PUSH  D    ⎬  in RAM
         PUSH  H    ⎭
         MVI   C,10      Set C to 10 to count number of areas
         LXI   H,1000H   Set HL address register to first sensor
EXAM:    LDA   1050H     Get reference temperature in A register
         MVI   B,8       Initialize B counter to number of sensors/area
         MVI   E,0       Clear Sensor low counter
ALOOP:   CMP   M         Compare reference value in A to sensor value
         JM    OK        If A ≤ M, sensor ok
         INR   E         If not, sensor is low — increment E
OK:      INX   H         Increment address to next sensor
         DCR   B         Decrement sensor counter
         JNZ   ALOOP     If counter ≠0 repeat loop
         MOV   A,E       Check E value by moving it to A,
         CPI   5         compare it to 5,
         CP    ON        If E ≥ 5, call the turn-on subroutine
         INX   H         If not, increment address to next sensor area
         DCR   C         Decrement area counter
         JNZ   EXAM      Repeat sequence for next area if counter ≠0
         POP   H    ⎫
         POP   D    ⎪      If counter = 0 all areas have been
         POP   B    ⎬      handled so restore registers from stack
         POP   PSW  ⎭
         EI              Enable interrupt system
         RET             Return to interrupted program
```

Figure 6-21.
ON Subroutine

ON:	OUT	0	Turn on furnace*
	LXI	D,4	load DE with distance between OUT instructions in instruction table. (4 bytes)**
	PUSH	H	Save HL contents (sensor address) in stack
	LXI	H,FIRST	Set HL address to first instruction in table
	MOV	B,C	Copy current area counter value into B
CHK:	DCR	B	Decrement counter
	JNZ	TABLE	If not zero, update instruction address in HL
	PCHL		If zero, jump to instruction indicated by HL
TABLE:	DAD	D	Add table displacement (4) to HL address value
	JMP	CHK	Go to decrement counter
FIRST:	OUT	10	
	POP	H	
	RET		
	OUT	9	
	POP	H	
	RET		
	OUT	8	
	POP	H	
	RET		
	:		
	::		Repeat this three instruction sequence for OUT 7 through OUT 2**
	:		
	OUT	1	
	POP	H	
	RET		

*It is assumed that the furnace and flow valve remains on for 5 minutes after it is turned on by the OUT 0 instruction. This time is controlled by a hardware timer as the time intervals between entering the CONTROL subprogram.

**Each instruction in the table takes 4 bytes of program memory as follows:

OUT	n	Turn on appropriate flow valve n (2 bytes)
POP	H	restore H to CONTROL subprogram value (1 byte)
RET		Return to CONTROL Subprogram (1 byte)

An 8-Bit
Microprocessor Application

ABOUT THIS CHAPTER

Thus far in the book only the applications of a 4-bit microprocessor and microcomputer have been considered. These units did not have interrupt capability so that they had to initiate the time they would receive an input from the outside world. This meant timer subprograms had to be used to determine when the microprocessor should check to see if external information was being sent on its input lines. This is a simple method of maintaining communications but it is not always effective. If an external signal occurs between the times the microprocessor examines the external inputs, the microprocessor would miss the external signal; or if more than one signal occurs between processor checks, one of the signals would be missed.

An interrupt-driven processor, one that has an interrupt signal input, can let the external signals tell the microprocessor when communication is needed. This way all inputs will be received and the processor only spends the time required to fetch an input. It does not waste time looking for inputs that are not there. Some 4-bit processors have the interrupt feature, and almost all 8-bit and 16-bit units have an interrupt capability. In this chapter an example application will be developed that depends almost entirely on the interrupt features of the TMS8080A microprocessor. Examining this application should provide insight into the features of the architecture and instruction set of a very popular 8-bit microprocessor.

WHY USE AN 8-BIT MICROPROCESSOR?

Most 8-bit microprocessors perform arithmetic and communications operations twice as fast as 4-bit microprocessors. This is not an advantage where 1 bit control lines are being handled, but it is a significant advantage for communicating 8-bit ASCII characters.

Since there are 4-bit microprocessors with an interrupt capability and a relatively extensive instruction set, why would an 8-bit microprocessor be used at all? The most obvious answer is that the 8-bit processor offers double the speed of handling arithmetic and communications operations over a 4-bit unit with the same instruction set and timing features. This is simply due to the fact that the 8-bit processor handles twice the information in a given instruction as a 4-bit unit. This would not be an advantage in simple control situations involving operations using single bits to 16 bits, but it becomes an important advantage in dealing with the transmission of 8-bit ASCII characters or in arithmetic operations requiring accuracies of greater than one part in 16. Even in machines that need decimal arithmetic, the 8-bit units process two decimal digits at once, as compared with the one-digit-at-a-time performance of 4-bit machines.

In summary, the applications that are easily handled by 8-bit microprocessors include:

Simple to Relatively Sophisticated Controllers

Medium-Accuracy Numerical Processing

Medium-Speed Communications Systems

Sophisticated Games involving Numerical Accuracy or Alphabetical Manipulation Capabilities

To better understand the features offered by 8-bit microprocessors that make them useful in applications in these areas, the TMS8080A will be examined as a representative 8-bit device.

WHAT ARE THE FEATURES OF A TYPICAL 8-BIT PROCESSOR?

The TMS8080A is a microprocessor that supports a relatively complete instruction set and a simple, effective interrupt structure. Its timing features are relatively straightforward, though not as simple as some other 8-bit and most 16-bit microprocessors. It depends primarily on register indirect addressing for locating data in memory, and it provides 7 general-purpose 8-bit registers internally for high-speed data manipulation. The internal features of the device will be examined first.

Internal Features

The registers available for use by the programmer are shown in *Figure 7-1*. The A register is the *accumulator* and is involved in all arithmetic and logic operations. The *status register* contains the zero, sign, carry, half-carry (used in BCD arithmetic with the DAA instruction), and parity flip-flops. The parity flip-flop is set equal to 1 when the number of ALU bits equal to 1 is even. There is also an interrupt flip-flop and an interrupt-enable flip-flop that is used to monitor and control the interrupt signalling for the microprocessor. Commonly, the B, C, D, E, H and L registers are used as general purpose 8-bit data registers; however, they can be used in pairs (B-C, D-E and H-L) to act as 16-bit data address registers (register indirect addressing mode). The *program counter* (PC) contains the instruction address.

A special set of memory locations are set aside as operating or working registers. This set of memory locations is usually called a stack. The name is derived from the fact that information is stacked one location on another. A specific register, used to keep track of where information is or can be stored in the stack, is called the *stack pointer* (SP). It contains the address of the currently available empty location in the stack. Information is normally pushed down the stack one location after the other or it is pulled up from the stack one location after another. In some microprocessors the stack of registers is located within the microprocessor; for the 8080A the stack of registers must be provided for in external RAM storage outside the microprocessor.

The TMS8080A locates data in its memory by using register indirect addressing. It has a simple interrupt structure and has 7 internal, general-purpose, 8-bit registers which allow high-speed data manipulation.

The 8-bit microprocessor has several types of registers. Besides the PC, register A is the accumulator, and registers B, C, D, E, H and L are general purpose 8-bit data registers. There is also a status register.

A separate set of memory locations, called a stack, are set aside as workspace, or temporary working storage. A stack pointer keeps track of the location of information, or where it can be stored.

Figure 7-1.
TMS8080A Internal
Registers Available to
the Programmer

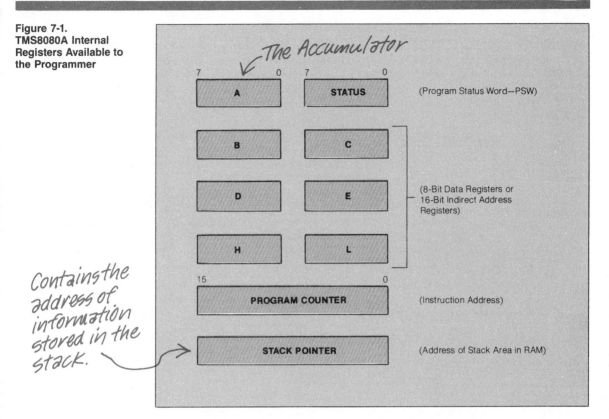

The Accumulator

Contains the address of information stored in the stack.

As subroutines are called, the address of the next instruction (program counter content) is saved in the stack. RETURN instructions restore the PC contents to complete the return from the subroutine call.

The programmer need only be concerned about the registers he can access with instructions.

Whenever a subroutine is called for in the program, the contents of the program counter needed for the next instruction after the call is saved in the stack. A RETURN instruction fetches this value off the stack and sends it to the program counter to effect the return from the subroutine. There are also instructions that allow the programmer to push the microprocessor registers to the stack 16 bits at a time and to pull them back from the stack 16 bits at a time.

In order to use these stack operation features, an additional storage area must be set aside in the RAM data memory. The address of this additional storage area (last byte in the area) must be loaded into the stack pointer when the processor goes through its first initialization procedures in order to load the correct initial values into the stack.

Of course, there are many registers and logic units in the microprocessor that are not shown in *Figure 7-1.* Obviously there must be an instruction register, instruction decoder, arithmetic-logic unit, as discussed for the general microprocessor. The user of the microprocessor knows these are present but need only be concerned with the registers that are accessible through the instructions and the operational features provided. Additional features that are of interest to the hardware designer are the timing and control signals that are sent and received by the processor.

Timing and Control Features

A status byte at the beginning of each operation alerts external components as to the function to be performed.

These features include the address and data signal timing, the interrupt signals, and the memory and input/output control signals. 65,536 memory locations can be addressed by the 16-bit address bus of the TMS8080A. In addition, the TMS8080A can address 256 input and output devices. The same address bus is used for selecting one of the input or output devices, but only the least 8 bits of the address are meaningful in input/output operations.

The TMS8080A alerts the external components as to which operations will occur at any given time by providing an 8-bit operational status byte at the beginning of each operation. This status byte contains the information that a memory write, a memory read, an input read, an output write, an interrupt acknowledge, and so on is in progress. These signals are not the enables themselves but are used as the source to provide the memory enables to turn on the memory subsystem and the input/output enables to turn on the input/output subsystems. As a result, the necessary read/write signals can be generated for each subsystem.

Read/Write Signals

The simplest way to generate these control signals is to use two peripheral integrated circuits designed especially for the 8080A. One is the SN74S428 System Controller and Bus Driver and the other is the SN74LS424 Clock Generator. The control structure is shown in *Figure 7-2.*

**Figure 7-2.
TMS8080A System
Timing and Control**

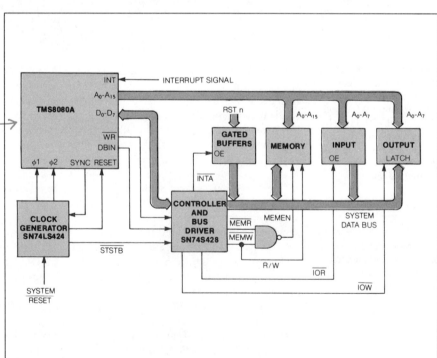

Alerts external componets through operational status byte.

DBIN is a read timing pulse. $\overline{\text{WR}}$ is a write timing pulse. When these signals are fed to the SN74S428 along with the operational status word on the data bus, the System Controller provides the correct control signals of the proper duration at the correct time to interface the TMS8080A to external memory or to external I/O units.

For example, MEMEN (memory enable) and R/W for external memory are shown in *Figure 7-2*. MEMEN is the NAND result of $\overline{\text{MEMR}}$ (memory read) and $\overline{\text{MEMW}}$ (memory write). R/W results directly from memory write, $\overline{\text{MEMW}}$. Similarly, $\overline{\text{IOR}}$ (Input/Output Read) out of the controller is used directly to control sending information from inputs to the microprocessor. In like fashion, $\overline{\text{IOW}}$ (I/O Write) is used to latch information coming from the microprocessor into an output unit. These signals are somewhat straightforward. The use of the $\overline{\text{INTA}}$ (interrupt acknowledge) signal is not so obvious, and requires an examination of the way the TMS8080A responds to an interrupt to fully understand its purpose.

When the status byte, along with operational timing pulses are fed into the system controller, it provides the control signals to interface the microprocessor to external units.

Interrupt Control

When the TMS8080A receives an interrupt signal on its INT pin, it will respond to that interrupt after it has finished its current instruction operations if the interrupt enable flip-flop has been set with the EI (enable interrupt) instruction. It responds to an interrupt by sending out an interrupt acknowledge signal and then waits for a special subroutine jump instruction to be returned to the microprocessor. This instruction is called a RESTART instruction (RST n) and must be generated by hardware external to the TMS8080A. The $\overline{\text{INTA}}$ signal provided by the controller is used to gate RST n onto the data bus for receipt by the microprocessor at the proper time. The format of the instruction is shown in *Figure 7-3*.

After an interrupt is received, the TMS8080A must complete its current instruction, acknowledge the interrupt, and send a RESTART (jump signal) to branch to the interrupt subroutine.

The 3-bit code in the RST n instruction is generated by the hardware and causes a jump to the address in ROM formed by the 3-bit code followed by three zeroes. Thus, if the 3-bit code is 000, a jump to location 0 in ROM will occur. If the 3-bit code is 001, a jump to location 8 will occur, and so on.

**Figure 7-3.
TMS8080A RESTART
Instruction Code and
Operation**

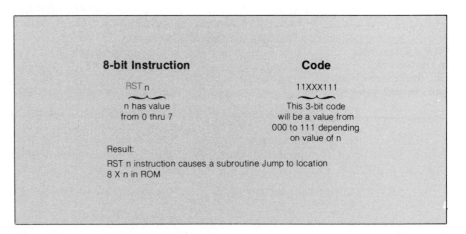

8-bit Instruction

RST n

n has value
from 0 thru 7

Code

11XXX111

This 3-bit code
will be a value from
000 to 111 depending
on value of n

Result:

RST n instruction causes a subroutine Jump to location
8 X n in ROM

At each of these addresses in ROM the programmer must provide instructions that start a subroutine to respond to a given interrupt situation so that the subsystem or the event that caused the interrupt can be serviced. When any of these subsystems need to interrupt the processor, the hardware designer must generate the INT signal and the correct restart code for each interrupting subsystem.

The EI (enable interrupt) instruction is used to initially allow an interrupt, then to re-enable the interrupt system once the interrupt has been serviced.

Once the subroutine has serviced the interrupt the TMS8080A will return to whatever it was doing in the program at the time of the interrupt, provided the programmer ends his interrupt subroutine with a RET instruction. Prior to the interrupt, the programmer had to enable the interrupt system with an EI (enable interrupt) instruction. After an interrupt, he must re-enable the interrupt system somewhere in his interrupt subroutine with an EI instruction. Otherwise the processor will ignore any INT signal until it does encounter an EI instruction. For all the interrupt procedures it is assumed that the hardware designer has provided a RAM storage area in data memory to save, in the register stack, the program information being executed before the interrupt occurred. It is with these interrupt related instructions of EI (enable interrupt), RST (subroutine jump to interrupt procedure) and DI (disable interrupt) which locks out an interrupt, that the communications with the TMS8080A system can be established and controlled. The rest of the TMS8080A instruction set provides the normal data manipulation and program control capabilities of a microprocessor.

INSTRUCTION SET

Data Movement Instructions

Like most processors the TMS8080A offers a variety of data movement, arithmetic, logical, comparison, and branch operations. Of these, the *data movement* instructions of *Figure 7-4* are the simplest to understand and use. The basic instruction is the MOV d,s where the source s and destination d can be one of the microprocessor registers A, B, C, D, E, H or L. S or d also can be the memory data location specified by the address in the HL 16-bit register, in which case the s or d operand will be denoted M. The result of the operation is that the data in the source location will be copied into the destination location.

MOV d,s is the basic instruction which copies data from a source location into a destination location.

There are also indirect addressing load and store operations of the accumulator through the LDAX rp and STAX rp instructions, in which rp is D (for the DE pair) or B (for the BC pair). The direct-addressing version of load and store accumulator is the LDA address and STA address with the address of the memory data location contained in the 3-byte instruction *(Figure 4-40)*. The INP address and OUT address instructions move data to the accumulator or from the accumulator to an input/output register specified by the address, which must represent a number between 0 and 255.

**Figure 7-4.
TMS8080A Data
Movement Instructions**

*The basic
move instruction*

Data Move Instruction:

MOV   d,s   s→d   Move contents of s to d.

s and d can be A,B,C,D,E,H,L, or M with M being the memory location whose address is in the HL register pair.

8-Bit Loads and Stores of the Accumulator:

INDIRECT ADDRESSING MODE:

LDAX   rp   Load the accumulator with data in memory whose address is in the register pair indicated.

STAX   rp   Store the accumulator contents in the memory at the address contained in the register pair.

rp can be the BC, DE, or the HL register pair.

DIRECT ADDRESSING MODE:

LDA   address Load the accumulator with data from the memory at the address contained in the instruction.

STA   address Store the accumulator into the memory at the address contained in the instruction.

Initializing Registers and Register Pairs:

8-BIT REGISTER INITIALIZATION:

MVI   d,data   Send data from instruction into register d with d being A,B,C,D,E,H,L, or M

16-BIT REGISTER INITIALIZATION:

LXI   rp,value Place 16-bit value from instruction into the register pair indicated. rp can be B,D,H, or SP.

16-Bit Transfers:

XCHG   Exchange contents of HL register pair with DE register pair
PUSH   rp   Push the register pair contents to the stack.
POP   rp   Pop the register pair contents from the stack.
SHLD   address Store the contents of the HL register pair in memory starting at the address in the instruction.
LHLD   address Load the HL register pair with the 16 bits in memory addressed by the address in the instruction.

Input/Output Transfers:

INP   address Input data to the accumulator from the input device at the location specified by the address in the instruction.
OUT   address Output the accumulator data to the device at the location specified by the address in the instruction.

Other special purpose movement instructions are available to exchange the contents of the DE pair with the HL pair (XCHG) and to load and store the contents of the HL pair in two successive memory bytes (LHLD address and SHLD address). Register pairs may be pushed to and down the stack with PUSH rp or popped from or off the stack into a register pair with POP rp. For stack operations the register pair (rp) can be specified as PSW (accumulator and status registers), D (DE), B (BC), or H (HL).

There are immediate addressing instructions for initializing registers or register pairs with data. The MVI d, data instruction causes the data in the 2-byte instruction to be loaded into the destination indicated by d (A, B, C, D, E, H, L, or M). The LXI rp, value causes 16 bits to be loaded into the register pair specified, which can include SP for stack pointer.

Arithmetic Instructions

The arithmetic operations add or subtract from accumulator data and store the results in the accumulator. They include increment, decrement, rotate and a DAA instruction for BCD addition.

The *arithmetic instructions* of *Figure 7-5* provide for addition to or subtraction from the accumulator data with the result stored in the accumulator. There are additions (ADD), addition with carry (ADC), addition of data from the instructions (ADI data and ACI data), subtractions (SUB), subtraction with borrow (SBB), and subtraction of data in the instruction (SUI data and SBI data). The increment register (INR), decrement register (DCR), increment register pair (INX), and decrement register pair (DCX) instructions are also a form of addition and subtraction, since one is added or subtracted from the operand data. The DAD rp instruction provides the addition of 16 bits of data from the BC, DE, or HL pairs to the 16 bits contained in the HL pair with the result stored in the HL pair. The DAA (decimal adjust) instruction provides for BCD addition. The four rotate instructions RAL, RAR, RLC, RRC are also a form of arithmetic operations, with the RAR (rotate right) and RAL (rotate left) rotating through the carry to provide for the possibility of multi-byte shifts.

Logical Instructions

Basic logic functions of AND, OR and XOR are performed by interacting with data in the accumulator and then storing the results in the accumulator.

The *logical operation* instructions *(Figure 7-6)* provide for the basic operations of the AND, OR, Exclusive OR, and complement to be performed with the data in the accumulator. The result is stored in the accumulator. The two operand instructions allow for the non-accumulator operand to be A, B, C, D, E, H, L, M, or instruction data. The mnemonics are ANA (AND), ANI (AND immediate), XRA (Exclusive OR), XRI (Exclusive OR Immediate), ORA (OR), ORI (OR Immediate) and CMA (Complement the Accumulator). With the immediate operations the data used is contained in the second byte of the instruction code. *(Figure 4-40)*

**Figure 7-5.
TMS8080A Arithmetic
Instructions**

Addition Instructions:

ADD   r   Add contents of register r to A register and place sum in A; r can be A,B,C,D,E,H,L, or M.

ADC   r   Add contents of register r plus the carry to the A register and place the results in A.

ADI   data   Add data in instruction to A and place sum in A.

ACI   data   Add data in instruction plus carry to A and place sum in A.

DAD   rp   Add 16 bits in register pair indicated to contents of HL pair and place sum in HL. rp can be B,D, or H.

INR   r   Add one to the contents of register r.

INX   rp   Add one to the 16-bit contents of the register pair.

DAA   Adjust the result of the previous addition so that both 4-bit codes in the A register are correct BCD codes.

Subtraction Instructions:

SUB   r   Subtract contents of register r from A and place result in A.

SBB   r   Subtract contents of register r and carry from contents of A and place result in A.

SUI   data   Subtract data in instruction from contents of A and place result in A.

SBI   data   Subtract data in instruction and carry from contents of A and place result in A.

DCR   r   Subtract 1 from contents of the register r.

DCX   rp   Subtract 1 from 16-bit contents of the register pair.

Rotations of the Accumulator Data:

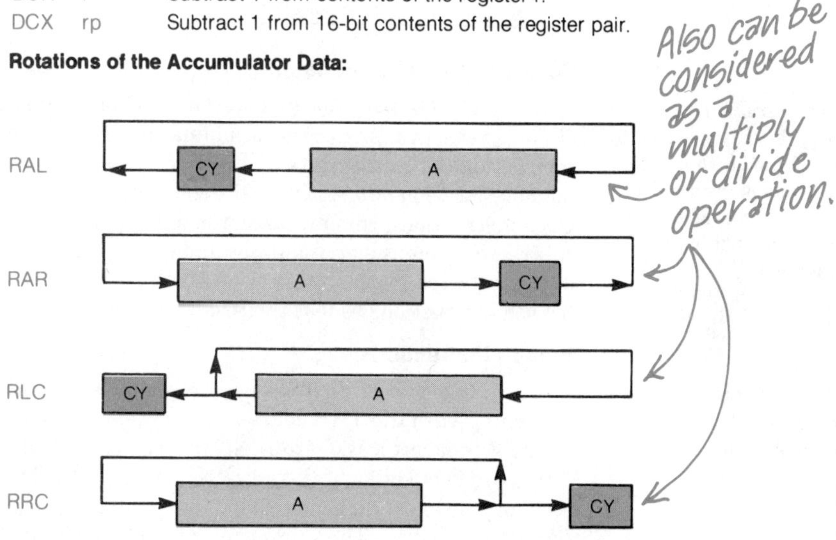

Also can be considered as a multiply or divide operation.

**Figure 7-6.
TMS8080A Logical
Instructions**

AND Instructions:

ANA   r   The contents of the register r are ANDed with the contents of the A
register; results to the A register. r may be A,B,C,D,E,H,L, or M.

ANI   data   The data in the instruction is ANDed with the contents of the A register
with the results to the A register.

OR Instructions:

ORA   r   The contents of the r register are ORed with the contents of the A
register and the results to the A register.

ORI   data   The data in the instruction is ORed with the contents of the A register
with the results to the A register.

Exclusive OR Instructions:

XRA   r   The contents of the register r are exclusive ORed with the contents of
the A register; results to the A register.

XRI   data   The data in the instruction is exclusive ORed with the contents of the A
register; results to the A register.

Complement

CMA   Complement the contents of A register, results to A register.

Results are stored in the accumulator [handwritten annotation]

Comparison Instructions

In comparison instructions, the data specified by the operand is subtracted from data in the accumulator which then affects the status bits, but not the data itself.

The *Comparison Instructions* are all arithmetic comparisons *(Figure 7-7)*. The data in the accumulator is compared to data in the instruction (CPI) or to data in one of the processor registers or in the memory location addressed by the contents of the HL register pair (the CMP instruction). In both cases, the data specified by the operand is subtracted from the accumulator and the status bits are affected. Neither data is affected by the comparison operation. It is left to the conditional branch instructions to test the results of the comparisons.

Branch Instructions

Branch instructions can be conditional or unconditional.

The *Branch Instructions (Figure 7-7)* provide for unconditional branching with the JMP address instruction or conditional branching with the JNZ (not zero), JZ (zero), JNC (no carry), JC (carry), JP (positive), JM (minus), JPO (odd parity), and JPE (even parity). The subroutine calls can similarly be unconditional (CALL) or conditional (CNZ, CZ, CNC, CC, CP, CM, COP, or CPE). The subroutine returns can be unconditional (RET) or conditional (RZ, RNZ, RNC, RC, RP, RM, RPO, or RPE). The restart instruction (RST n) discussed under timing and control is also a subroutine jump to address n∗8 (meaning n × 8) where n is a value from 0 to 7 as specified by the restart instruction (RST n). The PCHL is an indirect address unconditional branch since the contents of the HL register pair are loaded into the program counter to cause the jump.

Figure 7-7.
Comparison, Branch
and Miscellaneous
TMS8080A Instructions

Comparison Instructions:

CMP   r   The contents of the register r are subtracted from the contents of the
               accumulator affecting the status bits. r can be A,B,C,D,E,H,L, or M.

CPI   data   The data in the instruction are subtracted from the contents of the A
               register, affecting only the status bits.

Branch Instructions:

JMP   address The address in the instruction is loaded into the program counter.

Jcond address If the condition is true, the address in the instruction is loaded into the
               program counter. cond is Z (zero), NZ (not zero), C (carry), NC (no
               carry), P (plus), M (minus), PO (odd parity) or PE (even parity).

CALL   address The address is loaded into the program counter and the old program
               counter value for the next instruction is saved on the stack.

Ccond address A subroutine CALL operation occurs if the condition is met. Same
               condition possibilities as the Jcond.

RET   The top of the stack is sent to the program counter.

Rcond   If the condition is met, the top of the stack is sent to the program
               counter.

RST   n   The program counter value for the next instruction is saved in the stack
               and the program counter is loaded with n x 8.

PCHL   The program counter is loaded with the contents of the HL register
               pair.

Miscellaneous Instructions:

EI   Enable the interrupt signal.

DI   Disable the interrupt signal.

HLT   Halt the processor; wait for an interrupt or RESET.

NOP   No Operation; time delay of 4 x clock period.

CMC   Complement the carry flip-flop.

STC   Set the carry flip-flop.

Miscellaneous Instructions

In addition to the instructions surveyed thus far there are some
miscellaneous instructions *(Figure 7-7)* that are often used. The enable
interrupt system (EI) and disable interrupt system (DI) instructions have
already been discussed under the timing and control features of this
chapter. The CMC is used to complement the carry flip-flop and the STC is
used to set the carry flip-flop. The HLT or halt instruction causes the
microprocessor to stop executing instructions and wait for a reset or an
interrupt before continuing operations. The NOP is a no operation which is
inserted to use up time while waiting for some timer to end or some other
event to occur.

This instruction set is relatively complete, allowing the TMS8080A
to be used in a wide variety of applications with relative ease. One such
application will be examined in this chapter.

AN EXAMPLE APPLICATION

Assume a mechanical device has been built that will sort coins by denomination. Coins of a given denomination will be sent down a trough so that they interrupt a light beam as they pass a certain point in the trough on their way to an automatic packager. There is a need for a control and monitoring system that will start the sorter and maintain a running total of the value of all coins sorted. There also likely would be a need to maintain a running total of the number of each denomination sorted, however, in this example this task will not be considered as a part of the microprocessor system problem solution. The reader may develop this.

The system to be designed must respond to a given light beam interruption by adding an appropriate amount to the total. It must also provide for a switch that will command the system to display the total dollar value of the coins sorted. This switch could serve to turn off the sorter as well.

HOW COULD THE COIN SORTER HARDWARE BE DESIGNED?

Interrupt Signal Circuits

A coin interrupts a light beam to trigger a microprocessor interrupt. The interrupt subroutine adds the coin value to the total.

From *Figure 7-3* recall that the TMS8080A can handle 8 interrupt signals and that there are eight different restart instructions. Since there are only six light beams being interrupted by coins of six different denominations (penny, nickel, dime, quarter, half-dollar and dollar), these signals can be used to generate six different restart instructions as shown in *Figure 7-8*. The switch that requests a display of the total dollar value sorted can be used to generate a seventh restart instruction. Thus, a display switch will cause a subroutine jump (RST 7) to location 56 in memory, a penny detection will cause a jump to location 48 in memory, and so on up to a dollar detection causing a subroutine jump to location 8 in memory. Restart 0 is not used. Only a RESET signal will cause a jump to location 0 of memory. The subroutine programs that service the interrupts will cause the appropriate amount to be added to the accumulating total when a coin causes the interrupt or will cause the total to be displayed and the sorter stopped in case the display switch is activated. The INTA gates the generated restart code onto the data bus which is sent to the microprocessor.

The SN74148 is a priority encoder which converts 8 input lines to 3 output lines. It generates the restart address for the interrupt service routine.

The 8-line-to-3-line encoder SN74148 will generate a 3-bit code corresponding to the *complement* of the input line number that is brought low. If input line 0 is brought low, the 3-bit output will be 111. This will be the case for a display request interrupt. If input line 6 is brought low, the output will be 001 for a restart 1, which is used for the dollar coin detection. If more than one input line is brought low, the 3-bit output corresponds to the highest number input that is low. If the first six input lines are low, the output will be the code for input line 5 which is a 010. Thus the SN74148 is a priority encoder, with the input line 7 (output code 000) the highest priority.

The INT signal to the TMS8080A is received from the GS output of the encoder. This output is low everytime an input low signal is received.

Input Interface Circuits

The actual interrupt is generated by the coin interrupting the light beam, energizing an optical sensor and triggering a flip-flop.

With the restart generation circuitry of *Figure 7-8*, the input signals need to be developed and held low until the input has been responded to by the TMS8080A. A TIL147 (Optoelectronic Source-and-Darlington Sensor Assembly) can be used to detect the presence of a coin of a given denomination as shown in *Figure 7-9*. Only the penny detector, which is to generate an input 1 for the SN74148 priority encoder, is shown.The other coin detectors would be duplicates of this circuit. When the coin passes through the slot of the TIL147, the light beam is cut off and the transistor current changes from 4 mA to 0 mA, providing a 0 or low to the CLOCK input terminal of the D flip-flop. When the coin passes out of the slot, the transistor current is restored and the positive transition on the clock terminal of the flip-flop causes the 1 on the D input to set Q to a 1 and $\bar{Q}$ to a 0. The active low on $\bar{Q}$ is applied to input 1 of the SN74148 producing the INT signal and the restart code at the correct time to the TMS8080A. In the case of the display flip-flop an active low from a switch is applied to the $\bar{R}$ terminal of a $\bar{S}$-$\bar{R}$ flip-flop to reset Q to a 0. This low from Q (not $\bar{Q}$) is fed to input 0 to generate the restart code. (*Figures 7-8* and *7-11*).

**Figure 7-8.
Restart Generating
Circuits**

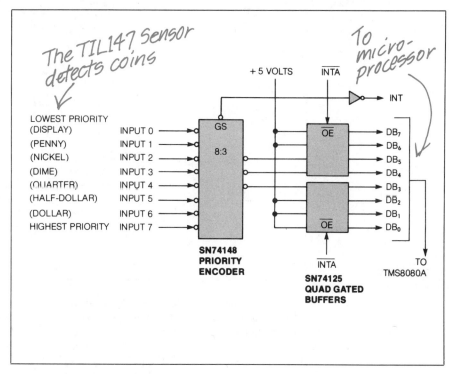

At the end of the interrupt service routine a signal identifies the coin detected and resets the circuits to recognize the next coin.

The restart code shifts the program to the subroutine located by the restart code address. Within the subroutine that performs the operations to recognize the coin detected (starting at address 48 in ROM for the penny) there is an OUTPUT instruction (OUT 1 for the penny). When executed by the TMS8080A, this instruction sends out an address code and an output enable signal that identifies that the coin has been recognized *(Figure 7-9)*. The address code is used to send an active low to the CLEAR terminal of the D flip-flop, clearing Q to a 0, $\overline{Q}$ to a 1 and releasing the active low signal on the priority encoder (on input 1 for the penny) so that it can recognize the next coin detected.

Figure 7-9.
Coin Detection Circuitry

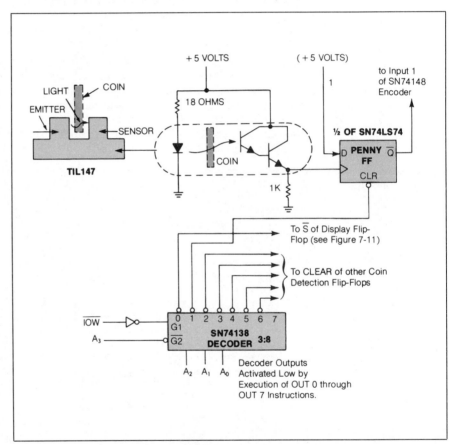

The active low for the CLEAR terminal is provided by an SN74138 3-line-to-8-line decoder as shown in *Figure 7-9*. It detects the address code and the enable signals produced by the OUTPUT operation and outputs the CLEAR signal on the appropriate line. G1, an active-high enable for the decoder, is provided by $\overline{\text{IOW}}$ and is ANDed with an active-low enable to G2 provided by the address bit A3. Thus, the decoder responds to output instruction addresses 0 through 7 when an output instruction is executed.

Output line 1 is shown connected to the D flip-flop in *Figure 7-9*. The other outputs of the decoder are connected to the appropriate CLEAR terminals of the D flip-flops for the other coins. For example, OUT 2 clears the nickel flip-flop, OUT 3 clears the dime flip-flop, and so on so that OUT 6 clears the dollar flip-flop. The display flip-flop is also set back to an uninterrupted condition by an OUT 0, but in a little different fashion. In this case the active low on line 0 goes to the $\overline{S}$ terminal of the display flip-flop to reset the Q output to a 1, releasing the input 0 of the priority encoder. After the coin detector and display switch detector flip-flops are cleared or set back they wait for a new coin or switch closure detection.

In all of these cases the circuits detect the execution of an appropriate output instruction by the TMS8080A and use this information to determine which flip-flop to clear. During this execution the accumulator data will be placed on the data line, but since neither the memory or display devices have been addressed the data will be ignored by these units.

Display Circuits

To display the accumulated coin totals, the BCD codes which represent the digits, are latched by logic circuits and displayed on the LED's.

The other output circuitry that must be devised is that required to display the dollar total of the coins sorted. This can be done by latching the BCD codes for the digits to be displayed into TIL308 LED displays with logic integrated circuits. The 8 bits on the data bus represent 2 BCD digits and come from the accumulator on an OUTPUT instruction. They can be latched into two TIL308's to display two decimal numbers. By assigning a total of 6 digits to the dollar amount and 2 digits to the cents amount, 8 TIL308's will be needed. If these four pairs of TIL308's are assigned the OUTPUT addresses 8, 9, 10, and 11, respectively, the instruction, OUT 11, will access the cents display (2 digits) and the instruction, OUT 8, will access the most significant dollar digits. Again a SN74138 3-to-8-line decoder can be used *(Figure 7-10)*. It is activated when A_3 is high and $\overline{IOW}$ is low to generate the latching signals for the TIL308's. Thus, it responds to addresses A_0 through A_3 during the execution of an output instruction. When an OUTPUT operation with address 1011 is being executed (as a result of an OUT 11 instruction) A_3 will be high, $\overline{IOW}$ will be low and output pin 11 of the SN74138 will be low, latching the available data to be displayed into the two TIL308's used for cents data. Corresponding address codes will latch data into the other three pairs of TIL308's.

The entire display can be turned on and off by controlling the signal applied to the BI inputs of the TIL308's. Thus, as shown in *Figure 7-10*, by performing an OUT 12 instruction (the output address code assigned to turning off the display), the decoder will deliver a low to the $\overline{R}$ terminal of a BI flip-flop which will cause Q and the BI line to be low and turn off the display. When an OUT 13 instruction is executed, the decoder output will send a low to the $\overline{S}$ terminal of the BI flip-flop to set Q and the BI line to a 1 turning the display on. Address code 13 is the one assigned to turn on the display.

**Figure 7-10.
Total Dollar Value
Display-Cents Digits**

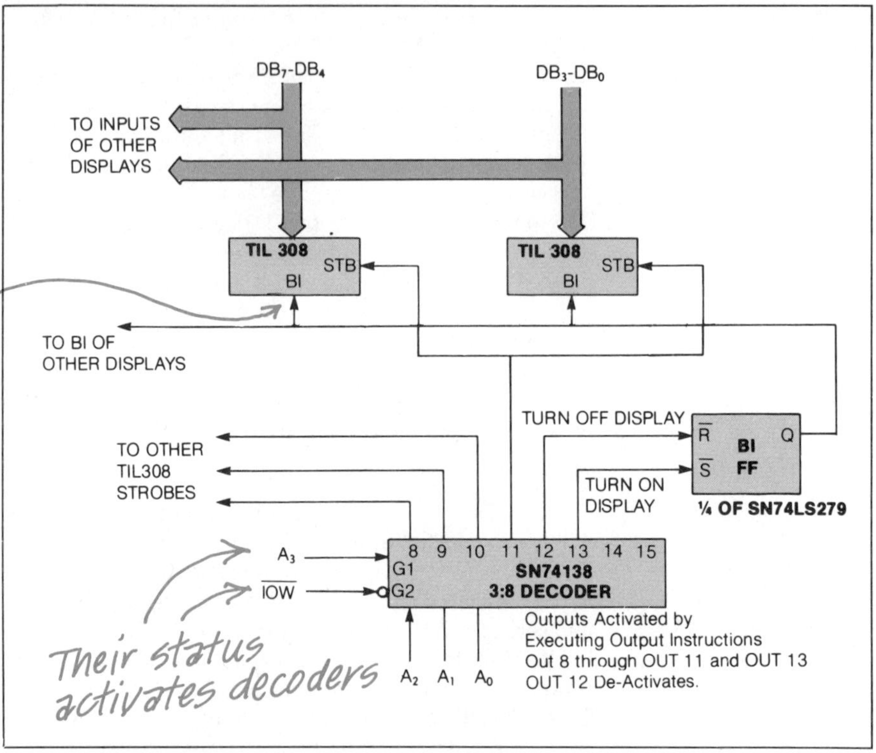

*Controlling
signal to BI
turns display
on or off.*

*Their status
activates decoders*

The request for a display is signalled as shown in *Figure 7-11* by pushing a momentary contact switch, which resets the Q output of the display flip-flop to an active low. Since this is connected to input 0 of the SN74148 priority encoder, as shown in *Figures 7-8* and *7-12*, a Restart 7 will be generated causing a subroutine branch to location 56 in ROM. If in that subroutine an OUT 0 instruction is executed, the output of the first SN74138 decoder will set the display flip-flop Q output back to a 1, a non-requesting state that would release the display.

Reset Sequence And Sorter Control

Pushing the RESET switch sends a reset signal to the microprocessor to begin at the program start and execute the instructions in ROM. It also resets a flip-flop to start the sorter.

The display request switch can also be used to turn the sorter off if it is used to control the sorter flip-flop as shown in *Figure 7-11*. When display is requested, sorter FF output Q will go low turning the sorter motor off. Q output of the sorter FF is also fed to an OR gate with the RESET signal. If the sorter is on, Q will be a 1 and a RESET cannot be generated. With Q at 0 (sorter off) an active low can be generated on the RESET line. When a RESET switch is pushed, a momentary reset signal is generated to force the TMS8080A to start executing instructions at location 0 in ROM. This RESET condition will also set the sorter flip-flop output to a 1 to turn the sorter on again. Thus, the RESET switch could be labeled a sorter-on switch and the display switch could be labelled a sorter-off/display switch.

Figure 7-11.
Display Interrupt and
Sorter Control
Connections

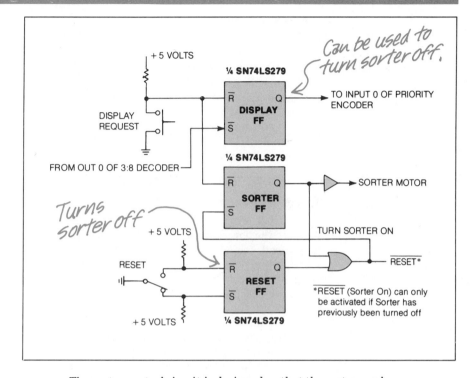

The sorter control circuit is designed so that the sorter can be started by the reset switch only after the sorter has been previously stopped by a display request. *To start the sorter for the first time the operator must first press the DISPLAY switch and then the RESET switch.*

Memory Design

As the coin sorter is based on interrupts, there is no need for stack information to be saved and no requirement for external RAM.

The problem as stated only needs four bytes of data storage for the 8-digit coin value total. The 6 8-bit registers provided within the TMS 8080A will be used for this purpose. If a more complicated program were required for the system, external RAM would have to be provided to save the information in the stack registers when a subroutine is required. This is so that the system will correctly continue with what it was doing before it was interrupted.

Since the coin sorter system uses a program structure that is totally dependent on interrupts there is no need to save the stack information and there is no need for external RAM in this present system design.

A single 256 byte PROM IC for the program provides all the external memory required.

The ROM memory design depends on the number of bytes required for the program, which cannot be determined until the program has been written. As will be seen later, the total program requirement for this system is less than 128 bytes. To allow for an expansion of the system capabilities, a 256 byte PROM will be used for the program memory using the SN74S471 Fuse-Link Programmable Memory. Thus, a single integrated circuit will provide more than enough memory for the coin sorter.

The Overall Design

If the individual circuit designs of *Figure 7-8* through *7-11* are combined into one overall diagram, the complete system design results as shown in *Figure 7-12*. This figure includes the ROM circuit, the SN74S471. To simplify the drawing, only block diagram representations of the circuits are shown. The details of the connections of these circuits can be found in *Figure 7-8* through *7-11*.

As stated previously, the TMS8080A provides more than enough data registers for the needs of the coin sorter. The internal registers B, C, D, and E will be used to store the sorted money total.

HOW WOULD THE PROGRAM BE DEVELOPED?

System Flow Chart

The program for the coin sorter is relatively straightforward, as shown in the flow chart of *Figure 7-13*. Each restart or interrupt subroutine simply loads the A register with the coin value to be added to the accumulating dollar total stored in registers B, C, D, and E. It then outputs a signal to the coin flip-flop CLEAR terminal with an OUT instruction, and jumps to a subprogram to perform the addition of the coin value in the A register to the total. Of course, the display subroutine must output the digits contained in the total storage area (registers B, C, D, and E) to the TIL308 display devices. Further, when the system is first turned on with the RESET switch, the contents of the processor registers and the state of the display must be cleared. Thus, six coin and one display interrupt subroutines, a subprogram that maintains a running total, and a sequence to set the initial conditions must be written.

Setting Initial Conditions

Since there is insufficient ROM memory between the reset address and the address for the first coin detection subprogram, the JMP CONT command is used to jump to a new memory location where enough memory is available to complete the operation.

When the RESET switch causes the program counter to clear to a ROM address of zero ("Reset" flow chart of *Figure 7-13*), the first instruction of *Figure 7-14*, OUT 12, turns off the total display. Then the A register is cleared with the XRA A instruction (when a register is XOR'ed with itself the result is all zeros in the register). Registers B through E are cleared by moving the A register contents (now all zeros) to these other registers. At the end of this sequence the interrupt signal is enabled with the EI instruction and a HLT (halt) instruction causes the processor to wait for an interrupt (or another RESET). Unfortunately this sequence would require 9 bytes of ROM and there are only 8 bytes available between address 0 where RESET starts and address 8 where the RST 1 subprogram for the first coin detection starts. Thus, after B and C have been cleared, a jump to a new location (80) in ROM is required. A JMP CONT is used to get to the MOV D,A and MOV E,A instructions which clear the D and E registers. These are followed by the instructions EI and HLT to complete the sequence.

**Figure 7-12.
Overall Coin Sorter
Design**

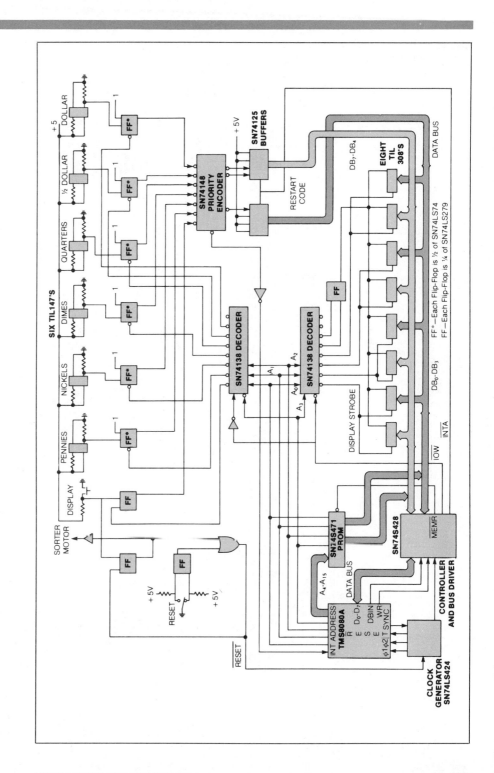

**Figure 7-13.
Coin Sorter Flow Charts**

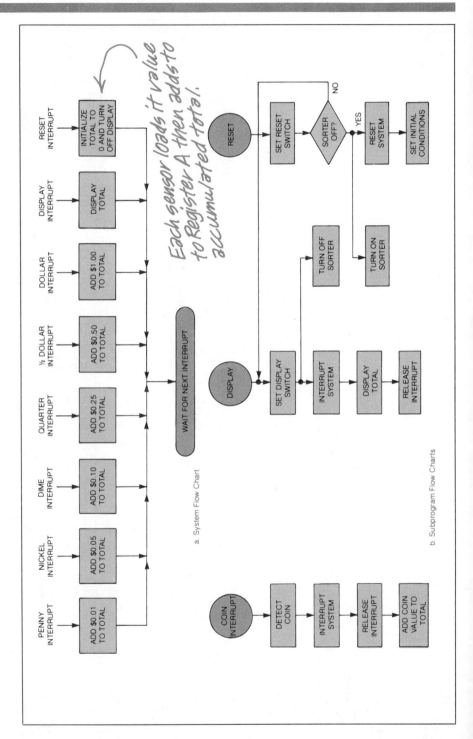

Each sensor loads it value to Register A then adds to accumulated total.

a. System Flow Chart

b. Subprogram Flow Charts

**Figure 7-14.
Initialization Sequence
for Coin Sorter**

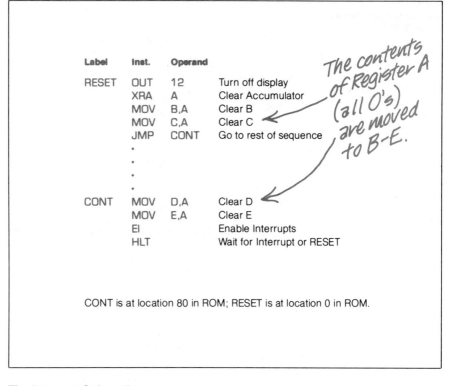

Label	Inst.	Operand	
RESET	OUT	12	Turn off display
	XRA	A	Clear Accumulator
	MOV	B,A	Clear B
	MOV	C,A	Clear C
	JMP	CONT	Go to rest of sequence
	.		
	.		
	.		
CONT	MOV	D,A	Clear D
	MOV	E,A	Clear E
	EI		Enable Interrupts
	HLT		Wait for Interrupt or RESET

The contents of Register A (all 0's) are moved to B-E.

CONT is at location 80 in ROM; RESET is at location 0 in ROM.

The Interrupt Subroutines

Coin Detection

For each coin, Register A is initialized to the coin value with a MVI A instruction. This is the value added to the total when the coin is detected.

All of the coin detection subroutines are of the same form shown in *Figure 7-15*. They begin by initializing the A register with the coin value to be added to the total. The MVI A, constant instruction is used for this. Thus, in the case of the penny the constant is 1, in the case of the nickel the constant is 5, and so on until for the dollar the constant $0A0_{16}$ (hexadecimal equivalent of binary 1010 0000) is loaded into the A register. The H on the end of the constant indicates to the TMS8080A that the number is a hexadecimal number. Once the constant is in the A register, an OUTPUT instruction clears the appropriate coin detection flip-flop $\overline{Q}$ output back to 1. For example, the dollar flip-flop is cleared with an OUT 6 instruction, the penny flip-flop is cleared with an OUT 1 instruction, and so on. Once the coin detection flip-flop has been cleared, a JMP TOTAL instruction causes a jump to the subprogram that will add the constant in the A register to the total in the B through E registers.

Figure 7-17.
Subprogram to Compute
Dollar Total

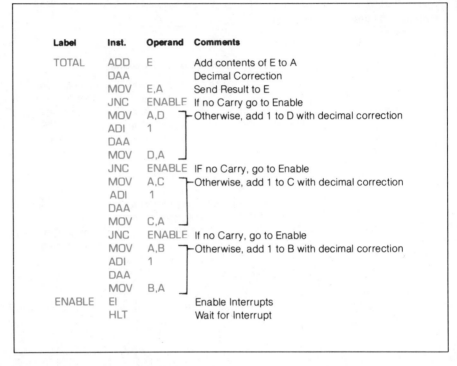

Label	Inst.	Operand	Comments
TOTAL	ADD	E	Add contents of E to A
	DAA		Decimal Correction
	MOV	E,A	Send Result to E
	JNC	ENABLE	If no Carry go to Enable
	MOV	A,D	Otherwise, add 1 to D with decimal correction
	ADI	1	
	DAA		
	MOV	D,A	
	JNC	ENABLE	IF no Carry, go to Enable
	MOV	A,C	Otherwise, add 1 to C with decimal correction
	ADI	1	
	DAA		
	MOV	C,A	
	JNC	ENABLE	If no Carry, go to Enable
	MOV	A,B	Otherwise, add 1 to B with decimal correction
	ADI	1	
	DAA		
	MOV	B,A	
ENABLE	EI		Enable Interrupts
	HLT		Wait for Interrupt

Summary

The program requirements are now complete. The system is simple
and straightforward, but very useful for organizations that must count
large numbers of coins and generate the total value in dollars and cents.
The features of the system are readily expandable. By adding a sequence of
instructions at the end of the DISPLAY subprogram that would cause the
total value to be sent out in serial ASCII character form, the system could
communicate directly with a bank computer. Of course, a serial-data
hardware interface would have to be added to the hardware design as an
output port 14, but this would be no real problem. If the number of each
coins counted were required, this circuitry and its display could be added.

Much of the simplicity of both the hardware and the software of
this example is due to the 8-bit microprocessor capability and the relative
efficiency of the instruction set of the TMS8080A. This is one of the
advantages of using an 8-bit processor for such a problem.

The program would have to be assembled before it can be used by
the system. That means that the mnemonic instructions would have to be
converted to their respective machine codes, all multiple byte instructions
locations included with their data and addresses, and all labels assigned
addresses. This normally would be done by computer but it can be done by
hand. An exercise has been included using the TOTAL subprogram of
Figure 7-17 to demonstrate the techniques used for assemblying a
program.

WHAT HAVE WE LEARNED?

- 8-bit microprocessors offer instruction and interrupt features that make them very useful for control, communications, and numerical computational problems that require medium-speed data transfers and relatively accurate numerical results.

- Microprocessors that have internal registers may provide enough on-chip data storage that external random-access data memory may not be needed for many applications.

- The availability of an interrupt system in a microprocessor can greatly simplify the exchange of information between the processor and external devices, resulting in simple hardware and programs.

- To provide the most cost-effective solution to any problem, the full capabilities of the microprocessor must be used in the most efficient way. Full use should be made of the high performance versatile integrated circuit support devices to simplify both the hardware and the software design.

- As with all processors, the overall design effort in developing an 8-bit system must be defined by a flow chart and then broken down into hardware subsystem designs and the development of their related subprograms.

WHAT'S NEXT?

In this chapter the advantages and applications of 8-bit microprocessors have been examined. But what about 16-bit microprocessors? Do these units offer advantages over the 8-bit processors just as the 8-bit processors have over the 4-bit units? The answer to this question will be the subject of the next chapter.

**Figure 7-15.
Interrupt Subprograms
for Coin Sorter**

Label	Inst.	Operand	Comments
DOLL	MVI	A,0A0H	Initialize A to 10100000
	OUT	6	Clear Dollar flip-flop
	JMP	TOTAL	Add $1 to total
FIFTY	MVI	A,50H	Initialize A to 50 cents
	OUT	5	Clear ½-dollar flip-flop
	JMP	TOTAL	Add 50 cents to total
QUART	MVI	A,25H	Initialize A to 25 cents
	OUT	4	Clear Quarter flip-flop
	JMP	TOTAL	Add 25 cents to total
DIME	MVI	A,10H	Initialize A to 10 cents
	OUT	3	Clear Dime flip-flop
	JMP	TOTAL	Add 10 cents to total
NICKEL	MVI	A,5	Initialize A to 5 cents
	OUT	2	Clear Nickel flip-flop
	JMP	TOTAL	Add 5 cents to total
PENNY	MVI	A,1	Initialize A to 1 cent
	OUT	1	Clear Penny flip-flop
	JMP	TOTAL	Add 1 cent to total

Note: An H *after* a number in the operand
indicates that it is a hexadecimal
number.

Display Request

Once all of the digits have been stored in the registers for the display, the display is turned on for a given amount of time.

The display request interrupt program of *Figure 7-16* at location 56 of ROM is more complicated than the other interrupt sequences. Basically, the E register contents are written (sent) to output port 11, the D register contents are written to output port 10, the C register contents are written to output port 9, and the B register contents are written to output port 8. Of course, since the contents of the A register are sent out on the data bus during an OUT instruction, the contents of the appropriate B, C, D, or E register must be moved over to the A register just prior to the OUT instruction. For example, to output the contents of the E register first a MOV A,E is used to get the contents of E over to A. Then an OUT 11 instruction sends this data out to the two least significant digit LED's (the cents display). Once all outputs have been sent to the displays, the OUT 13 instruction turns on the display. Next, after a program delay sequence, an OUT 0 instruction clears the display request to avoid an endless display request loop. Then an EI and HLT sequence re-enables the interrupt system and causes the processor to wait for a new interrupt or a RESET.

**Figure 7-16.
Display Subprogram for
Coin Sorter**

Label	Inst.	Operand	Comments
DISPLAY	MOV	A,E	Move Register E to A
	OUT	11	Output cents digits to display
	MOV	A,D	Move Register D to A
	OUT	10	Output two least-significant dollar digits to display
	MOV	A,C	Move Register C to A
	OUT	9	Output next most-significant dollar digits to display
	MOV	A,B	Move Register B to A
	OUT	8	Output most-significant dollar digits to display
	OUT	13	Turn on Display
DELAY	LXI	B, 08F9H	Load BC with Hex Counter value
DIS	DCR	C	Decrement LS byte of Counter
	JNZ	DIS	Jump if not zero
	DCR	B	Decrement MS byte of Counter
	JNZ	DIS	Jump if not zero
	OUT	0	Set Display Request flip-flop
	EI		Enable Interrupts
	HLT		Wait for Interrupt or Reset

The program provides for a 15 millisecond delay starting at the LXI instruction to allow time for the display switch to stop bouncing before the microprocessor releases the interrupt input from the display flip-flop. Otherwise, there would be a number of continuous display interrupt requests. In addition, this delay is accomplished with software rather than hardware so it can be adjusted easily if need be.

Subprogram For Maintaining A Total

The summing of all coins placed in the sorter is performed by the total subprogram. Each register, B through E, is first added to register A, totalled, corrected by a BCD adjust DAA instruction, and then stored in the appropriate register.

The TOTAL subprogram shown in *Figure 7-17* performs the operation of adding the constant loaded into the A register by one of the interrupt subprograms to the current total contained in registers B, C, D, and E. It does this by first adding E to A, with the result stored in A (ADD E). A decimal adjust (DAA) instruction corrects the 2 4-bit BCD codes and makes the addition decimally correct; at which time the result is stored in E with the MOV E,A instruction. A condition jump on no carry (JNC) to ENABLE occurs if there is no carry out of this first byte addition. If there is a carry, 1 must be added to the contents of D by using the MOV A,D to bring D to A, followed by the ADI 1 for the addition to A and the DAA instructions for the necessary correction. The result in A is sent to D with the MOV D,A operation. Similarly, another jump conditioned on a carry (JNC) is used to see if the program is to jump to ENABLE or add 1 to the contents of C with similar program steps as for register D. If 1 is added to C, the carry must again be checked to see if the program is to jump to ENABLE or add 1 to the contents of B. Once the complete sum is formed, the program re-enables the interrupt system with the EI instruction at location ENABLE followed by a HLT to force the processor to wait for the next coin or display interrupt.

Assembly Exercise

Write the machine code for the TOTAL subprogram of *Figure 7-17*
by filling out the table of *Figure 7-19*. The following information will be
helpful:

1) A given instruction may require one, two, or three bytes as shown in
Figure 4-40a.

2) The OP CODES for the TMS8080A instructions used in TOTAL are given
in *Figure 7-18*.

3) The location of the first instructions of the coin sorter subprograms are as
follows:

Subprogram or Label	Location (Base 10)	Location (Base 16)
RESET	0	0
CONT	80	50
DOLL	8	8
FIFTY	16	10
QUART	24	18
DIME	32	20
NICKEL	40	28
PENNY	48	30
DISPLAY	56	38
TOTAL	96	60

4) In determining the machine code for the three bytes of JNC ENABLE, the
address for the location called ENABLE will not be known until the entire
machine code program has been written.

**Figure 7-18.
TMS8080A Instruction
Codes for TOTAL
Subprogram**

Instruction	OP CODE	Number of Instruction Bytes
ADD E	83	1
ADI	C6	2
DAA	27	1
EI	FB	1
HLT	76	1
JNC	D2	3
MOV A,B	78	1
MOV A,C	79	1
MOV A,D	7A	1
MOV B,A	47	1
MOV C,A	4F	1
MOV D,A	57	1
MOV E,A	5F	1

Figure 7-19.
Work Table

Address	Code	Instruction
60		
61		
62		
63		
64		
65		
66		
67		
68		
69		
6A		
6B		
6C		
6D		
6E		
6F		
70		
71		
72		
73		
74		
75		
76		
77		
78		
79		
7A		
7B		

Figure 7-20.
Computer Assembly
Solution

Address	Code	Label	Instruction	Operand
0060			ORG	60H
0060	83	TOTAL:	ADD	E
0061	27		DAA	
0062	5F		MOV	E,A
0063	D27B00		JNC	ENABL
0066	7A		MOV	A,D
0067	C601		ADI	1
0069	27		DAA	
006A	57		MOV	D,A
006B	D27B00		JNC	ENABL
006E	79		MOV	A,C
006F	C601		ADI	1
0071	27		DAA	
0072	4F		MOV	C,A
0073	D27B00		JNC	ENABL
0076	78		MOV	A,B
0077	C601		ADI	1
0079	27		DAA	
007A	47		MOV	B,A
007B	FB	ENABL:	EI	
007C	76		HLT	

Exercise Solution (Codes in hexadecimal)

Figure 7-21.
Hand Assembly Solution

Address	Code	Instructions
60	83	ADD E
61	27	DAA
62	5F	MOV E,A
63	D2	JNC ENABLE*
64	7B*	
65	00*	
66	7A	MOV A,D
67	C6	ADI 1
68	01	
69	27	DAA
6A	57	MOV D,A
6B	D2	JNC ENABLE*
6C	7B*	
6D	00*	
6E	79	MOV A,C
6F	C6	ADI 1
70	01	
71	27	DAA
72	4F	MOV C,A
73	D2	JNC ENABLE*
74	7B*	
75	00*	
76	78	MOV A,B
77	C6	ADI 1
78	01	
79	27	DAA
7A	47	MOV B,A
7B (ENABLE)	FB	EI
7C	76	HLT

*ENABLE was determined to be 007B only after the entire code was listed, reserving two bytes for each ENABLE address in the JNC instructions. Then, once ENABLE was determined, this value was filled in the reserved bytes. Compare your solution to the Computer Assembled Solution in b.

A 16-Bit Microcomputer
Application

ABOUT THIS CHAPTER

In the last chapter an application of a typical 8-bit microprocessor
was examined, with a survey of the applications areas that would be
compatible with 8-bit processing. In this chapter a similar survey of 16-bit
microprocessor applications is examined concluding with a 16-bit
microcomputer system application example. An opportunity exists to carry
through this application with "hands on" work by using a microcomputer
completely assembled on a printed circuit board (a microcomputer module).
In this way the complete range of microprocessors and microcomputer
devices will have been examined, starting with a 4-bit microprocessor, SAM,
in Chapter 5, continuing with the 8-bit application in Chapter 7, and ending
with the 16-bit microcomputer application in this chapter. Such a range
spans the integrated circuit technology from LSI to VLSI.

WHY SELECT A 16-BIT MICROPROCESSOR OR MICROCOMPUTER?

The advantages of a 16-bit
over an 8-bit microcom-
puter includes faster computation, more extensive
instruction set and ex-
panded capability.

Some of the reasons for selecting 16-bit microcomputers have
already been explored in the last two chapters. Generally, processing data in
longer bit groups provides for faster system operation, whether the system
is oriented towards control, communications, or requires a great deal of
computation. Further, a longer bit-length processor usually offers a more
extensive instruction set with expanded capability. Thus, for any given
operation, twice to four times as much information can be processed by a
16-bit device, and often instructions that accomplish more complete
operations are available, resulting in shorter and more efficient programs.
If these advantages in system performance are important in a given
application, then the selection of a 16-bit microcomputer is the reasonable
approach, and selection of a 4-bit or an 8-bit system would be difficult to
justify.

Application Areas

Figure 8-1 lists a number of the areas of application that benefit
from 16-bit processing in terms of lower program requirements and
improved system operating speed. Foremost are the application areas that
require high computational accuracy or complex computations. Obviously
when the system is to be used as a computer such as minicomputers,
personal computers or "smart" terminals, this requirement may well be
overriding.

**Figure 8-1.
Applications Areas for
16-Bit Processors**

Minicomputers
Personal Computers
"Smart" Terminals
Complex Controllers
Display Terminals
  Plotters
  Graphics Terminals
High-Speed Communications Networks
Word Processing Systems
Special Military Systems
Diagnostic Systems
Advanced Games

Even if the system is not obviously a "number-cruncher" type of system, it may still require fast and accurate numerical performance of its processing element. Controllers that require mathematical expressions to be evaluated or precise numerical control information to be generated are examples of such systems, and missile and other vehicle controllers are prime examples that fall into this category. Even special purpose display terminals such as flat-bed or drum plotters or cathode ray tube (CRT) curve plotters usually require the high speed and complex numerical computational capability offered by 16-bit systems.

Additional applications occur in systems that must provide high-speed data or alphabetical communications with another system. Communications switching networks that operate under constantly changing priorities and interrupt conditions are examples of such systems.

Word processing, diagnostic systems, and special military systems are additional examples. Advanced games that interract with players through alphanumeric commands and instructions and with complicated game displays may be designed with 8-bit systems but would be designed best with 16-bit systems. Certainly computers which offer high-level language capabilities (BASIC, FORTRAN, APL, and so on) would be simpler to implement using 16-bit systems.

Expansion For the Future

When designing a system, even though initial operating requirements do not dictate it, it may be best to design around a 16 bit computer to accommodate future expansion.

When selecting a microprocessor or microcomputer element for a given application, it would be well to keep in mind that future system performance requirements may dictate the use of a 16-bit device. Even if present system operation does not absolutely require a 16-bit element, future expansions of the system may cause the system to evolve into a 16-bit version. In that case, it may be better to design the initial system with 16-bit devices, so that expansions and improvements do not require any major redesign costs. Additional benefits occur when family units are used that keep the same software as the system expands.

A 16-bit microprocessor or microcomputer can do all the operations that a 4-bit or an 8-bit unit can do. However, the reverse is not necessarily true and each application should be examined carefully. If the 16-bit system makes sense, given comparable costs and availability, the 16-bit microprocessors or microcomputers are a better buy. The question would be which type of 16-bit element to buy: a microprocessor, a microcomputer, or a microcomputer module?

WHAT ADVANTAGES DO MICROCOMPUTERS AND MICROCOMPUTER MODULES OFFER?

Microprocessor Approach

The microprocessor-based system is flexible to design, but assembly testing and implementation can be difficult and lengthy.

Figure 8-2 shows a comparison of the advantages and disadvantages available to a microprocessor system designer when using any one of three approaches. Microcomputers and microcomputer modules offer certain advantages to the system designer that are not available when the system design starts with a microprocessor. An advantage of the microprocessor approach is that it allows the designer to custom design the memory and input/output structure to meet the present and future system needs. However, once such a design has been developed on paper, the designer must design an interconnect system, assemble the parts, and test the system to arrive at a working system. This can be a time-consuming, tedious, and expensive exercise, especially if only a few copies of the system are to be built.

**Figure 8-2.
Comparison of
Microcomputer
Alternatives**

Approach	Advantages	Disadvantages
Microprocessor	Can be configured to meet any system requirements.	Must be assembled into final system form.
Microcomputer	Single-chip systems with low assembly costs possible.	Fixed input/output configurations. Memory is not easily expandable.
Microcomputer Modules	Pre-wired as a microcomputer module with provisions for memory and input/output expansion. Ideal for initial low cost start on small system.	Relatively expensive if large numbers of identical systems are required.

Microcomputer Approach

The microcomputer-based system is similar to the microprocessor-based system, except that it is likely to yield a simpler, less expensive system. It may be limited, however, in memory capacity if expansion is required.

The same steps must occur, perhaps, to a lesser extent, when a single-package microcomputer integrated circuit is used. The main difference is that since the memory and processor are contained within the microcomputer, there are few circuits to assemble and wire together. However, because the memory and I/O are contained in the microcomputer the memory and input/output structure is limited by the microcomputer architecture. If the microcomputer does offer sufficient on-chip memory and if the input/output structure of the device is easily adaptable to the system requirements, then the microcomputer approach will result in a simpler and less expensive system than is possible with the microprocessor approach. However, the problem of assembling and testing the final system still remains even with the microcomputer approach.

Microcomputer Module Approach

The microcomputer module based system is designed around proven self-contained computer modules that can be ready for use very quickly.

The microcomputer module is a completely wired and tested microcomputer, containing the microprocessor, read-only-memory, (sometimes containing a monitor program to allow for assembling and running user programs), a limited amount (typically 1 to 2k locations) of RAM for data memory and program development, and an input/output structure dedicated to inputting information from a keyboard and outputting information to a display. The advantage of such a module is that it is already wired and tested and can be used immediately for program development and verification. In many cases it can then be modified slightly and used in the intended system application. Such an approach offers the simplest and quickest way of building small numbers of systems. It may even be the least expensive way to develop limited production systems.

The microcomputer module is excellent for start-up projects when the quantity of units is small, but it may be expensive when used for systems that are to be produced in large quantities.

However, there are also disadvantages to the approach. Once designed, it is not the least expensive way to build a large number of copies of a given system. The microcomputer module may have been set up primarily as a developmental tool. This may make it awkward to match the fixed module structure to the system requirements. However, for most designers dealing with small numbers of a given type of system, the module approach is the easiest, most inexpensive, and least time-consuming approach available. The savings of the time and effort required to construct an operating system usually outweighs the structure limitations and initial cost disadvantages of the microcomputer module approach.

Even if a large number of copies of a system are to be made, the development of the first design can be made easily and quickly with the microcomputer module. This design then can be converted to the appropriate microprocessor or microcomputer version as required for producing the large number of copies inexpensively. Since this approach is likely to be the easier design procedure for the beginning designer, it will be used to develop the concepts and problem solution for the 16-bit system application contained in the remainder of the chapter.

WHAT ARE THE FEATURES OF A TYPICAL 16-BIT MICROCOMPUTER MODULE?

One example of a 16-bit microcomputer module is the Texas Instruments TM 990/U89 microcomputer board shown in *Figure 8-3*. The block diagram of this module is shown in *Figure 8-4*. The basic hardware features of this module can be summarized by examining this block diagram.

**Figure 8-3.
TM 990/U89 Board
Layout**

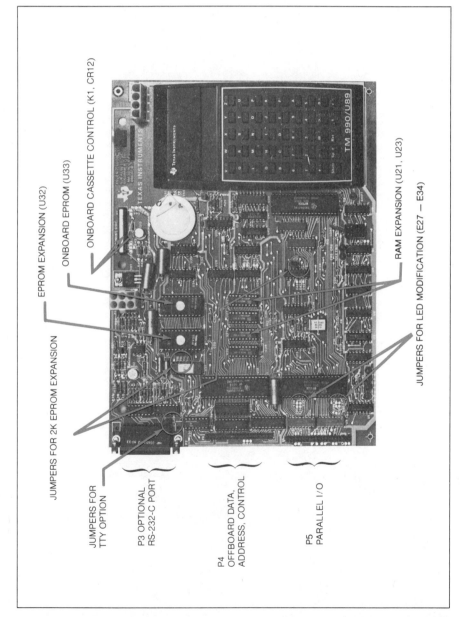

Figure 8-4.
TM 990/U89 System
Block Diagram

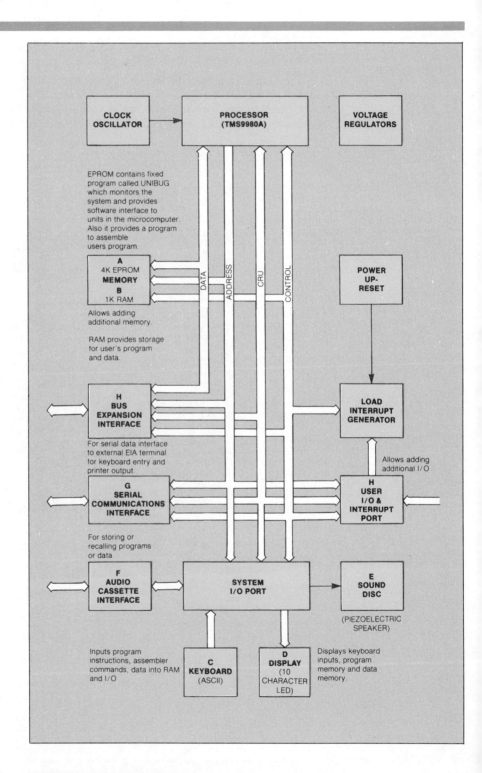

CLOCK
OSCILLATOR

PROCESSOR
(TMS9980A)

VOLTAGE
REGULATORS

EPROM contains fixed
program called UNIBUG
which monitors the
system and provides
software interface to
units in the microcomputer.
Also it provides a program
to assemble
users program.

A
4K EPROM
MEMORY
B
1K RAM

DATA
ADDRESS
CRU
CONTROL

POWER
UP-
RESET

Allows adding
additional memory.

RAM provides storage
for user's program
and data.

H
BUS
EXPANSION
INTERFACE

LOAD
INTERRUPT
GENERATOR

For serial data interface
to external EIA terminal
for keyboard entry and
printer output.

Allows adding
additional I/O

G
SERIAL
COMMUNICATIONS
INTERFACE

H
USER
I/O &
INTERRUPT
PORT

For storing or
recalling programs
or data

F
AUDIO
CASSETTE
INTERFACE

SYSTEM
I/O PORT

E
SOUND
DISC

(PIEZOELECTRIC
SPEAKER)

Inputs program
instructions, assembler
commands, data into RAM
and I/O

C
KEYBOARD
(ASCII)

D
DISPLAY
(10
CHARACTER
LED)

Displays keyboard
inputs, program
memory and data
memory.

Hardware Features

The TM990/U89 micro-
computer module inputs 8
bits at a time, although its
operation is that of a 16-bit
system. It has all of the
hardware of a standard
computer, including ROM
and RAM memory, full
keyboard, a LED display,
an audio transducer, provisions for an audio cassette
interface, a serial data interface, and memory and
I/O expansion capability.

The central feature of the module is the microprocessor, the
TMS9980A, which behaves like the TMS9900 family 16-bit microprocessors
and microcomputer in that its instruction set operates on 16-bit words in
memory. In the case of the TMS9980A, data and instructions are
transferred in the system 8 bits at a time on the 8-bit data bus. This makes
the basic architecture of the data bus similar to 8-bit microprocessor.
However, as far as the person that programs the system is concerned, the
device is behaving as if it were a 16-bit microprocessor. Any program
developed on the TMS9980A will run on the TMS9900 family of devices with
a 16-bit data bus or on the TMS9940 16-bit microcomputer.

In addition to the TMS9980A microprocessor, the TM 990/U89
microcomputer module has the following components:

A) 4k ROM/EPROM, which contains a monitor called UNIBUG which
provides a symbolic assembler and the software interfacing to the input/
output components on the board. There is room on the board to directly
expand this ROM/EPROM memory by an additional 2k by simply mounting
another memory circuit on the board.

B) 1k RAM which can be used for data or user program storage. There is
room on the board for an additional 1k of RAM.

C) A keyboard that allows alphanumeric entry of program instructions,
assembler commands, and data into the RAM and input/output locations.
This keyboard resembles that of an advanced scientific calculator with
many of the keys devoted to alphanumeric characters and system
commands. Full ASCII character entries are possible.

D) A 10-character LED display for displaying the information inputted
through the keyboard or for displaying program and data memory
information as commanded by the keyboard entries. Not all alphanumeric
characters are displayed in true form. Some have symbols that can be
accommodated by the display. Thus, it is called a psuedo ASCII display.

E) A piezoelectric speaker for outputting audio information such as
prompting tones to the programmer/user.

F) An audio cassette interface that allows the user to connect a standard
audio tape recorder to the module for storing or recalling program or data
information. This allows the user to add bulk memory easily and
inexpensively.

G) A serial data interface for connecting the module to an external EIA
terminal for keyboard entry and printer output.

H) Memory and input/output expansion connectors provide for adding
additional memory and input/output boards to the microcomputer module
for expansion of memory and input/output to the full addressing capability
of 16k bytes of the TMS9980A microprocessor.

While the basic board structure and features tend to make the TM 990/U89 a system development and laboratory component, the expansion connector features allow the board to act as the central microcomputer of a complete special or general purpose system. The designer simply has to define the on-board program memory and the additional memory and input/output board designs to match the requirements of the system being built. Once the program is developed for the system and the module is to be included in the operating system, the program can be written into the EPROM or ROM circuits on the TM 990/U89. If there is not enough memory space additional memory boards can be used as needed.

Architecture Of Microprocessor

The 9900 series of devices all use a memory-to-memory architecture in which all program data is stored in memory and not in the processor circuit. While the processor contains various working registers, arithmetic-logic-unit circuits, decoders, and so on, the programmer is only concerned with the three registers that are used to locate data and instructions in memory and save the status information. These registers are shown in *Figure 8-5*. However, 16 working registers contained in the workspace are defined by the workspace pointer and can be addressed by the programmer.

Although the micro-processor contains many operating blocks, to do a task, the programmer is only concerned with how information can be used in the Program Counter (PC), the Status Register (ST), the Workspace Pointer (WP) and its 16 registers.

**Figure 8-5.
9900 Family Memory-to-Memory Architecture**

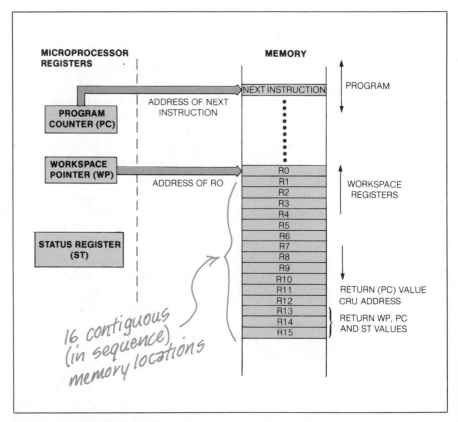

The PC stores the address of the instruction; the ST stores the results of the previous instruction; and the WP stores the address in memory in the workspace registers.

The (PC) program counter maintains the address of the instruction to be executed. The (ST) status register keeps track of the results of the previous instruction. The (WP) workspace pointer stores the address of the first of 16 successive locations in data memory, called workspace registers. These workspace registers are actually memory locations, though they are treated by the processor as if they were registers in the processor. They can be used to store data or data addresses. They may be used as index registers for indexed addressing *(Figure 4-44)*.

Special workspace register locations have dedicated purposes for programming inputs and outputs, and for keeping track of branch instructions.

Certain of the workspace register locations have special dedicated purposes. For example, register 12 contains the address of the serial input/output bit that is accessed through a serial data link called the CRU (Communications Register Unit). Special instructions to execute such operations are called CRU instructions. Register 11 contains the program counter value of the main program while a subroutine (BL called) is being executed. Registers 13, 14, and 15 contain the program counter, workspace pointer, and status register values as they existed before a subroutine call (BLWP instruction). By using the information in register 11 or registers 13, 14, and 15, the program can return back to the main or calling program from a subroutine.

Addressing Modes

The 9900 family of devices support the following addressing modes:

Register Addressing
The workspace register indicated in the instruction by a number between 0 and 15 contains the data.

Register Indirect Addressing
The workspace register indicated by an asterisk (*) followed by a number between 0 and 15 is used as an address register to hold the address of the data. If the number is followed by a plus (+) in the instruction mnemonic coding, the contents of the address register are incremented following the instruction. This causes the address register to act as a data counter that contains the address (points) to successive data locations as the instruction is executed.

Direct Addressing
The address in the instruction is the location in memory to be used by the instruction. The mnemonic coding used to indicate this type of addressing is @ followed by the direct address value or symbol.

Indexed Addressing
The address of data is formed by adding the offset contained in the instruction to the value contained in the index register specified (registers 1 through 15). The mnemonic coding for this type of addressing is @ followed by the offset value or label followed by the register number in parenthesis.

Examples of the mnemonic assembly language coding for these addressing modes for the CLR (clear) instruction are shown in Figure 8-6. This instruction will cause 16 zeroes to be sent to the location specified by the addressing mode in the instruction.

Figure 8-6.
Addressing Modes for
16-bit Microprocessor
(TMS9900 Family)

Addressing Mode	Mnemonic Coding for CLR Instruction	Effect of Instruction if R1 Contains 100_{16}
Register	CLR R1	R1 cleared to all zeroes.
Register Indirect	CLR *1	Location 100_{16} is cleared to all zeroes, R1 not effected
	CLR *1 +	Location 100_{16} is cleared to all zeroes. The contents of R1 are incremented to 102_{16}.
Index	CLR@ >10 (R1)	The location $100_{16} + 10_{16}$ or 110_{16} is cleared to all zeroes. R1 is not changed.
Direct	CLR@ >200	The location 200_{16} is cleared to all zeroes.

Notes: the symbol > denotes a Base 16 (hexadecimal) value

Instruction Set

The base instruction set for the TMS9900 microprocessor family can utilize immediate, register, register indirect, direct and indexed addressing modes.

The instructions available on the 9900 family devices are summarized in *Figure 8-7*. Most of these operations can use all the addressing modes listed in *Figure 8-6* and *8-7*, though there are exceptions. For example, immediate operations (those whose mnemonics end in I) use *immediate addressing* to indicate data constants that are to be loaded into registers. The data is contained right in program memory as the second word of the instruction. *Register addressing* is used to locate a data variable from a workspace register involved in an instruction. The multiply and divide instructions use register addressing for the destination data locations, that is, the product or quotient/remainder are stored in two successive workspace registers. The shift operations use register addressing only. The jump instructions use a special kind of indexed addressing called *program-counter relative addressing*. In this case the displacement contained in the instruction is added to the contents of the program counter (acting as the index register) to determine the instruction address to which the program jumps.

Arithmetic Instructions

The arithmetic operations of the 9900 family devices include addition and subtraction (byte (8-bit) or word (16-bit) operations), negation, absolute value, increment and decrement (by one or two), and multiplication and division. Absolute value means the unsigned value of the number.

**Figure 8-7.
16-bit Microprocessor
(TMS9900 Family) Base
Instruction Set***

Arithmetic Operations

Addition	A, AB, AI
Subtraction	S, SB
Negation	NEG
Absolute Value	ABS
Multiply (16 bit x 16 bit)	MPY
Division (32 bit ÷ 16 bit)	DIV
Increment	INC, INCT
Decrement	DEC, DECT

Logic Operations

Invert	INV
OR	ORI, SOC, SOCB
AND	ANDI, SZC, SZCB
Exclusive OR	XOR

CRU I/O

Single Bit	TB, SBO, SBZ
Multiple Bit	STCR, LDCR

Data Movement

Move Data	MOV, MOVB, SWPB
Store Registers	STST, STWP

Compare Operations

Compare to Constant	CI
Compare	C, CB
Masked Compare	COC, CZC

Initialization

Clear	CLR
Set (all ones)	SETO
Load Immediate	LI
Load Registers	LWPI, LIMI

Special Operations

Execute Instruction out of Sequence	X
Extended Operation	XOP

Branch Operations

Unconditional Branches	B, JMP, RTWP
Subroutine Call	BL
Context Switch	BLWP
Conditional Branches	JEQ, JNE, JGT, JOP, JOC, JNC, JNO, JLT, JH, JHE, JL, JLE

Control

Reset	RSET
Idle	IDLE
Condition	

Addressing Modes

Register
Register indirect, without Autoincrementing
Register Indirect, with Autoincrementing
Indexed
Direct
Immediate
Relative (Used in jump instructions)

Shift Operations

Arithmetic Shifts	SLA, SRA
Logical Shift Right	SRL
Circular Right Shift	SRC

*Meaning of Mnemonic Endings: B—Byte I—Immediate T—by two

Data Movement Instructions

The TMS9900 family has an exceptionally broad instruction set that includes multiply and divide instructions and twelve condition jump operations.

The data movement operations include byte and word movement instructions and instructions to store the status and workspace registers.

Initialization Instructions

Initialization operations include clearing a data word to all zeroes or setting a data word to all ones. The workspace pointer, interrupt mask, (this is a special interrupt control) and workspace registers can all be loaded with constants from the program with Load instructions.

Logical Instructions

Logical operations include the OR, AND, Invert, and Exclusive-OR operations as well as some special logical OR operations (SOC, SOCB).

Compare Instructions

Memory data can be compared to a constant or to another memory byte or word. Again special compare provisions are provided in COC and CZC to select specific words or bits to check system limits or status of subsystems.

Shift Instructions

The shift operations include arithmetic shifts left or right, logical shift right, and a circular right shift (right circulate).

Branch Instructions

There are two types of subroutine calls and two types of unconditional branches. There are twelve conditional jump operations that can check status bits for conditions of carry, parity, equal, and arithmetic and logical greater than, less than, and so on.

Input/Output Instructions for CRU

Special Communications Register Unit (CRU) instructions move data serially from inputs to microprocessor to outputs.

There are some special instructions that can move data serially over an input and output serial data link which is called the Communications Register Unit. With the CRU the same type of serial data input performed by SAM in Chapter 5 can be performed with the CRU Instructions. Individual bits can be tested at an input with TB or set or cleared with SBO or SBZ. Multiple bits (and the number can be programmed) can be stored in memory from the CRU or loaded into the CRU with the STCR or LCDR instructions, respectively.

All of these instructions are available on the TM 990/U89 microcomputer module, which permits programmers to enter these instructions directly in mnemonic form.

Interrupt Features

The TMS9980A has up to 8 levels of interrupt priorities, all of which can be masked off. A three bit interrupt code selects the priority.

Unlike the TMS8080A which has one interrupt input, the TMS9980A has an interrupt structure which allows 8 levels of interrupts, which can be given a priority and any of which can be made non-active (masked off) by the programmer. The interrupt levels are indicated to the processor by a 3-bit interrupt code whose bits are IC_0, IC_1, and IC_2. These signals are generated by a TMS9901 Programmable Systems Interface circuit on the TM 990/U89 board. This interface circuit is especially designed to mate to the TMS9980A. By these means the user can control which interrupts are to be active and what they mean.

The microprocessor responds to the interrupt by jumping to the particular subroutine that is reserved in memory and designed to service that interrupt. A provision is made to link back to the main program after the interrupt is serviced.

The TMS9980A responds to a given interrupt by performing a "context switch." This is a form of subroutine jump to a subprogram designed to service the interrupt. When the interrupt occurs and the context switch is made, the program goes to the reserved location in memory specified by *Figure 8-8* for the respective interrupt code. (For interrupt 1 the location is 0004 for the workspace pointer and 0006 for the program counter.) The contents of these memory locations contain the values for the workspace pointer and at the next adjacent location the value for the program counter. The program counter value addresses the first instruction of the subprogram to service the interrupt. The workspace pointer value defines the location of the workspace registers to be used by the subprogram. Recall in the discussions on subroutines and interrupts that a provision is made to link back the main program after a subroutine is completed. The values of the workspace pointer, program counter, and status register that existed at the time of the interrupt are saved in registers 13, 14, and 15 of the new workspace for the subprogram. Then, at the end of the subprogram, an RTWP instruction causes these values to be restored to the three processor registers to provide the link back and to cause program execution to resume from the interrupted point in the system program.

Figure 8-8.
16-bit Microprocessor
(TMS9980A) Interrupt
Codes

Interrupt Code IC_0 IC_1 IC_2	Function	Location of Address of 1st Instruction (PC Value)	Location of Workspace Pointer (WP Value)
0 0 0	Reset	0002	0000
0 0 1	Reset	0002	0000
0 1 0	Load	3FFE	3FFC
0 1 1	Interrupt 1	0006	0004
1 0 0	Interrupt 2	000A	0008
1 0 1	Interrupt 3	000E	000C
1 1 0	Interrupt 4	0012	0010
1 1 1	—		

One interrupt level that is of special interest in *Figure 8-8* is Interrupt 1. Within the TM 990/U89 microcomputer, any input signal that initiates a signal on the INT 3 input of the TMS9901 triggers Interrupt 1, or it can be initiated when an interval timer inside the TMS9901 has been decremented to zero. The Interval timer reaching zero generates an INT 3 out of the 9901 which is interpreted by the TMS9980A as an Interrupt 1. This particular feature will be used in the application example of this chapter.

Input/Output Features

One feature of the CRU instructions that makes the 9900 family instruction set so powerful is the fact that individual input and outputs can be controlled bit by bit.

Some of the input/output features of the TM 990/U89 module have been mentioned already, such as the cassette interface which is controlled by a keyboard input that is monitored and responded to by the monitor program stored in EPROM in the system. Most of the components on the board and many single-bit control or input lines off the board are accessed by using the CRU instructions of the TMS9980A. Control signals and signals placed on the address lines are used to locate I/O units as well as memory cells. Each individual bit in the system input/output structure is assigned a CRU address just like memory locations are assigned addresses. Their addresses are made relative to a base address of a particular I/O unit. These bits can be accessed one bit per input/output instruction using the single bit CRU instructions SBO (Set CRU Bit to One), SBZ (Set CRU Bit to Zero), and TB (Test value of CRU Bit). The address of the bit accessed is contained in a special place — bits 4 through 14 of workspace register 12.

A Single-Bit Example

As an example of such an operation, the piezoelectric speaker is assigned the CRU address $21E_{16}$ in the TM 990/U89 system. Thus, to turn the speaker on the following instruction sequence would be used:

Label	Mnemonic	Operand	Comment
	LI	12, >43C	Set up $43C_{16}$ (twice $21E_{16}$) in R12
	SBO	0	Set Bit $21E_{16} + 0$ to a one

The signed displacement in the instruction (0 in this case, n in the general case) is added to the CRU address in R12 (1/2 of the value loaded into R12) to form the address of the CRU bit to be set to one. The CRU address is 1/2 the value in R12 because bit 15 is disregarded. This is just like shifting bits right one position (Remember, this divided a binary number by 2). The overall addressing procedure is shown in *Figure 8-9*.

If the instruction had been SBO 5, then 5 would have been added to the base address in *Figure 8-9* to set the 6th bit to a 1.

Similarly, a SBZ 0 instruction with $43C_{16}$ in R12 would turn the speaker off.

**Figure 8-9.
Single-Bit CRU
Addressing**

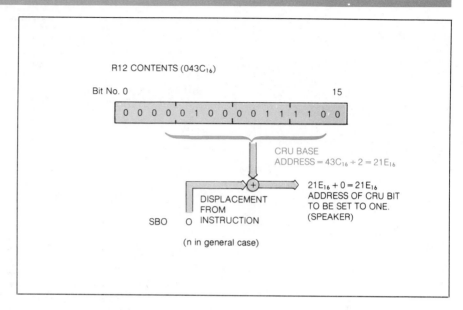

R12 CONTENTS (043C$_{16}$)

Bit No. 0   15

0 0 0 0 0 1 0 0 0 0 1 1 1 1 0 0

CRU BASE
ADDRESS = 43C$_{16}$ ÷ 2 = 21E$_{16}$

21E$_{16}$ + 0 = 21E$_{16}$
ADDRESS OF CRU BIT
TO BE SET TO ONE.
(SPEAKER)

DISPLACEMENT
FROM
SBO   0   INSTRUCTION

(n in general case)

Multiple-Bit Example

This input/output bit control is demonstrated with an interval timer example.

      The individual CRU bits can be accessed several bits at a time with the multiple-bit CRU instructions LDCR (Send the number of bits specified to successive CRU locations (obtained from a RAM location called out in the instruction), starting at the base address contained in R12) and STCR (receive the number of bits specified from the CRU, starting at the location specified in R12, and send the successive bits to the memory location specified in the instruction).

      As an example of such an operation, *Figure 8-10* illustrates the procedure for initializing the interval timer in the TMS9901 at position U10 in the TM 990/U89 microcomputer for a 500 millisecond (0.5 second) time interval. The bits for initializing the timer, are assigned the CRU addresses 1 through 14. To gain access to the timer, a requirement of the 9901 is that CRU bit 0 must first be set to a one. Thus, the first operation is to initialize R12 to 0 with the LI R12,0 instruction. The timer value is to be initialized to >3D09$_{16}$.

      This value arises from the fact that the interval time is given by:
$$T = Timer/31250 \text{ seconds}$$
For 0.5 seconds, Timer must equal 15625 (base 10) or 3D09$_{16}$. Then, the 3D09$_{16}$ is placed in R1 in bits 1 through 14, with bit zero a 0 and bit 15 a 1 as shown in *Figure 8-10*. With this bit combination, 7A13$_{16}$ is the number loaded into R1 with the LI R1,>7A13 instruction. With the instruction LDCR R1,15 the 15 bits are loaded into the CRU bits to set the timer register in the TMS9901. The 1 in CRU bit zero gains access to the timer.

      The three remaining instructions of *Figure 8-10a* are required to enable the INT3 signal (generated by the internal timer in the TMS9901 going to zero) to pass through to the TMS9980A as an interrupt.

**Figure 8-10.
Multiple-Bit CRU
Transfer**

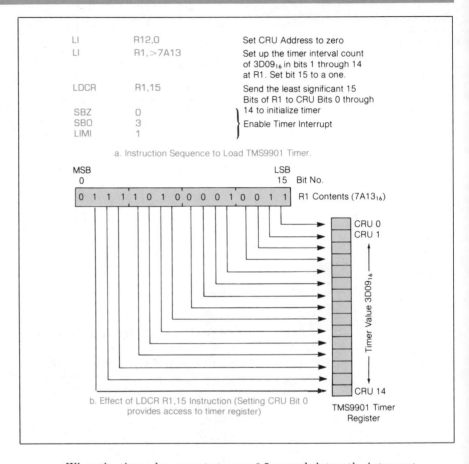

LI	R12,0	Set CRU Address to zero
LI	R1,>7A13	Set up the timer interval count of $3D09_{16}$ in bits 1 through 14 at R1. Set bit 15 to a one.
LDCR	R1,15	Send the least significant 15 Bits of R1 to CRU Bits 0 through 14 to initialize timer
SBZ	0	
SBO	3	Enable Timer Interrupt
LIMI	1	

a. Instruction Sequence to Load TMS9901 Timer.

MSB 0   LSB 15 Bit No.

`0 1 1 1 1 0 1 0 0 0 0 1 0 0 1 1` R1 Contents ($7A13_{16}$)

CRU 0
CRU 1

Timer Value $3D09_{16}$

CRU 14

TMS9901 Timer
Register

b. Effect of LDCR R1,15 Instruction (Setting CRU Bit 0
provides access to timer register)

The workspace pointer defines 16 contiguous (all in a row) memory locations that are used as temporary storage registers (workspace) as the microprocessor runs through the program.

When the timer decrements to zero 0.5 seconds later, the interrupt level 1, properly enabled, will cause the program to jump to the subprogram address contained in memory location 0006. At the same time it sets up the 16 workspace registers defined by the workspace pointer value contained in memory location 0004. The current workspace pointer, program counter, and status register values will be saved in registers 13, 14, and 15 of the subprogram workspace so that this information is restored when the program returns.

Other components on and off the board can be similarly accessed with the CRU instructions. The off-board expansion modules, if used, can be made active by addressing the appropriate assigned CRU addresses $0C00_{16}$ through $0C3E_{16}$.

Not all of the microcomputer features have been discussed but it can be seen from this brief discussion the TM 990/U89 microcomputer module it is a very versatile unit. It has considerable on-board system development capabilities as well as offering easy expansion of memory and input/output to allow the unit to be directly applied to a microcomputer system problem.

WHAT WOULD BE A TYPICAL APPLICATION OF A MICROCOMPUTER MODULE?

The BASIC program consists of interrupts controlled by timers.

Since the microcomputer module is a self-contained computer, it can be applied to any system problem that is compatible with the operating speed of the microcomputer. In fact, it can be used to handle any number of tasks by using the interrupt signals to notify the microcomputer when a task needs attention.

As a simple example, consider using the TM 990/U89 as a simple version of a "grandfather clock," which chimes out the hour count on the hour. The application could be designed to be much more complicated. For example, the system could be designed to play certain tunes on the 15 minute intervals, maintain an hour and minutes display, and chime and play a tune on the half hour. All of these features can be illustrated by just considering what's involved in the version that on the hour simply chimes the hour count.

Since a microcomputer module is being used, there is no need for any hardware design in this application, especially since the module already contains a piezoelectric speaker and interval timers on the board. All that really has to be considered is the program that will access these various components in the appropriate manner. It also serves to show how easy it is to begin applying a microcomputer by using the microcomputer modules.

HOW WOULD THE PROGRAM BE DEVELOPED?

Most of the programming required in this application will set various timers to determine when system conditions need to be changed.

System Flow Chart

One possible flow chart description of system activities is shown in *Figure 8-11*. First, the programmer must allow for the system to be started initially at the current hour and minutes when the system is turned on. In other words, the "clock" must be set. Then the programmer can cause the program to start executing by setting the TMS9901 interval timer to 0.5 seconds and waiting for the timer to interrupt the processor with a level 1 interrupt. While the processor is waiting for this interrupt, it can be handling other system operation tasks. When the interrupt occurs, the 1/2 second counter will be decremented. If it is not zero, the 0.5 second interval timer in the 9901 will be reinitialized and another wait for interrupt will occur. If the 1/2 second counter is zero, the hour is up so that the chimes must be sounded.

The subprogram to operate the chimes involves microprocessor timing loops performed by software generating tones that are maintained for specific time periods.

Assume that the chime tones are to be 1 kilohertz notes, so that the speaker is on for 0.5 millisecond and then is off for 0.5 millisecond. This pattern is to be repeated to sustain the tone for 1 second. There will then be one second of silence, and, if necessary, another tone will be sounded for 1 second, until the number of 1 second tones equals the hour count. Once all required tones have been sounded, the ½ second counter will be reinitialized and the sequence repeated for the next hour.

**Figure 8-11.
Grandfather-Clock Flow
Chart**

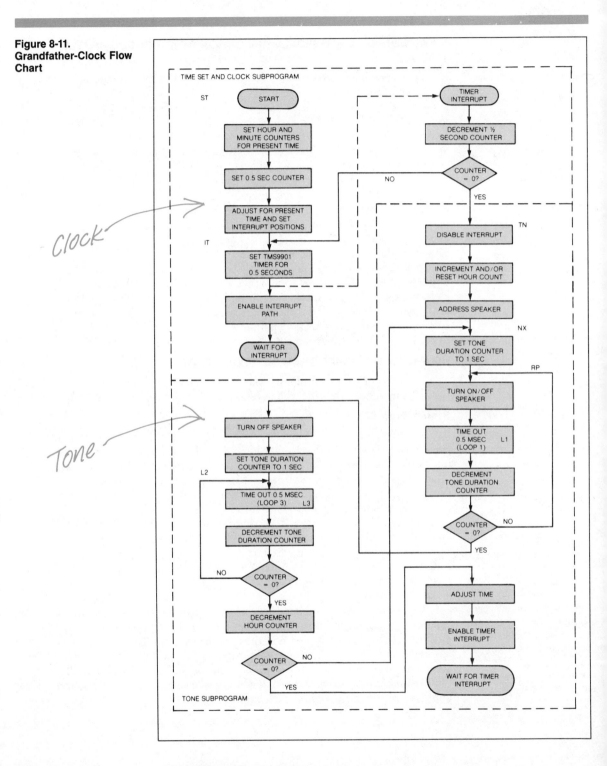

The tone sounding sequence involves processor timing loops performed with software instead of the hardware timing available in the TMS9901. Every 0.5 millisecond the speaker is changed from on to off or from off to on. This is repeated until there have been 2000 such changes (1 second tone duration). Then the hour counter is decremented. If it is not zero, the tone generation sequence is repeated.

Data Requirements

Most of the data requirements for this flow chart are associated with the timer and counter functions required. One possible assignment of the workspace registers and memory locations is shown in *Figure 8-12*. Registers 0 through 5 contain the basic timer and interval values used for control in the problem. Register 6 contains the hour counter used in the program while register 5 keeps the hour value. Register 7 is used to hold the current minute count when the time is initially set. Register 12 must be used to hold the CRU address value, and Registers 13 through 15 are used to hold the return values for the workspace pointer, program counter, and status register that existed at the time of the 0.5 second interrupt (interrupt level 1).

**Figure 8-12.
TM 990/U89 Memory Allocation**

General Use	Memory Location (Starting Address)
Time Set and Clock Subprogram	200_{16}
Tone Subprogram	250_{16}
Workspace	300_{16}
Interrupt Transfer Vector	
(WP)	0004
(PC)	0006

Workspace Register	Address	Use
R0	300	1/2 counter 7200_{16}
R1	302	TMS9901 Interval Timer value 3009_{16}
R2	304	0.5 millisecond timer value
R3	306	1-second counter 2000_{10}
R4	308	Speaker Control
R5	30A	Hour Counter
R6	30C	Hour Counter Copy
R7	30E	Minutes-Set Register
.	.	
.	.	
.	.	
R12	318	CRU Address
R13	31A	Main Program Workspace Pointer Value
R14	31C	Main Program Program Counter Value
R15	31E	Main Program Status Value

b. Workspace Register Allocation.

The workspace is located in RAM addresses 300_{16} through $31E_{16}$. The timesetting program sequence is assumed to start at location 200_{16} in RAM, while the 9901 interrupt service subprogram starts at address 226_{16} in RAM.

The Program

The total program contains a time set, clock subprogram and a tone subprogram. Each subprogram tracks the flow chart. The initial input by the programmer is the value for the hours and the minutes converted to hexadecimal.

The program for the flow chart of *Figure 8-11* is shown in *Figure 8-13*. This is relatively straightforward implementation of the flow chart, beginning with the time-setting sequence at the label ST(Set) (which would be at location 200_{16}). Before executing the program, the programmer defines the values for HOUR and MIN (Minutes). Hour and minutes values of 10 or greater must be converted to their hexadecimal equivalents before entering. He would load the program counter with 200_{16} and the workspace pointer with 300_{16} and press the execute command of the keyboard to run the program. This will be discussed later.

Once the current hour and minutes values are initialized into R5 and R7 the LI 9,120 and MPY 7,9 instruction convert current minutes to current ½ seconds. Multiplying two 16-bit numbers results in a 32-bit product which is placed in R9 and R10. R10 will be the significant part and it is moved to R7 which then holds the current number of 1/2 seconds. R0 is then

**Figure 8-13a.
Time Set and Clock
Subprogram —
Grandfather Clock**

ST	LI	5,HOUR	Set R5 with current hour value at 202_{16}
	LI	7,MIN	Set R7 with current minutes value at 206_{16}
	LI	9,120	Set R9 to ½ seconds in a minute
	MPY	7,9	Multiply current minutes by 120 for ½ seconds
	MOV	10,7	Move current ½ seconds (in R10) to R7
	LI	0,7200	Initialize R0 with number of ½ seconds in hour
	S	7,0	Subtract current ½ seconds to get those left
	LI	9,>300	Load R9 with WP value to be used by interrupt
	MOV	9,@4	Send this value to transfer vector location
	LI	9,>226	Load R9 with PC value for interrupt sequence
	MOV	9,@6	Send this value to transfer vector location
IT	LI	12,0	Set R12 to 0 (CRU Base Address for 9901 Timer)
	LI	1,>7A13	Load R1 with timer access (bit 15 a one) and timer value of $3D09_{16}$ in bits 1 through 14.
	LDCR	R1,15	Send R1 contents to CRU to initialize timer to ½ second
	SBZ	0	⎫
	SBO	3	⎬ Enable User 9901 Timer Interrupt
	LIMI	1	⎭
	DEC	0	Decrement ½ second counter R0
	JEQ	TN	If zero, go to tone sounding sequence
	IDLE		If not, wait for next interrupt

**Figure 8-13b.
Tone Subprogram —
Grandfather Clock**

```
TN    LIMI    0            Disable Timer Interrupt
      INC     5            Increment current hour count
      CI      5,13         Compare hours to 13
      JLT     OK           If less than 13, hours OK
      LI      5,1          If not, reset hour count to 1
OK    MOV     5,6          Copy hour count to R6
      LI      12,>43C      Set up Speaker address in R12
      LI      4,>AAAA      Set alternating 1-0 pattern in R4
NX    LI      3,2000       Set 0.5 millisecond counter (tone duration) in R3
RP    LDCR    4,1          Send bit 7 of R4 to speaker
      SRC     4,1          Shift bit pattern in R4 to complement bit 7
      LI      2,>22        Set speaker on or off time to 0.5 milliseconds
L1    DEC     2            Decrement speaker on/off counter
      JNE     L1           If not zero, continue timing
      DEC     3            Decrement tone duration counter
      JNE     RP           If not zero, continue sounding tone
      SBZ     0            If zero, turn speaker off
      LI      3,2000       Set tone off counter to one second value
L2    LI      2,>22        Set up 0.5 millisecond timer value
L3    DEC     2        ⎫
      JNE     L3       ⎬   Implement 1 second time delay
      DEC     3        ⎪
      JNE     L2       ⎭
      DEC     6            Decrement hour count
      JNE     NX           If not zero, sound another tone
      MOV     5,7          If zero, move number of tones sounded to R7
      LI      9,4          Initialize R9 with number of ½ seconds/tone
      MPY     7,9          Multiply by number of tones to get time used by tones
      MOV     10,7         and get this value into R7
      LI      0,7200       Load R0 with number of ½ seconds per hour
      S       7,0          Subtract time used by tones to get ½ seconds
                           remaining into R0
      LIMI    1            Turn on Timer interrupt
      IDLE                 Wait for timer interrupt
```

initialized to 7200 (the number of ½ seconds in an hour). The current ½ second value is then subtracted from R0 to get the 1/2 seconds remaining in the hour. The next four instructions load the workspace pointer value of 300_{16} into memory location 4 and the program counter value of 226_{16} into memory location 6. The interrupt level 1 procedure uses those values in jumping to the sequence beginning at IT(Interrupt).

When the timer causes an interrupt level 1 of *Figure 8-8*, the 300_{16} stored in location 0004 and the 226_{16} stored in location 0006 of RAM cause the microcomputer to start executing instructions at location 226_{16} (label IT) using the workspace starting at location 300_{16}. In the IT sequence the timer is reinitialized and the interrupt enabled as shown in *Figure 8-10*. Next, the register 0 counter is decremented. If it is not zero, IDLE causes the program to wait for the next interrupt. If the ½ second counter is zero, the program jumps to the tone generating sequence starting at TN(Tone).

Tone Subprogram

The Tone Subprogram produces a 1,000 cycle note by executing a timing loop with software that turns on the tone for 0.5 millisecond and turns off the tone for 0.5 millisecond.

At TN the interrupt is disabled with the LIMI 0 instruction then the hour count is incremented. If the hour count has been incremented to 13 it is reset to 1 with the next three instructions. The hour count is copied to R6 to use as a counter for the number of tones, preserving R5. Register 12 is set to the speaker address ($43C_{16}$), and register 4 is initialized to a pattern of alternating 1's and 0's ($AAAA_{16}$). The tone duration is set at one second in R3 with LI R3,2000. At RP(Repeat), the least significant bit of the first byte of R4 (Bit 7 which is initially a zero) is sent to the speaker with the LDCR R4,1 instruction. The register 4 is circulated (SRC 4,1) to complement the least significant bit (now bit 7 is a 1). R2 is the counter that determines the time of the half-period of the tone. With 22_{16} loaded in R2 and the time it takes to execute the instructions starting at RP through LI 2,>22, the half-period time is 0.5 milliseconds. The two instruction loop beginning at L1(loop 1) is used to time the 0.5 millisecond half-period, either on or off, for the 1000 cycle tone. After L1, register 3 is decremented to see if the tone has been sounded for 1 second. If it hasn't, the program jumps to RP to change the speaker input and time out the next half-period. If it has, the next seven instructions are used to keep the speaker off for 1 second, at which time the hour count in register 6 is decremented and checked for zero.

If not enough tones have been sounded, the sequence is repeated starting at NX(Next). If enough tones have been sounded, RO is initialized to 7200 minus 4 times the number of tones sounded. Thus, the instructions from MOV 5,7 to S 7,0 are correcting the next ½ second hour count for the time it took to sound the tones. The interrupt is again enabled with the LIMI 1 instruction so that the next 9901 time interval will generate an interrupt. The IDLE causes the processor to wait for the next timer interrupt.

Running the Program

The loading of this program into memory, the initialization of the memory locations 202_{16} (for the current hour), and 206_{16} (for the current minutes) and the starting of the program execution at address 200_{16} once these locations have been set, are all accomplished by the keyboard commands supported by the monitor program of the TM 990/U89 microcomputer. This monitor offers several program execution and debugging capabilities that would allow this program to be verified and implemented with a minimum of time and effort.

To run the program, the board must be supplied with the correct dc voltages, the program must be entered via a keyboard procedure, the PC and WP must be set to appropriate values, and the initial hours and minutes values entered.

The first step in setting up the U89 microcomputer for any application is connecting the ± 12 volt and $+5$ volt power supplies to the board. Once the board displays CPU READY, the programs and constants can be entered into the microcomputer with the following procedure:

1. Press Return

2. When board displays ? Press A200 and Return. When the board displays 0200, the label for that address can be entered as a two letter symbol such as ST for SET. Once the label is entered the mnemonic can then be entered. If the instruction does not have a label, the label is omitted by pressing the space key followed by the instruction mnemonic, once the instruction address has been displayed.

3. After each instruction is entered, its assembled code will be displayed. Pressing successive returns will get the address to the next instruction location. Instructions and their assembled code can continue to be entered and displayed until the entire program of *Figure 8-13* has been entered.

4. To enter the current time data, the user presses the M key followed by the address code and the data code. Thus, to enter the hour value in location 202_{16} and the minute value in location 206_{16}, the following sequence would be used.

> M202
> Return
> Hour Value
> Space
> Space
> Minute Value
> Return

5. The program is started by first setting the program counter (PC) to 200_{16} and the workspace pointer (WP) to 300_{16} and pressing the execute key:

P
Return
200
Return
W
Return
300
Return
E
Return

The program will run without further user control unless the user decides to modify the time or program sequence.

6. To stop the program or to start over in entering a program enter a system RESET.

HOW COULD THE SYSTEM PERFORMANCE BE IMPROVED AND EXPANDED?

Once the basic clock program has been written, it would be a relatively simple matter to add subprograms that would maintain hours and minutes and seconds displays. Similarly, the microcomputer clock could be used to time events such as cooking time or lawn watering times and so on. The musical capability of the clock can be improved by adding subprograms that will generate tunes instead of just sounding a steady tone. By generating a sequence of tones of different pitch and duration (and even different sound levels), any tune could be played by the microcomputer. The programming would be very similar to that of *Figure 8-13*, just more extensive timing sequences, all controlled by the values contained in the tone period generation registers and the tone duration registers.

A decimal-to-binary conversion subprogram could be added to allow the user to enter current hour and minute values in familiar decimal form. The development of such a program is saved as an exercise for the reader at the end of this chapter.

Since programs that run on the TMS 990/U89 microcomputer will also run on other 9900 family devices, the clock system could be implemented with a TMS9940 single-chip microcomputer with almost no extra components.

Programming for music synthesis is possible using additional sound source electronics controlled by the CRU bit of the microcomputer.

If in addition to a clock the user wants to go into music synthesis with the TM 990/U89 (or other 9900 family devices), the same basic procedures used in the clock can be used. The main difference is that since several tones would need to be sounded at once, probably with different intensities and waveforms, these tones would have to be generated by a bank of oscillators, whose on-off, output level, and waveform could be controlled by the CRU bits of the microcomputer. In this case the cassette interface capability would be very convenient since different musical compositions (different programs) could be stored onto magnetic tapes or read from magnetic tapes, just as a player piano uses paper rolls to store the piano control patterns. In fact, the complexity of the application features are limited only by the time the U89 board user is willing to spend on the project.

Other applications areas would be similarly expandable, limited only by the imagination of the user. Games is one obvious example of such an applications area. Control of home lighting, heating, burglar alarms, are other examples of an area with almost limitless possibilities. In all these areas the advantage of using the U89 microcomputer is that it allows the designer to concentrate on the application and not on the details of interconnecting integrated circuits together.

WHAT WE HAVE LEARNED?

- 16-bit microprocessors and microcomputers are required in high performance systems such as those requiring high numerical accuracy or high-speed communications.
- 16-bit microcomputers would be chosen for applications requiring high performance with minimum assembly costs.
- 16-bit microcomputer modules would be chosen for high performance systems that are to be produced in limited quantities.
- 16-bit microcomputer modules save the user time in developing both the system hardware (its already built) and system software.
- The TMS 990/U89 is an example of a microcomputer module that can be used as a learning tool, as a software development system and has the potential to be used for an actual system application.

PROGRAMMING EXERCISE

Write a subprogram called CONVERT that will convert the hour BCD value (0 through 12) in R5 to its binary equivalent. It will also convert the BCD number minutes entry (0 through 59) stored in R7 to binary form.

A simple algorithm for converting the hour value of 0 through 12 to its binary equivalent of 0 through C is as follows:

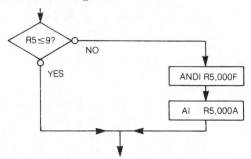

If the contents of R5 are less than 10, the number in R5 is correct. If the contents of R5 are 10 or more, remove the tens digit and add A to the units digit.

A comparable algorithm exists for converting a two digit decimal code to its binary equivalent. The only difference is that A is added to the units digit the number of times represented by the tens digit. Again, the tens digit is removed from the number before these additions are performed.

Solution

CONVERT	MOV	5,8	Copy Hour value into R8
	ANDI	5,>F	Remove tens digit from contents of R5
	ANDI	8,>F0	Remove units digit from contents of R8
	CI	8,>10	Compare tens digit in R8 to 1
	JNE	OK	If digit 0, number in R5 is binary equivalent
	AI	5,>A	If not, add A to R5 to get binary equivalent
OK	MOV	7,8	Copy minutes value into R8
	ANDI	7,>F	Remove tens digit from contents of R7
	SRL	8,4	Get tens digit into least four bits in R8
LOOP	CI	8,0	Is tens digit 0?
	JEQ	FIN	If it is, conversion of minutes is complete
	AI	7,>A	If not, add A to contents of R7
	DEC	8	Decrement tens counter in R8
	JMP	LOOP	Go Check current value of tens counter
FIN	RTWP		Conversion complete, return to calling program

> means base 16 constant

NOTE: When this subprogram is completed it may be added to the end of the main program inserting the instruction BL CONVERT after the first two instructions of the Time Set and Clock Subprogram of *Figure 8-13a* and substituting B *11 for RTWP in the last instruction of the above solution.

Glossary

Address: A pattern of characters that identifies a unique storage location.

Adder: A building block which provides a sum and a carry when adding two numbers.

Algorithm: A term used to describe a set of procedures by which a given result is obtained.

ALU: Arithmetic and Logic Unit. A subsystem that can perform arithmetic and logical operations on words sent to it.

Analog: Analog circuitry, also called "linear" circuitry, is circuitry that varies certain properties of electricity continuously and smoothly over a certain range.

AND Gate: A device or circuit with two or more inputs of binary digital information and one output, whose output is 1 only when all the inputs are 1.

ASCII: (American National Standard Code for Information Interchange, 1968). See USASCII.

Assembler: A computer program that prepares a machine language program from a symbolic language program.

Base Address: A given address from which a final address is derived by combination with a relative address.

Baud: A unit of signaling speed equal to the number of signal events per second.

Binary Number System or Code: A method of writing numbers by using two numeral digits, 0 and 1. Each successive bit position in a binary number represents 1, 2, 4, 8, and so forth.

Binary Coded Decimal (BCD): A binary numbering system for coding decimal numbers in groups of 4 bits. The binary value of these 4-bit groups ranges from 0000 to 1001, and codes the decimal digits "0" through "9".

Bit: The smallest possible piece of information. A specification of one out of two possible alternatives. Bits are written as 1 for "yes" and 0 for "no."

Borrow: An arithmetically negative carry in subtraction operations.

Branch: A program is said to "branch" when an instruction other than the next instruction in the program sequence is executed.

Bus: Two or more conductors running in parallel used for carrying information.

Byte: A sequence of adjacent binary digits operated upon as a unit – usually 8 bits.

Carry: When the sum of two digits is equal to or greater than 10, then 10 is subtracted from this sum, and 1 is added to the next more significant digit of the sum.

Central Processor Unit (CPU): Part of a computer system which contains the main storage, arithmetic unit, and special register groups. It performs arithmetic operations, controls instruction processing, and provides timing signals.

Character: A symbol whose image is formed by a display system for representation of information. Examples are numerals, letters, decimal point, punctuation marks, and special symbols indicating status of an electronic system.

Clear: To remove data and return all circuitry to an initial condition, usually "0."

Chip-Enable Input: A control input that when active permits operation of the integrated circuit and when inactive causes the integrated circuit to be inactive.

Clock Input: An input terminal on a building-block typically used for receiving a timing control-clock signal, but used in some applications for a control signal or even data.

Clock Generator: A building block that generates clock signals.

Compiler: A program that prepares a machine language program from a program written in another language.

Code: A set of meanings or rules assigned to groups of bits. Each combination of bits has a certain meaning based on following certain rules.

Complement: Usually means the "ones complement" of a bit, which is simply the inverse of the bit. To "complement" a number means to subtract it from a certain number (from one, in the case of ones complement).

Computer: A digital computer consists of at least one CPU, together with input, output, and memory units.

Conditional Jump: A jump that occurs if specified criteria are met.

CRU: Communications Register Unit: A bit addressable serial data link for I/O interface.

Cycle: 1. An interval of space or time in which one set of events or phenomena is completed. 2. Any set of operations that is repeated regularly in the same sequence.

Data: Another name for information.

Data Bus: One method of input-output for a system where data are moved by way of a group of wires forming a common bus.

Decimal Digit: In decimal notation, one of the characters 0 through 9.

Decimal Number System or Code: Also called "Arabic" number system. A method of writing numbers by using ten numeral digits. The "decimal digits" are 0, 1, 2, 3, 4, 5, 6, 7, 8, and 9.

Decoder: A combinational building-block receiving several parallel inputs, which "recognizes" one or more combinations of input bits and puts out a signal when these combinations are received.

D Flip-Flop: A clocked flip-flop with one data input (called "D"), whose "true" output changes at a clock signal to the state maintained at D during the clock signal.

Digital: Information in discrete or quantized form; not continuous.

Direct Addressing: Method of programming that has the address of data contained in the instruction that is to be used.

Dopant, Doping: A substance added to semiconductor material to make it p-type or n-type.

Edit: To modify the form or format of data, e.g., to insert or delete characters.

Effective Address: The address that is derived by applying any specified indexing or indirect addressing results to the specified address and that is actually used to identify the current operand.

EPROM: Eraseable and programmable read-only memory. An IC memory chip whose stored data can be read at random. The data can be erased and new data can be stored.

Error: Any discrepancy between a computed, observed, or measured quantity and the true, specified, or theoretically correct value or condition.

Exclusive-OR Gate: A device or circuit with two (not more) inputs of binary digital information and one output, whose output is 1 when either input is 1 and 0 if neither or both inputs are 1.

Execute: That portion of a computer cycle during which a selected instruction is accomplished.

Fetch: That portion of a computer cycle during which the next instruction is retrieved from memory.

Flip-Flop: A building-block having two stable states that stores one bit by means of two gates (ordinarily NAND or NOR gates) "cross-coupled" as a latch, with the output of each forming an input to the other.

Flow Chart: A graphical representation for definition, analysis, or solution of a problem, in which symbols are used to represent operations, data, flow, equipment, etc.

Format: The arrangement of data.

FORTRAN: (FORmula TRANslating system) A language primarily used to express computer programs by arithmetic formulas.

Frequency: How often regular waves or pulses occur in a circuit or other transmission medium such as radio. Frequency is measured in hertz (cycles per second).

General-Purpose Computer: A computer that is designed to handle a wide variety of problems.

IC: See "Integrated Circuit"

Immediate Address: Pertaining to an instruction which contains the value of an operand.

Indexed Address: An address that is modified by the content of an index register prior to or during the execution of a computer instruction.

Indirect Addressing: The initial address is the storage location of a word that contains another address used to obtain the data to be operated upon.

Input/Output Devices (I/O): Computer hardware by which data is entered into a digital system or by which data are recorded for immediate or future use.

Instruction: A statement that specifies an operation and the values or locations of its operands.

Instruction Cycle: The period of time during which a programmed system obeys an instruction.

Integrated Circuit ("IC"): A small package with electrical terminals, containing a chip of silicon. The surface of the silicon is processed to form hundreds or thousands of transistors and other devices that are connected to make an electronic circuit.

Interrupt: To stop a process in such a way that it can be resumed.

Inverter: A binary digital building-block with one input and one output. The output state is the inverse (opposite) of the input state.

Jump: A departure from the normal sequence of executing instructions in a computer.

Label: One or more characters used to identify a statement or an item of data in a program.

Language: A set of representations, conventions, and rules used to convey information.

LED: See "Light-emitting diode."

Light-Emitting Diode (LED): A semiconductor "light bulb" made of semiconductor material (such as gallium phosphide) that makes light when electric current is passed through it in a particular direction, by way of two terminals.

Linear Circuitry: See "Analog."

Load: In Programming, to enter data into storage or working registers.

Logic Gate: See "AND, OR, NAND, NOR, NOT, and Exclusive-OR."

Logic Symbol: A symbol used to represent a logic element graphically.

LSB or LSD: Least-significant bit or digit. The bit or digit at the end of a number which has the smallest numerical value.

Machine Code: An operation code that a machine is designed to recognize.

Mask: 1. A pattern of characters that is used to control the retention or elimination of portions of another pattern of characters. 2. See photomask.

Memory: In a digital system, the part of the system where information is stored.

Microcomputer: A computer in the lowest range of size and speed, generally smaller, slower, and less sophisticated than a "minicomputer."

Microprocessor: An IC (or set of a few ICs) that can be programmed with stored instructions to perform a wide variety of functions, consisting at least of a controller, some registers, and some sort of ALU (that is, the basic parts of a simple CPU).

Minicomputer: A computer in a certain range of size and speed, generally smaller, slower, and less sophisticated than a "computer."

MOS Integrated Circuit: A digital integrated circuit whose transistors are MOS transistors. Varieties include n-channel MOS, p-channel MOS, and CMOS.

MSB or MSD: Most-significant bit or digit. The bit or digit at the end of a number which has the largest numerical value.

NAND Gate: A binary digital building-block that acts as an AND gate followed by an inverter.

NOR Gate: A binary digital building-block that acts as an OR gate followed by an inverter.

NOT Gate: Occasionally used to mean "inverter."

Object Code: Output from a compiler or assembler which is itself executable machine code or is suitable for processing to produce executable machine code.

OR Gate: A device or circuit with two or more inputs of binary digital information and one output, whose output is 1 when any one or more inputs are 1.

Output: An information signal going out of a system or a part of a system.

Output Enable: A signal that when true connects the outputs of a storage cell to the output lines of the device.

Parity Check: A check to see if the number of ones in an array of binary digits is odd or even.

PC: Program Counter.

Photomask: A transparent glass plate carrying an intricate, very precise pattern of microscopically small opaque (dark) spots photographically reduced from a larger pattern.

Photoresist: A liquid that, when spread in a thin film and dried, quickly hardens into a tough plastic substance when struck by ultraviolet light. When the unhardened areas have been washed away, the material beneath is exposed for etching by an acid.

Priority Interrupt: A method of providing some commands to have precedence over others.

Program: A series of actions proposed in order to achieve a certain result.

Programmable Read-Only Memory (PROM): A fixed program, read only, semiconductor memory that can be programmed after packaging.

Programmed System: A system that operates by following a series of stored instructions.

Pushdown Stack: A set of registers which implement a pushdown list.

RAM: A random-access memory where words may be "written" (stored) or "read" (recovered) in any order at random.

Refresh: To refresh a dynamic storage unit means to restore its charge to the desired voltage level.

Register: A certain type of temporary storage unit for digital information.

Relative Address: The number that specifies the difference between the absolute address and the base address.

Reset: To "reset" a stored bit means make it a "0."

ROM: A read-only memory containing data permanently stored when the unit was made.

Routine or Programmed Routine: A series of instructions followed by a programmed system in doing a particular job. Usually contained within a main program.

Semiconductor: Semiconductor material such as silicon.

Serial Data Transmission: Two or more bits of a group are said to be transmitted "in series" when one at a time is transmitted through the same wire.

Set: To "set" a stored bit means make it a "1."

Shift: A movement of stored data right or left.

Shift Register: A register in which the stored data can be moved to the right or left.

Significant Digit: A digit that is needed to preserve a specific accuracy or precision.

Simulator: A computer program that represents the behavior of a system.

Software: A set of computer programs, procedures, and possibly associated documentation concerned with the operation of a data processing system, e.g., compilers, library routines, manuals, circuit diagrams.

Source Code Program: A computer program written in a source language.

Stored Program: A set of instructions in memory determining the order of the problem solution.

Substrate: The semiconductor material of a slice or chip that lies beneath the diffused and expitaxially deposited regions.

Subroutine: A routine that is part of another routine.

Subsystem: A smaller system inside a larger system. Each subsystem can be thought of as a separate system with its own job to do.

Sum: In arithmetic, the result of an addition.

Terminal: A computer terminal is an input (usually a keyboard) or output device (usually a printer or CRT screen) operated by a person.

Truth Table: A table showing the logic state of each output that results from each combination of logic states at the inputs. The logic states are 1 (yes, true) and 0 (no, false).

TTL or T²L: Transistor-transistor logic.

USACII: See "ASCII." A standard code for alphanumeric characters.

Word: A group of bits handled as a unit usually stored at a certain address in a RAM.

Workspace: In the 9900, a set of 16 consecutive words of memory used as registers.

Index

Answers to Quizzes

Chapter 1
1. a. **False**
   b. **True**
   c. **False**
   d. **True**
   e. **True**
   f. **False**
   g. **True**
   h. **True**
2. a. **a**
   b. **d**
   c. **b**
   d. **f**
   e. **c**
   f. **e**

3. a. **a**
4. **d**
5. **e**
6. a. **B, 3**
   b. **E, 5**
   c. **A, 4**
   d. **C, 2**
   e. **D, 1**
7. **d**
8. **b**
9. a. **c**
   b. **d**
   c. **a**
   d. **b**
10. **a**

Chapter 2
1. a. **3**
   b. **2**
   c. **4**
   d. **1**
2. a. **c**
   b. **e**
   c. **a**
   d. **d**
   e. **f**
   f. **g**
   g. **b**
3. **c**
4. **b**
5. **c**
7. **e**
8. **i**
9. **c**

Chapter 3
1. **e**
2. **f**
3. **3**
4. **e**
5. **d**
6. **e**
7. **a**
8. **f**

Chapter 5
1. **f**
2. **c**
3. **e**
4. **a**
5. **c**
6. **b**
7. **d**
8. **b**

Exercise Solutions are at the end of Chapters 4, 6, 7 and 8.